How to Raise STARTUP FUNDING in India

From Idea to IPO:
What startup founders need to know

Karminder Ghuman, MBA, PhD & Sahil Makkar, CA

BLUEROSE PUBLISHERS
India | U.K.

Copyright © Dr Karminder Ghuman & CA Sahil Makkar 2023

All rights reserved by author. No part of this publication may be reproduced, stored in a retrieval system or transmitted in any form or by any means, electronic, mechanical, photocopying, recording or otherwise, without the prior permission of the author. Although every precaution has been taken to verify the accuracy of the information contained herein, the publisher assumes no responsibility for any errors or omissions. No liability is assumed for damages that may result from the use of information contained within.

BlueRose Publishers takes no responsibility for any damages, losses, or liabilities that may arise from the use or misuse of the information, products, or services provided in this publication.

For permissions requests or inquiries regarding this publication,
please contact:

BLUEROSE PUBLISHERS
www.BlueRoseONE.com
info@bluerosepublishers.com
+91 8882 898 898
+4407342408967

ISBN: 978-93-5819-927-7

Cover design: Shivam
Typesetting: Namrata Saini

First Edition: October 2023

Gratitude and Acknowledgement

I am deeply grateful to the following professionals and students who contributed towards he development of the manuscript through their inputs and insights.

Mr. Vineet Khurana, CEO, Startup Accelerator Chamber of Commerce (SACC) for his inputs regarding the manuscript.

Mr. Rahul Sharma, Manager, Venture Lab, Thapar Institute of Engineering & Technology, Patiala for provision of research-based content for the development of the manuscript.

Mr. Aneesh, an entrepreneur, Product Manager, Business Consultant, and startup mentor, for his contribution towards the manuscript.

Dr. Kavitha, Assistant Professor, LM Thapar School of Management, for her valuable suggestion regarding the content with respect to financial analysis.

Ms. Anisha Jain, HR Executive, TCS, for her contribution towards the compilation of valuation methods.

Sukriti Sharma, Ankita Gupta, Harshita Arora, and Rimpy Mishra, Teg Mahip Kaur, and Isha the MBA students at LM Thapar School of Management, for their contribution towards undertaking research for few chapters for the manuscript.

Contents

What makes a Venture a Startup?..1
Startup Ecosystem...8
Social Entrepreneurship..15

Government Departments: Startups & Innovation 25
Startup Incubation Ecosystem 33
GIFT City Gujarat..48

What is Startup Finance?..54
Financial Skills an Entrepreneur Needs..56
Startup Journey 58
Startup Stages and Financial Implications..60

Business Model Canvas 67
Revenue and Cost Drivers..74
Budgeting 77
Financial Reserves before Starting a Startup..80
Organization Structures: Financial Implications..................................82

Cost of Capital..84
Capital Structure..87
Financial Leverage 93

Incubator Grant Schemes..95
Incubator Seed Funding Schemes 96
Incubator Soft Loan Schemes..98

Types of Business Loans..101
Concessional Bank Loans for Small Businesses 104
Feasibility Report for a Bank Loan...107
Credit Rating: Startup Finance 108
Peer 2 Peer Lending 111
Crowdfunding...113

Readiness for Funding from Angel Investors......................................118
Employee Stock Options (ESOPs)...122
Key Metrics for Pitching...125
Valuation of a Startup...140

Angel Investor Ecosystem in India..153
Pitching..159
Exit Strategy of Investors...169
Term Sheet..171
Business Plan 186

Tax on Investment in Startups in India 193

VC Funding 195
VC Funding Ecosystem in India 203
Fund of Funds for Startup 215
Accredited Investors 216
When Funding Stops: Innovative Strategies to Overcome Financial Constraints 218

Transition from Startup to Corporate 219
Modern CFO: A Function in Transition 223
Mergers & Buyouts 227
Private Equity Investment 233

Startup Platforms on BSE and NSE 236
Profitability before IPO 239
IPO 242

FOUNDER'S AGREEMENT: A TEMPLATE 251
Term Sheet: A Template 259

What makes a Venture a Startup?

"A big business starts small."–
Richard Branson, English business magnate, investor, author, and philanthropist

What is a Startup?

A startup is a newly established business that is typically characterized by innovation, scalability, and a focus on rapid growth. It is often associated with technology-driven ventures operating in various industries. Startups aim to develop and bring disruptive or novel products, services, or business models to the market. Hence, it's a new enterprise that has a scalable business model and intends to grow beyond the solo founder.

CRED, Vernacular.ai, PharmEasy, Digit Insurance, Meesho, Groww, Nykaa, Udaan, Dream11, Swiggy, Instamojo, PostMan, Delhivery, Slice, InMobi, Practo, Boat, Skyroot Aerospace, LivSpace, Ather, PhonePe, Licious, PolicyBazaar, Razorpay, Paytm were the top 25 startups in India in 2023.

How a Startup is different from Traditional Business?

Here are some key differences between startups and traditional businesses:

1. **Innovation and Disruption**: Startups are often driven by innovation and disruption. They aim to introduce new and groundbreaking ideas, technologies, or approaches to solve existing problems or meet untapped market needs. Traditional businesses, on the other hand, may focus on established products or services and incremental improvements.
For instance, Uber reshaped urban transportation, Netflix, transformed our viewing habits, the iPhone revolutionised communication, and now ChatGPT challenging stalwarts like Google by disrupting traditional business models. Indian startup **Meesho** has made deliveries from more than 1,00,000 registered suppliers, generating more than Rs.500 Cr i.e., $68 million in income for the homepreneurs.

2. **Growth Potential**: Startups typically have a high growth potential and aspire to scale rapidly. They aim to capture significant market share and expand their operations locally, nationally, or globally. Traditional businesses may prioritize stability and steady growth over rapid expansion.
For example, **PharmEasy** tied up directly with over 3,000 manufacturers and over 90,000 retailers across India to deliver medicines to customers in the shortest time possible. **DREAM 11** the India's first Unicorn startup, with a valuation of $5 billion, has grown at a CAGR of 230 percent in 3 years from 2020 onwards. The food delivery services startup **Swiggy**, which started with just 5

delivery boys and 25 restaurant partners in 2014 when Zomato was already there in the market is serving in 27 cities and has partnered with more than 40,000 restaurants. The company's target market has also grown to 50 million. **InMobi**, which was founded in 2011, has 22 offices spread across 12 nations and 5 continents, with about 1,500 individuals working there.

3. **Scalability**: Startups seek to build scalable business models that can grow exponentially without proportional increases in costs. They often leverage technology, automation, and network effects to achieve scalable growth. Traditional businesses may have more limited scalability due to resource constraints or operational limitations.
   CRED, the youngest Indian startup to be valued at around $2.2 billion has more than 6 million customers and about 22% of all credit card holders in just 4-years. **Groww** founded in 2016, has more than 15 million users registered till 2023, and more than 60% of the company investors belong to smaller cities of India that have never invested before. **Dream 11** took three years to hit the mark of first 1 million users, and post that, it crossed the 3 million user mark in less than 2 months. The company had around 75 million users before the COVID-19 pandemic started in India, and in 2023 reached 100 million users.

4. **Risk and Uncertainty**: Startups operate in an environment of high risk and uncertainty. They face challenges such as market validation, product-market fit, competition, and securing funding. Traditional businesses, especially established ones, may have more predictable markets, established customer bases, and proven business models, reducing some of the inherent risks.

5. **Lean and Agile Approach**: Startups often adopt a lean and agile approach, emphasizing quick iterations, experimentation, and customer feedback. They are adaptable and willing to pivot their strategies based on market insights. Traditional businesses may have more structured processes and decision-making hierarchies.

6. **Funding and Investment**: Startups often rely on external funding to fuel their growth. They may seek investments from angel investors and venture capitalists (VCs) or participate in incubator or accelerator programs. Traditional businesses may rely on traditional financing methods such as bank loans or personal investments. For example, **Nykaa** raised Rs.2,396 crore from anchor investors ahead of IPO. and raised USD 715 million in India's first D2C startup IPO in 2021.

7. **Culture and Work Environment**: Startups tend to have a dynamic and entrepreneurial culture. They often have flat organizational structures, encourage creative thinking, and foster a culture of innovation. Traditional businesses may have more hierarchical structures and established processes. Culturally also a professionally managed startup is very different from a "Lala" mindset company based on following parameters:

Difference between Lala Company and Professional Company Mindset vis-à-vis Employees

	Lala Company Mindset	Professionally Managed Startup Company Mindset
Salary	Depends on the whims and fancies of the owner	Performance management system and career paths are in place with rewards and recognitions pre-decided for a given period
Bills	Owner clears all bills and signs all cheques	System for making payments with various positions having different signing authorities
Recruitment	Preference for owner's friends, relatives for senior positions	Recruitment happens on merit and professionals occupy key positions
Presence at Events	Owner attends all major events, conferences with participation fee or delivers media interviews	Professionals heading various departments represent organization at prestigious events and interact with external stakeholders
Career trajectory	Significantly affected by accessibility to the owner	Career growth decided based on attainment of key performance indicators (KPIs)
Focus	Owners focus more on closest competitors & wants to dominate the segment by any means	The focus is more on customer delight and customer relationship management
Exit	At the time of resignation, there can be many issues like clearance of dues, experience certificate, etc.	There exists a procedure regarding exit of employees and dues are cleared within a few days of the no-dues procedure
Demand from Family members	Family members can expect support for their personal works	Family members rarely make unexpected demands from employees of organization
Consistency	Policies usually do not exist in writing, there can be inconsistencies or contradiction within a short period of time	There is a consistency in terms of plans and activities in the short term
Office Timing	Arrival time is fixed, but the going home timing depends on when the owner leaves the office, and timings revolve around owner's office timings	There are policies like overtime or flexitime in addition to official duty hours. Employees do know that they shall be rewarded for the extra hours they are putting in.

Source: Adapted from: Are You working in a " Lala Company"? Beware - Know this proactively. ! https://www.linkedin.com/posts/sameer-kaul-a70b705_3-million-views-are-you-working-in-a-activity-6047016360759021568--Klv/?trk=public_profile_like_view

These differences represent general characteristics, and there can be variations among startups and traditional businesses. Additionally, startups may eventually evolve into more traditional businesses as they mature and establish themselves in the market.

DPIIT recognised Startup

As per government notification, entities are recognised as 'startups' under Startup India initiative by the Department for Promotion of Industry and Internal Trade (DPIIT). Till 28th February 2023, DPIIT has recognised 92,683 entities as startups since the launch of Startup India initiative in 2016.

Eligibility Criteria to become DPIIT recognised Startup

In order to be eligible for tax holiday under the Income Tax Act, the startup must be a Private limited company or an LLP and become DPIIT recognised.

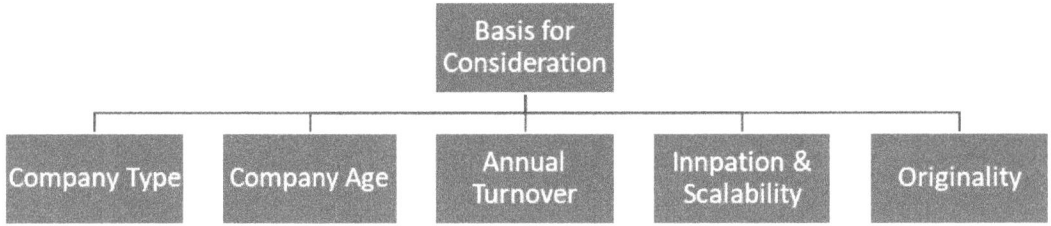

Startup founders should ensure that their startup meets the following eligibility criteria set by DPIIT:

a. The entity should be incorporated as a private limited company or registered as a partnership firm or a limited liability partnership (LLP) in India.
b. The startup should be working towards innovation, development, deployment, or commercialization of new products, processes, or services driven by technology or intellectual property, or it is a scalable business model with a high potential for employment generation or wealth creation.
c. The entity should not be older than ten years from the date of incorporation.
d. Annual turnover should not have exceeded INR 100 crores (approximately USD 14 million) in any preceding financial year since incorporation/ registration.
e. The entity should have obtained a recommendation letter from a startup incubator, or an accelerator recognized by the Government of India or meet certain funding criteria.
f. It should not be an entity formed by splitting up or reconstruction of a business already in existence. It is not formed by the transfer to a new business, or the machinery or plant previously used for any purpose. (33 B)

Process to become DPIIT recognised Startup:
To become a DPIIT (Department for Promotion of Industry and Internal Trade) recognized startup in India, you need to follow the process outlined below:

1. **Register Your Business**: First, you need to register your startup as a legal entity. It can be registered as a Private Limited Company, Partnership Firm, Limited Liability Partnership (LLP), or Registered Partnership.

2. **Register on the Startup India Portal**: Visit the Startup India portal (www.startupindia.gov.in) and create an account. Provide the required information about your startup, including details about the founders, business model, and financials.
3. **Self-Certification**: Complete the self-certification process by declaring that your startup meets the eligibility criteria specified by DPIIT.
4. **Upload Required Documents**: Upload the necessary documents, including the Certificate of Incorporation, Memorandum of Association, Articles of Association, and relevant documents related to your startup's legal entity.
5. **Recommendation Letter (if applicable)**: If your startup has received a recommendation letter from a recognized startup incubator or accelerator, upload the letter verifying that your startup meets the specified criteria as part of the application process.
6. **Review and Approval:** The application is then reviewed by the DPIIT and if meets the criteria and requirements, you will receive the DPIIT recognition for your startup.
7. **IMB (Inter Ministerial Board) Certificate:** Certification issued by the DPIIT, which makes the startups eligible for various benefits and recognition, including eligibility for government schemes and programs (Discussed in subsequent section).

Note: The process and criteria for DPIIT recognition may evolve over time. It is advisable to visit the official Startup India portal (www.startupindia.gov.in) or consult with professionals or legal experts for the most up-to-date information and guidance regarding the DPIIT recognition process.

Benefits for DPIIT recognised Startups

Being recognized by the DPIIT in India as a startup provides the following benefits and advantages:

1. **Tax Benefits**: Recognized startups are granted an IMB Certificate and are exempted from income tax on profits and gains for a period of 3 consecutive years out of 10 years since incorporation. They are exempted from the "angel tax" on funds raised from recognized angel investors or registered VC funds. A DPIIT recognised startup is eligible for exemption from section 56(2)(viib) of the Income Tax Act and the maximum limit is Rs.25 cr.
2. **Fast-track Patent Examination**: Startups recognized by DPIIT can expedite their patent application process through the Fast Track Mechanism. This allows them to receive quicker examination and approval for their patents, enabling faster protection of their intellectual property.
3. **Easier Winding-up Process:** DPIIT-recognized startups have access to a simpler and faster winding-up process under the Insolvency and Bankruptcy Code, 2016. The Government has notified Startups as 'fast track firms', enabling them to wind up operations within 90 days vis-à-vis 180 days for other companies.
4. **Government Procurement Benefits:** DPIIT-recognized startups can participate in public procurement processes and avail benefits, such as exemptions from

prior experience/turnover requirements, earnest money deposits, and other qualifying criteria for government tenders. Central Ministries/ Departments have been directed to relax conditions of prior turnover and prior experience in public procurement for all DPIIT recognised startups subject to meeting quality and technical specifications. This opens up opportunities for startups to access government contracts and projects. Government e-Marketplace (GeM) Startup Runway has also been developed as a dedicated corner for government approved startups to sell products and services directly to the Government.

5. **Access to Startup India Hub**: Recognized startups gain access to the Startup India Hub, a comprehensive platform for networking, mentorship, and knowledge sharing. The hub provides a forum to connect with other startups, mentors, investors, and industry experts, fostering collaborations and business opportunities. The Online Hub hosts startups, investors, funds, mentors, academic institutions, incubators, accelerators, corporates, government bodies, and more.

6. **Simplified Compliance:** DPIIT-recognized startups are allowed to self-certify their compliance under 9 Labour and 3 Environment laws for a period of 3 to 5 years from the date of incorporation. This reduces regulatory burden and compliance costs for the startups.

7. **Access to Funding**: DPIIT recognition can improve startups' access to funding opportunities. They become eligible for various government schemes, grants, and funds dedicated to supporting and promoting startups. The recognition status enhances their chances of attracting investment from angel investors, VC firms, and other funding sources. Startup India Seed Fund Scheme (SISFS) provides financial assistance to startups for proof of concept, prototype development, product trials, market-entry, and commercialization. Rs. 945 crores have been sanctioned under the SISFS Scheme for a period of 4 years, starting from 2021-22.

8. **Credit Guarantee Scheme for Startups**: It provides access to credit guarantees to loans extended to DPIIT recognised startups by Scheduled Commercial Banks, Non-Banking Financial Companies (NBFCs), and Venture Debt Funds (VDFs) under SEBI registered Alternative Investment Funds up to Rs.5 crores.

9. **Support for Intellectual Property Protection**: Startups are eligible for fast-tracked patent application examination and disposal. The Government launched Start-ups Intellectual Property Protection (SIPP) which facilitates startups to file applications for patents, designs, and trademarks through registered facilitators at appropriate IP offices. Facilitators under this Scheme are responsible for providing general advice on different IPRs, and information on protecting and promoting IPRs in other countries. The Government bears the entire fees of the facilitators for any number of patents, trademarks, or designs, and startups only bear the cost of the statutory fees payable. Startups are provided with an 80% rebate in the filing of patents and a 50% rebate in the filing of trademarks vis-à-vis other companies.

10. **International Market Access**: Through international Government to Government partnerships, participation in international forums, and hosting of global events. Startup India has launched bridges with over 15 countries (Brazil, Sweden, Russia, Portugal, UK, Finland, Netherlands, Singapore, Israel, Japan,

South Korea, Canada, Croatia, Qatar, and UAE) that provides a soft-landing platform for startups from the partner nations and aid in promoting cross-country collaboration.
11. **Startup India Showcase**: Startup India Showcase is an online discovery platform for startups in the country.
12. **Networking and Exposure**: Being recognized by DPIIT offers startups increased visibility and recognition. They can showcase their recognition status to stakeholders, enhancing their credibility and attracting potential collaborations. Startups may also get opportunities to participate in national and international startup events, exhibitions, and trade fairs organized by the government.
13. **Skill Development and Incubation Support**: Recognized startups can benefit from skill development programs, incubation support, and mentoring initiatives offered by the government.

Note: The specific benefits and eligibility criteria may vary over time and should be verified from the relevant authorities. Startups should consult the official Startup India website or seek guidance from professionals to stay updated on the latest benefits and requirements associated with DPIIT recognition.

Startup Entity and Tax Benefits

		Partnership firm	LLP	Pvt Ltd
Tax holidays	80 IAC	No	Yes, but MAT applies	Yes, but MAT applies
Capital gain exemption	54 GB	No	No	Yes
Angel tax	56(2)(viib)	No	No	As per Section 56(2)(viib)
Presumptive tax	44 AD	Yes	No	No
Source of fund	1st proviso of Sec 68	NA	NA	Applicable
IMP certification	IMP for 80 IAC	No	Yes	Yes
Startup Recognised by DPIIT	Imp for 80 IAC 54GB 56(2)(viib)	No	Yes	Yes

Startup Ecosystem

"What do you need to start a business? Three simple things: know your product better than anyone, know your customer, and have a burning desire to succeed."
–Dave Thomas, Founder, Wendy's

According to the Economic Survey 2021–22, India has emerged as the third-largest environment in the world for startups. Startup India initiative was launched on 16th January 2016; since then, there are over 99000+ startups recognized by the government of India as of May 2023. The number of recognized Startups was 452 in 2016 and 84,012 as on 30th November 2022. Nearly half of them have a base in Tier 2 - Tier 3 cities.

Number of Enterprises Recognised as Startups by DPIIT in different Years

Year	2018	2019	2020	2021	2022
Startups Recognised	8,635	11,279	14,498	20,046	26,542

The government, too, is making serious endeavours both at the level of policymaking as well as financial support. India continues to demonstrate resilience concerning growth of startups and attracting global investors as the following structural enablers are driving a positive economic outlook creating a long runway for growth:

- Solid macro-fundamental
- Large consumption potential because of favourable demographics
- Sizeable workforce entering the formal economy
- Inclusive growth led by scale digital adoption of the decentralised "India Stack,"
- Effective fiscal and monetary policy discipline limiting inflationary growth,
- Economic activity shifting away from China.
- Low leverage,
- Increasing tech adoption leading to a digitally enabled population
- Deepening innovation ecosystem

According to a report published by IAMAI and Kantar Research, India's internet users are expected to reach 900 million by 2025 from 622 million in 2020. The rollout of 5G, digital payments, UPI, and voice assistants are laying down the necessary infrastructure that is fuelling the launch and growth of startups in India.

Looking at the big deals between companies in India, e.g., Walmart and Flipkart (having Myntra and PhonePe), India is growing up as a hub of the biggest startups. One 97 Communications (PayTM), Ola cabs, Dream 11, Swiggy, and Razorpay are a few of the richly valued Indian startups across the world. The country is now getting more startup unicorns, including companies from the sectors like Healthtech, social commerce, finance, and more. According to Inc42, India got its 10 startups listed in the list of Unicorns in 2023.

The recognised startups in India are spread across 56 diversified sectors, with around 4,500 startups recognised in emerging tech, such as the Internet of Things (IoT), robotics, artificial intelligence, analytics, etc. 13% recognized startups are from IT services, 9% from healthcare and life sciences, 7% from education, 5% from agriculture and 5% from food & beverages. With 15 times increase in the total funding of startups, 9 times increase in the number of investors, and 7 times increase in the number of incubators, Indian startup ecosystem has seen exponential growth from 2015 onwards.

India had about 25 unicorns till January 1, 2020, and Indian startups had received $14.5 billion funding. In June 2023 India had 108 unicorns (Startups that value more than $ 1 billion) with a total valuation of $ 340 billion. Out of these, 44 unicorns with a total valuation of $93.00 Bn were born in 2021, and 21 unicorns with a total valuation of $26.99 Bn were born in 2022. In the period of Jan-March 2021, investors have infused around $4.4 billion into Indian startups, and this amount is 26% more than the investments made in 2020 in the same quarter.

However, one prominent challenge lies in the transacting user growth, especially in categories like fashion, beauty and personal care, e-grocery, e-retailing, and mobility. Although total number of internet transactors in India is about 350 million, the growth of mature online transactors who are frequent buyers has plateaued at around 40-45 million.

Classification of Startups

Startups can be broadly classified into various categories based on different criteria. Here are some common classifications of startups:

A. **Industry Focus:**
   On the basis of industry focus, startups can be classified as:

   a. **Deep-Tech Startups:** Focus on developing and commercializing innovative technologies and operate in areas such as artificial intelligence, machine learning, virtual reality, blockchain, etc. Despite past turbulence, India's internet economy is projected to maintain a steady 25% compound annual growth rate (CAGR) until 2030.
   b. **HealthTech Startups:** Biotech and healthcare startups focus on developing new medical treatments, drugs, diagnostics, medical devices, or healthcare solutions, biotechnology research, telemedicine, or health IT. According to market research firm, International Data Corporation (IDC), India is the third-largest consumer of wearable devices globally and the wearable market in India grew 144.3 percent year-over-year (YoY) in 2020.

- c. **CleanTech Startups:** Focus on renewable energy, energy efficiency, or sustainable solutions for the environment.
- d. **FinTech Startups:** These startups leverage technology to offer innovative financial services, such as mobile payments, online banking, peer-to-peer lending, or cryptocurrency, investment platforms, or insurance technology. It comprises of many sub-themes: insurtech, embedded lending, and wealthtech.

    The top gainers in the funding deals in 2020-21 were the Fintech and Financial Services companies (123), followed by Retail and Ecommerce companies (99) and EdTech companies (84).
- e. **EdTech Startups:** Develop technology-based solutions for education by creating online learning platforms, educational apps, tools for classroom management, or specialized software to enhance teaching and learning experiences.
- f. **E-commerce Startups:** Operate online platforms for buying and selling products or services. They facilitate transactions between buyers and sellers and often specialize in specific product categories, such as fashion, electronics, home goods, or niche markets.

    According to Redseer, India's GDP is projected to be at $6.5 trillion by 2030, with a retail market size of $2 trillion, and a per capita GDP of $4,300, indicative of a robust digital ecosystem. In April 2023, there were more than 2,890 DPIIT Recognised startups in the Retail sector. Comparison Shopping, Retail Technology, and Social Commerce formed 77% of all retail startups, Amazon, Flipkart, Lenskart, Nykaa, Vahdam Teas, are leading examples of e-commerce startups. Till April 2023, Retail startups generated employment of over 28,000.
- g. **AgriTech Startups**: Focus on bringing technology to modernize or digitalize the traditional agricultural process with a focus on transforming agriculture into agribusiness.
- h. **MediaTech Startups:** India's Media & Entertainment industry is expected to reach $30.9 bn by 2024. The media sector in India has seen a massive transformation in the last decade, with the proliferation of digital media and the rise of social media. Media and entertainment sector is amongst the top 5 unicorn sectors with 7 unicorns from the sector.
- i. **Lifestyle Startups:** Lifestyle startups aim to provide products or services that enhance people's lifestyles or cater to specific interests. They may focus on areas such as fitness, wellness, fashion, food and beverage, travel, or entertainment.
- i. **Service Startups:** Service startups provide various types of services to clients, leveraging technology or expertise in a specific domain. Examples include consulting firms, marketing agencies, software development companies, design studios, healthcare service providers, etc.

B. **Business Model**

Based on business models, startups can be classified as:
- a. **Cloud Service Model Startups (XaaS)**

- **Infrastructure as a Service (IaaS):** These startups provide users with computing infrastructure resources on-demand. Users can purchase virtual servers, storage, networking components, and other infrastructure elements from a cloud provider. The resources are accessed and managed remotely through the internet. With IaaS, users have control over their operating systems, applications, and data, while the cloud provider is responsible for maintaining the underlying infrastructure.
- **Platform as a Service (PaaS)**: PaaS startups offers a complete development and deployment environment in the cloud. It provides developers with a platform to build, test, and deploy applications without the need to manage the underlying infrastructure. PaaS providers offer a range of tools, frameworks, and runtime environments to facilitate the development process. Developers can focus on coding and application logic, while the PaaS provider handles the infrastructure, scalability, and security aspects.
- **Software as a Service (SaaS)**: SaaS delivers software applications over the internet on a subscription basis. Users can access and use the software through a web browser or a thin client interface without the need for local installation. The software and its associated data are centrally hosted and managed by the SaaS provider. Users typically pay a recurring fee to access and use the software, and updates and maintenance are handled by the provider. SaaS allows users to utilize software without the need for extensive hardware and software management. SaaS startups develop and provide software solutions that cater to a wide range of industries and business needs. These solutions can include customer relationship management (CRM) software, project management tools, collaboration platforms, human resources management systems, accounting software, and many others. Software-as-a-service (SaaS) and fintech continued to see momentum relative to 2021, growing in salience from 25% to 35% of total funding in 2022.

b. **Product Startups:** Develop and sell physical products or software applications. They may create consumer goods, electronics, medical devices, software tools, or other tangible products for specific industries or market segments.

c. **Service Startups:** They provide services or solutions to clients, often leveraging technology to deliver their services more efficiently.

d. **Platform Startups:** Create platforms that connect users or businesses, facilitating transactions, collaborations, or exchanges of goods and services.

e. **Marketplace Startups:** Build online platforms that connect buyers and sellers, enabling transactions between them. They may focus on specific industries, such as real estate, transportation, freelance services, or B2B procurement.

Overview of Leading Indian Startups

Startup	Business Model	Industry	Valuation (2023)	Year Established
CRED	Platform	FinTech	$2.2 billion	2018
Digit Insurance	Insurance	FinTech		2016
Groww	Investing platform	Fintech		2016
Vernacular.ai	Voice automation and AI platform	AI-First SaaS business		2016
PharmEasy	Online pharmacy and medical store	MedTech		2015
Meesho	Reseller platform	e-commerce distribution	$2.1 billion	2015
Nykaa	Fashion e-commerce platform	Online beauty store	$1.2 billion	2012
Udaan	B2B e-commerce solutions	Connecting sellers	$3.1 billion	2016
DREAM 11	Fantasy gaming platform	Gaming	$5 billion	2008
Swiggy	Food delivery platform		$5 billion	2014
InMobi	Native Ads platform			2011
Practo	Find doctors, book appointments	Healthtech		2008
Boat	Stylish & affordable electronic goods			2016
Skyroot Aerospace	Space launch startup	Aerospace		2018
LivSpace	Interior design			2014
Ather Energy	Electric vehicles			2013
Licious	Raw food delivery	Foodtech		2015
PhonePe	Digital payments and financial services platform	Fintech		2016
Policybazaar	Online insurance aggregator	Fintech		2008
Razorpay	Payment gateway	Fintech		2014
Paytm	Digital payment & financial services	Fintech		2010

C. Development Stage

Based on the stage of development, startups can be classified as:

a. **Early-stage Startups:** These startups in their early stages of development, typically focused on product or market validation, securing funding, and building a team.
b. **Growth-stage Startups:** These startups have already validated their product or service and are experiencing significant growth in terms of customers, revenue, and market presence.
c. **Scale-ups:** These startups have achieved substantial growth and are focused on scaling their operations and expanding into new markets.

For instance, 32% of Retail startups in India were in the validation stage, while 33% were in the early traction stage till April 2023.

D. Social Impact

Based on the degree of social impact, startups can be classified as:

a. **Commercial Enterprise:** The startups have been created to generate profit and shareholder wealth maximization. The social impact of their commercial activities is a by-product but not a part of the mission.
b. **Social Enterprise:** These startups have a primary goal of creating a positive social or environmental impact while generating sustainable revenue. They often address pressing global challenges such as poverty alleviation, education, healthcare access, environmental sustainability, community development, etc. These startups are driven by a mission to address a social or environmental issue, and their primary focus is on achieving their mission rather than generating profits.

E. The Team

Based on who is managing the show, the enterprises can be classified as:

a. **Weekend/evening Side Hustle/Gig**
b. **Employee/member of Family business building a startup**
c. **Intrapreneur: Employee of a corporate entity building a startup within the corporate entity**
d. **Part-time Solopreneur**
e. **Full-Time Solopreneur**
f. **Part-time Entrepreneur with co-founders**
g. **Full-Time Entrepreneur with co-founders**

The investors give a significant consideration to this classification concerning startup founders in addition to the usual classification of startups based on business models, technology, etc. Investors definitely are more comfortable when they see a well-settled full-time team rather than a solopreneur. The team might constitute of: Advisor, Mentor, Co-founder Investor, Strategic Investor.

In the context of a startup, the terms advisor, mentor, co-founder, investor, and strategic investor refer to different roles and relationships with the company. Here's a breakdown of the differences:

- **Advisor:** An advisor is an individual who provides guidance and expertise to the startup based on their specific knowledge and experience. Advisors typically have subject matter expertise in a particular domain related to the startup's industry. They offer advice on various aspects such as business strategy, operations, marketing, and fundraising. Advisors may or may not have a formal or legal role within the company, and their involvement can vary in terms of time commitment and compensation.
- **Mentor**: A mentor is someone who shares their knowledge, experience, and guidance with an entrepreneur or a startup founder. Mentors play a vital role in providing support, advice, and helping entrepreneurs develop their skills and navigate challenges. They often have a more personal and long-term relationship with the individual they are mentoring. Mentoring can cover a broad range of topics, including business strategy, leadership, networking, and personal development.
- **Co-founder:** A co-founder is one of the individuals who initiates the formation of a startup and is actively involved in its establishment and growth. Co-founders are typically involved in the early stages of the company's development, contribute to its vision, and often have complementary skills and expertise. They are crucial in shaping the startup's strategy, building the team, and securing resources. Co-founders often have a significant ownership stake in the company and share responsibilities in decision-making and operations.
- **Investor**: An investor is an individual or entity that provides financial resources to a startup in exchange for ownership equity or other financial instruments. Investors can be individuals (angel investors) or institutional entities (venture capital firms, private equity firms, etc.). Their primary objective is to generate a return on their investment by supporting startups with growth potential. Investors may provide funding in different stages of a startup's lifecycle, ranging from early seed funding to later-stage funding rounds.
- **Strategic Investor:** A strategic investor is a specific type of investor who not only provides capital to a startup but also brings strategic value beyond the financial investment. Strategic investors often have expertise or resources that are directly relevant to the startup's industry or business model. They may offer market insights, industry connections, access to distribution channels, or other strategic advantages. Strategic investors typically seek to align their interests with the startup's success and may take a more active role in shaping its direction.

It's important to note that there might be transition between these roles as the startup evolves.

Social Entrepreneurship

"Social entrepreneurs are not content just to give a fish or teach how to fish. They will not rest until they have revolutionized the fishing industry." – **Bill Drayton, Founder, Ashoka**

Social entrepreneurship refers to the practice of using entrepreneurial skills and approaches to create a positive social or environmental change. It combines the principles of business entrepreneurship with a focus on addressing social issues and improving the well-being of communities.

Social entrepreneurs are individuals or organizations that identify societal problems, such as poverty, inequality, environmental degradation, or lack of access to basic services, and develop innovative and sustainable solutions to tackle these challenges. Unlike traditional entrepreneurs who primarily seek to generate profits for themselves or their shareholders, social entrepreneurs prioritize creating social impact as their primary goal. They apply business principles and strategies to build enterprises that are financially sustainable while also addressing social needs. This may involve developing innovative products or services, implementing new business models, or creating organizations that operate in a socially responsible and ethical manner.

Social entrepreneurs often work in areas where market forces have failed to adequately address social problems. They aim to fill gaps in society by providing solutions that can lead to systemic change and sustainable development. Their initiatives can range from nonprofit organizations, social enterprises, cooperatives, or hybrid models that blend social and commercial objectives. Key characteristics of social entrepreneurship include:

a. **Social Mission**: Social entrepreneurs are driven by a clear social or environmental mission, seeking to make a positive impact and improve lives.
b. **Innovation**: They employ innovative approaches, technologies, or business models to create effective solutions to social problems.
c. **Sustainability**: Social entrepreneurs strive for financial sustainability to ensure the longevity and scalability of their initiatives.
d. **Systems Thinking**: They take a holistic approach to address underlying systemic issues rather than focusing solely on the symptoms.
e. **Collaboration**: Social entrepreneurs often work with various stakeholders, including government agencies, nonprofits, businesses, and communities, to achieve their goals.
f. **Measurement of Impact**: They emphasize measuring and evaluating the social or environmental impact of their initiatives to assess their effectiveness and drive continuous improvement.

Social Entrepreneurship and SDG

Social entrepreneurship plays a crucial role in contributing to the achievement of the United Nations Sustainable Development Goals (SDGs). The SDGs are a set of 17 global goals designed to address the world's most pressing social, economic, and environmental challenges by 2030. Social entrepreneurs, with their innovative and sustainable approaches, aim to drive progress towards these goals. Here's how social entrepreneurship intersects with the SDGs:

a. **Poverty alleviation (SDG 1)**: Social entrepreneurs develop innovative solutions to tackle poverty, focusing on creating income-generating opportunities, providing access to basic services, and promoting economic empowerment.
b. **Zero hunger (SDG 2)**: Social entrepreneurs work on initiatives related to sustainable agriculture, food security, reducing food waste, and improving farmers' livelihoods, contributing to achieving food security and ending hunger.
c. **Good health and well-being (SDG 3)**: Social entrepreneurs develop healthcare innovations, improve access to quality healthcare services, and address health disparities, ultimately promoting well-being and ensuring healthy lives for all.
d. **Quality education (SDG 4)**: Social entrepreneurs create innovative educational models, improve access to education for marginalized communities, develop educational technology solutions, and promote skill development to ensure inclusive and equitable quality education for all.
e. **Gender equality (SDG 5)**: Social entrepreneurs promote women's empowerment, address gender-based discrimination, and create opportunities for women's economic and social advancement, contributing to achieving gender equality and empowering all women and girls.
f. **Clean water and sanitation (SDG 6)**: Social entrepreneurs focus on clean water and sanitation solutions, such as innovative water purification technologies, community-based sanitation initiatives, and promoting water conservation practices.
g. **Affordable and clean energy (SDG 7)**: Social entrepreneurs drive the adoption of renewable energy technologies, promote energy access in underserved areas, and develop sustainable energy solutions, contributing to affordable and clean energy for all.
h. **Decent work and economic growth (SDG 8)**: Social entrepreneurs create employment opportunities, support microenterprises and cooperatives, and promote inclusive economic growth, aiming to foster sustainable and inclusive economic development.
i. **Industry, innovation, and infrastructure (SDG 9)**: Social entrepreneurs drive innovation and develop sustainable business models, particularly in areas like clean technology, renewable energy, sustainable agriculture, and affordable housing, contributing to building resilient infrastructure and promoting inclusive and sustainable industrialization.

j. **Reduced inequalities (SDG 10)**: Social entrepreneurs address social and economic inequalities by empowering marginalized communities, promoting inclusive business models, and working towards social inclusion and equal opportunities for all.
k. **Sustainable cities and communities (SDG 11)**: Social entrepreneurs develop solutions for affordable housing, urban waste management, access to basic services, and community development, contributing to creating sustainable and inclusive cities and communities.
l. **Responsible consumption and production (SDG 12)**: Social entrepreneurs promote sustainable production practices, reduce waste, develop circular economy models, and encourage responsible consumption, contributing to sustainable consumption and production patterns.
m. **Climate action (SDG 13)**: Social entrepreneurs develop climate change mitigation and adaptation solutions, promote renewable energy adoption, sustainable agriculture practices, and conservation efforts, contributing to urgent action to combat climate change and its impacts.
n. **Life below water (SDG 14) and Life on land (SDG 15)**: Social entrepreneurs work on initiatives related to marine and terrestrial conservation, sustainable fisheries, reforestation, land restoration, and biodiversity preservation, contributing to the protection and sustainable use of marine and terrestrial ecosystems.
o. **Peace, Justice, and Strong Institution (SDG 16)** Social entrepreneurs promote peaceful and inclusive societies, providing access to justice for all and building effective, accountable, and inclusive institutions at all levels. They ensure people everywhere should be free of fear from all forms of violence and feel safe as they go about their lives whatever their ethnicity, faith, or sexual orientation.
p. **Partnerships for the goals (SDG 17)**: Social entrepreneurs collaborate with various stakeholders, including governments, corporations, nonprofits, and communities, fostering partnerships to leverage resources, knowledge, and expertise towards achieving the SDGs.

By combining business principles with a social mission, social entrepreneurs play a vital role in tackling global challenges and creating a more sustainable and inclusive future.

Social Entrepreneurship and CSR Funding

Social entrepreneurship and corporate social responsibility (CSR) funding are two distinct but interconnected approaches to addressing social and environmental challenges. While they have some similarities, they differ in their primary focus and the ways they mobilize resources. Here's how social entrepreneurship and CSR funding relate to each other:

A. **Focus and Objectives:**
   - **Social Entrepreneurship**: Primarily focuses on creating sustainable, innovative, and impactful solutions to address social and environmental

challenges. It aims to combine business principles with a social mission, emphasizing long-term systemic change and self-sustainability.
- **CSR Funding**: Initiatives and activities undertaken by businesses to positively contribute to society and the environment by allocating a portion of a company's profits or resources towards social and environmental causes, typically through grants, donations, or community development projects.

B. **Approach to Social Impact**:
- **Social Entrepreneurship**: Entrepreneurial approach to social impact, leveraging market-based strategies, innovative business models, and sustainable practices to address societal needs. They aim to create scalable and systemic solutions that generate both social and financial returns.
- **CSR Funding**: Focused on supporting social and environmental causes through financial contributions by providing grants or donations to nonprofit organizations, funding community development projects, supporting education or healthcare initiatives, or addressing specific social or environmental issues.

C. **Revenue Model:**
- **Social Entrepreneurship**: Develop revenue-generating models through the sale of products or services. They aim to create financially sustainable enterprises that reinvest profits into their social mission and reduce reliance on external funding sources.
- **CSR Funding**: Provided by established corporations as a part of their philanthropic efforts. It is not driven by a revenue-generating model but rather by the company's commitment to giving back to society and supporting social and environmental causes.

D. **Scale and Impact:**
- **Social Entrepreneurship**: Potential for significant scale and impact by leveraging entrepreneurship, innovation, and market-based approaches. Social entrepreneurs often focus on creating systemic change and addressing root causes of social and environmental challenges.
- **CSR Funding**: Tends to have a more localized or targeted impact, focusing on specific projects, initiatives, or communities. While it can create positive change within its scope, the scale of impact may be limited compared to the potential of scalable social entrepreneurship models.

E. **Collaboration**:
- **Social Entrepreneurship**: Social entrepreneurs often collaborate with multiple stakeholders, including governments, nonprofits, businesses, and communities, to achieve their goals. They seek partnerships that can leverage expertise, resources, and networks to drive impact.
- **CSR Funding**: Corporations engaging in CSR funding often collaborate with nonprofits or community organizations to implement initiatives or projects. These collaborations can help align the company's resources and expertise with the specific needs and expertise of the nonprofit sector.

Leading Social Enterprises in India

There are several leading social enterprises in India that have made significant contributions to addressing social challenges and creating positive impact. Here are a few notable examples:

a. **SELCO Foundation**: SELCO Foundation works towards sustainable energy access for underserved communities in India. They focus on designing and deploying decentralized solar energy solutions and promoting entrepreneurship in the renewable energy sector.
b. **Aravind Eye Care System**: Aravind Eye Care System is a network of eye hospitals that provides high-quality, affordable eye care services in India. They have developed an innovative model that combines efficient processes, technology, and cross-subsidization to make eye care accessible to all, regardless of their ability to pay.
c. **Husk Power Systems**: Husk Power Systems addresses the energy needs of rural communities by providing clean and affordable electricity using biomass gasification technology. They convert rice husks into gas and generate electricity, powering off-grid villages in rural India.
d. **Goonj**: Goonj is a nonprofit organization that focuses on addressing rural poverty and promoting sustainable development. They work on various initiatives, including disaster relief, community development, and transforming urban waste into resources for rural communities.
e. **Fabindia**: Fabindia is a well-known social enterprise that promotes traditional Indian handicrafts and empowers rural artisans. They create a market for handmade, sustainable products while preserving traditional skills and providing livelihood opportunities.
f. **Chototel**: Chototel aims to provide affordable housing solutions to low-income individuals and families. They develop micro-homes using cost-effective construction techniques and offer essential amenities at affordable rates, enabling access to dignified living conditions.
g. **Bhartiya Micro Credit (BMC)**: BMC is a microfinance institution that provides financial services and support to women in rural and underserved areas. They offer microloans, savings programs, and entrepreneurship training, empowering women to start and grow their own businesses.
h. **Vaatsalya Healthcare**: Vaatsalya Healthcare operates a chain of hospitals in rural and semi-urban areas, focusing on providing affordable and quality healthcare services to underserved communities. They employ innovative models to make healthcare accessible and address the gaps in rural healthcare infrastructure.
i. **Kalinga Institute of Social Sciences (KISS)**: KISS is a residential institute that provides education, accommodation, and healthcare to tribal children in Odisha. It aims to eradicate poverty and empower tribal communities through education and skill development.
j. **D.light**: D.light designs and manufactures affordable solar lighting and power products for off-grid communities. Their products provide clean and safe lighting solutions, replacing kerosene lamps and improving the lives of people without access to reliable electricity.

Select Social Enterprises: Revenue Models & Funding

Social Enterprise	Problem	Solution	Funding Source	Future Planning
ARVIND EYE CARE	Increase in needless blindness	Make compassionate and quality eye care affordable to all.	Cross-subsidization (40% patients charged full payment; that money used to provide free of cost treatment to poor)	Eliminate needless blindness from India by providing large volume high quality affordable care to needy.
SELCO	Lack of access to reliable energy sources in rural areas	Providing reliable Solar lighting energy service to poor in a sustainable way in rural areas	Don't have institutional or angel investors. (50% of portfolio is secured with long term fund raising)	Develop affordable innovations & improvements in products that enhance livelihood of low-income villagers.
HUSK POWER	Lack of clean energy services in rural areas	Husk Power serves the entire rural economy, with mini grids at the center of the company's business model.	Raised three rounds of equity, totalling about $30 million. (Revenue model for customers is pay-as-you-go).	Signed UN Energy Compact, with a commitment to build 5,000 mini-grids by 2030 and displacing 700 million gallons of diesel for gensets
FAB INDIA	Unemployed rural crafts people	Retail store chain with handmade products by craftspeople. Works closely with artisans: providing design, quality control, raw materials and production coordination	Funded by Lighthouse Funds. Closed its last funding round in 2019 from a private equity round.	Further scale up its business by adding 50 new stores in Indian and international markets every year.
CHOTOTEL	Clean, safe and affordable accommodation	Chain of super-budget hotels to eradicate homelessness. (price per night ranges $2 to $5)	Funded by friends and family and they are in process of their first round of funding.	Mission is to provide budget-friendly accommodation with uninterrupted utilities clean, potable water
VAATSALYA	Child protection	Achieving development and child protection aligned with SDGs	Raised an initial funding of Rs 1 crore from angel investors based in the US and Europe.	To prevent child abuse, exploitation, ensure quality care, rehabilitation & social reintegration of children.

These social enterprises represent a diverse range of sectors and approaches, but all share a common commitment to addressing social challenges and improving the lives of marginalized communities in India.

Section 8 Company

In India, a Section 8 company under the Companies Act, 2013, is a legal entity that is incorporated for promoting art, science, commerce, education, religion, charity, social welfare, sports, or any other useful purpose.

The primary objective of a Section 8 company is to promote a specific social or charitable cause, and its profits or income, if any, are applied towards achieving those objectives.

These companies have a distinct legal framework that enables them to operate as non-profit organizations and access certain benefits and exemptions provided under the Companies Act.

Here are some key characteristics and features of a Section 8 company:

a. **Non-Profit Nature:** A Section 8 company is established with the intention of promoting charitable or social causes rather than generating profits for its members or shareholders. Any income generated by the company is utilized for the fulfilment of its objectives.
b. **Name of the Company:** The name of a Section 8 company typically ends with words like "Foundation," "Association," "Society," "Council," "Organization," or other suitable terms that indicate its non-profit nature.
c. **No Share Capital**: Unlike other companies, a Section 8 company may be formed without having a share capital. It can be registered as a company limited by guarantee or as a company without share capital.
d. **Limited Liability**: Like other forms of companies, a Section 8 company has the benefit of limited liability for its members. The personal assets of the members are generally protected in case of any liabilities or debts incurred by the company.
e. **Statutory Restrictions**: Section 8 companies are subject to certain restrictions outlined in the Companies Act, 2013. These restrictions are designed to ensure that the activities of the company remain focused on the specified social or charitable objectives and that its assets and income are not utilized for the benefit of its members.
f. **Regulatory Compliance**: Section 8 companies must comply with the regulations and provisions of the Companies Act, 2013. They are required to file annual financial statements, annual returns, and other necessary documents with the Registrar of Companies (ROC) to maintain legal compliance.

It is important to consult legal professionals or refer to the Companies Act, 2013, for detailed information and guidance specific to Section 8 companies in India.

How can social entrepreneurs raise finance?

Social entrepreneurs have various options for raising finance. Here are some common methods used by social entrepreneurs to secure funding:

a. **Incubators and Accelerators**: Joining incubator or accelerator programs tailored to social enterprises can provide access to funding, and networking opportunities. These programs often connect social entrepreneurs with potential investors and help refine their business models.
b. **Grants and Donations**: Social entrepreneurs often rely on grants from foundations, government agencies, and philanthropic organizations. These grants are provided to support specific projects or cover operational expenses.
c. **CSR Funding:** social entrepreneurship and CSR funding can complement each other and create synergies. Some corporations may choose to support social entrepreneurs through CSR funding, recognizing their innovative approaches and potential for creating sustainable social impact.
d. **Corporate Partnerships**: Collaborating with corporations can provide social entrepreneurs with financial support, in-kind resources, and access to expertise and networks. Corporate social responsibility initiatives or strategic partnerships can offer funding and other forms of support.
e. **Revenue Generation**: Social entrepreneurs can generate income through sale of products/services. By developing sustainable business models, they can reinvest profits and reduce dependency on external funding sources.
f. **Impact Bonds**: Impact bonds or social impact bonds are financing instruments where private investors provide upfront capital to finance social ventures. If the predetermined social outcomes are achieved, the government or another outcome payer repays the investors with a financial return.
g. **Crowdfunding**: Online crowdfunding platforms allow social entrepreneurs to raise funds from many individuals who contribute small amounts. This approach leverages the power of crowd and can help raise funding for social enterprise.
h. **Impact Investors**: Impact investors are individuals, organizations, or funds that seek to invest in enterprises generating both social impact and financial returns. Social entrepreneurs can approach impact investors who align with their mission and demonstrate potential for social and financial outcomes.
i. **Social Impact Funds**: These funds pool investments from multiple investors and allocate capital to social enterprises. These funds usually have a focus area or geography and provide financing, and support to social entrepreneurs.
j. **Debt Financing**: Social entrepreneurs can secure loans from banks, financial institutions, or microfinance institutions. They may need to provide collateral or demonstrate creditworthiness to access traditional debt financing.
k. **Social Venture Capital**: Social venture capital funds specialize in investing in social enterprises. These funds provide capital in exchange for equity or other forms of financial instruments. Social entrepreneurs with scalable and high-growth potential models can explore this avenue.

It's important for social entrepreneurs to identify the most appropriate funding sources based on their specific needs, stage of development, and target impact. Building relationships, networking, and showcasing the social and financial potential of their initiatives are crucial for successfully raising finance.

Impact Investing

Impact investing refers to the practice of making investments with the intention of generating positive social or environmental impact alongside financial returns. It is an approach that seeks to align financial goals with social and environmental objectives, emphasizing the idea that investments can be a force for good.

While traditional investing primarily focuses on financial returns, impact investing takes into account the broader effects of investments on society and the planet. Impact investors actively seek opportunities that address social and environmental challenges while also generating competitive financial returns. Key characteristics of impact investing include:

a. **Intentionality**: Impact investors have a clear intention to generate positive social or environmental impact through their investments. They proactively seek out opportunities that align with their impact goals.
b. **Measurable Impact**: Impact investing emphasizes the measurement and assessment of the social or environmental impact of investments. Investors aim to understand and track the outcomes and effects of their investments, using metrics and frameworks such as the UN Sustainable Development Goals (SDGs) or Environmental, Social, and Governance (ESG) criteria.
c. **Financial Returns**: Impact investments are not purely philanthropic; they also aim to generate financial returns. While the exact financial expectations may vary, impact investors seek to achieve competitive returns that are commensurate with the risk involved.
d. **Diverse Sectors**: Impact investing covers a wide range of sectors, including but not limited to renewable energy, sustainable agriculture, affordable housing, healthcare, education, clean technology, and microfinance. The focus is on sectors that address social and environmental challenges and provide sustainable solutions.
e. **Blended Finance**: Impact investors often use a blended finance approach, combining different types of capital, such as grants, debt, equity, and guarantees, to address funding gaps and attract additional investors to projects with a social or environmental impact.
f. **Collaborative Approach**: Impact investing often involves collaboration among investors, philanthropic organizations, governments, and nonprofits. By leveraging collective resources and expertise, stakeholders can create a greater impact and address complex challenges more effectively.
g. **Risk and Return Trade-off**: Impact investing recognizes that pursuing positive social or environmental impact may involve taking on additional risk or accepting potentially lower financial returns. However, impact investors aim to strike a balance where both impact and financial performance are optimized.

Impact investing has gained significant momentum in recent years as investors increasingly recognize the potential to create positive change while achieving financial goals. It offers an opportunity to channel investment capital towards addressing pressing global issues and fostering sustainable development.

Leading Impact Investment Funds in India

There are several leading impact investment funds operating in India that focus on supporting socially and environmentally responsible enterprises. Here are some prominent impact investment funds in India:

1. **Aavishkaar Group**: Aavishkaar Group is a pioneer in impact investing in India. They manage multiple funds that invest in sectors such as financial inclusion, agriculture, healthcare, clean energy, and education. Some of their funds include Aavishkaar India Micro Venture Capital Fund, Aavishkaar Bharat Fund, and Aavishkaar Frontier Fund.
2. **Elevar Equity**: Elevar Equity is an impact investment firm that focuses on investing in scalable and sustainable enterprises serving underserved communities in India and other emerging markets. They invest in sectors such as financial services, agriculture, healthcare, and education.
3. **Acumen**: Acumen is a global impact investment fund that operates in India and other countries. They invest in enterprises that provide solutions to tackle poverty, focusing on sectors like agriculture, energy, healthcare, and education. Acumen supports companies at different stages of growth and provides patient capital to drive long-term impact.
4. **Omidyar Network India**: Omidyar Network India is an impact investment firm that invests in businesses, nonprofits, and social enterprises addressing critical social challenges in India. They focus on sectors like financial inclusion, digital identity, education, property rights, and governance.
5. **Unitus Ventures:** Unitus Ventures (formerly Unitus Seed Fund) is an early-stage impact investment fund that backs startups working on sectors such as healthcare, education, fintech, and agriculture. They provide seed and early-stage capital along with mentorship and support to entrepreneurs.
6. **Ankur Capital**: Ankur Capital is an early-stage venture capital fund that invests in startups leveraging technology to address challenges in healthcare, education, agriculture, and sustainability. They support entrepreneurs driving innovation for underserved populations.
7. **Menterra Venture Advisors:** It is an impact investment fund that invests in early-stage social enterprises focusing on sectors such as education, healthcare, agriculture, and clean energy. They provide both financial and non-financial support to help enterprises scale and achieve impact.
8. **Caspian Impact Investment Adviser**: It is an impact-focused investment management company that provides debt and equity capital to enterprises addressing the needs of underserved communities. They invest in sectors like microfinance, agriculture, healthcare, and renewable energy.

These impact investment funds are actively supporting and nurturing socially and environmentally responsible enterprises in India. They play a vital role in bridging the gap between traditional financing and socially impactful ventures, driving positive change and sustainable development in the country.

Government Departments: Startups & Innovation

"An entrepreneur without funding is a musician without an instrument."
— **Robert A. Rice Jr.**

In addition to the Startup India programme, several government departments have also launched different programmes and schemes to provide the necessary boost to research, innovation, and startups in India. Startup founders can make use of schemes launched by these departments/government agencies to get financial support for their startups at an early stage when it is so crucial for both R&D and survival. Some of the initiatives by different government department are as follows:

1. **DST Scheme for Startups:** The Department of Science and Technology (DST) in India has implemented several schemes to support startups and innovation in various scientific and technological domains.
    a. **Technology Development Board (TDB)**: TDB, under the DST, supports agricultural innovation and technology development. It offers financial assistance through various schemes, such as the Seed Support Scheme and the Technology Development and Demonstration Program, to promote research, development, and commercialization of agricultural technologies.
        - **Seed Support System (SSS)**: The SSS scheme aims to support early-stage startups and innovative projects by providing financial assistance for proof-of-concept studies, prototyping, and testing in technology-intensive areas develop and commercialize innovative products or processes. It aims to bridge the gap between idea generation and commercialization.
    b. **National Initiative for Developing and Harnessing Innovations (NIDHI)**: The Innovation & Entrepreneurship division of DST, Government of India, launched an umbrella programme called NIDHI in 2016 for startups for nurturing ideas and innovations (knowledge-based and technology-driven) into successful startups. NIDHI aims to nurture start-ups through scouting, supporting, and scaling innovations. The key stakeholders of NIDHI include academic and R & D institutions, mentors, financial institutions, angel investors, VCs, and private sectors.
    Nidhi-Prayas: DST-NIDHI's PRomoting and Accelerating Young and ASpiring technology entrepreneurs (PRAYAS) is a pre-incubation initiative specifically to support young innovators to turn their ideas into proof of concept (PoC). Under this scheme support is available for both R&D of ideas and commercialization of products, especially at select Science and Technology Entrepreneurship Parks (STEPs) and Technology Business Incubators (TBIs) promoted by National Science and Technology Entrepreneurship Development Board (NSTEDB) of DST, Government of India. It is implemented through a Program Management Unit (PMU) and the incubators selected for implementing the PRAYAS progam known as the PRAYAS Centres (PCs).

2. **Biotechnology Industry Research Assistance Council (BIRAC)**: BIRAC is a public sector enterprise that supports startups and innovation in the biotechnology sector. It provides funding, mentorship, and networking opportunities through the following schemes:

    a. **Biotechnology Ignition Grant (BIG):** The BIG scheme aims to support early-stage startups and entrepreneurs in the biotechnology sector. It provides financial assistance to convert innovative ideas into proof-of-concept and prototype models. The grant covers activities, such as feasibility studies, market assessment, IP evaluation, and prototype development.
    b. **Biotechnology Ignition Scheme (BIS)**: It provides funding support to startups and entrepreneurs for establishing and scaling up biotech ventures. The scheme covers various stages, from ideation and technology validation to commercialization and market launch.
    c. **BIRAC AcE Fund:** The AcE (Accelerating Entrepreneurs) Fund is a dedicated funding program for startups in the biotechnology sector. It aims to provide financial support to high-potential startups and early-stage companies to accelerate their growth and commercialization. The fund supports activities such as product development, clinical trials, regulatory approvals, and market expansion.
    d. **BioNEST**: BioNEST is a BIRAC-supported incubation program that focuses on nurturing and supporting startups in the biotechnology domain. BioNEST provides incubation facilities, mentorship, training, networking opportunities, and access to specialized infrastructure to promote the growth and success of biotech startups.
    e. **Bioincubators**: BIRAC supports the establishment and operation of bioincubators across the country. These bioincubators provide dedicated infrastructure, technical support, and mentoring to biotechnology startups. They serve as hubs for fostering innovation, collaboration, and commercialization of biotech products and technologies.

3. **Innovation and Agri-entrepreneur development**: The Centre government's "Innovation and Agri-entrepreneur development" programme promotes innovation and agri-preneurship.

    a. **Agribusiness grants through - NIAM**: Startups and innovators receive transformational support. The selected individuals and groups participate in mentoring and coaching with technical experts, and business and thought leaders. The participants' prototype is passed through multiple technical validations, business assessments, IP, and other checks to create a feasible, viable, and scalable product ready for the market. Finally, the participants get to pitch their product to our panel of experts, and the selected startups can get incubation with a Grant-in-Aid of up to INR 25,00,000 to commercially launch their product. They are mentored to run and sustain their business, grow their market linkages & connections, and

develop a plan for scaling up. The start-ups also get field trials and pilot opportunities alongside.
   b. **Department of Agriculture, Cooperation & Farmers Welfare**: This department, provides support through various programs, including the Rashtriya Krishi Vikas Yojana (RKVY) and the Paramparagat Krishi Vikas Yojana (PKVY), which aim to enhance agricultural productivity and promote organic farming.
   c. **National Bank for Agriculture and Rural Development (NABARD)**: NABARD is a development finance institution that focuses on agriculture and rural development. It offers financial assistance and credit facilities to agricultural startups through various schemes, such as the NABARD Entrepreneurship Development Program (NEDP) and the NABARD Venture Capital Scheme.
   d. **Small Farmers' Agri-Business Consortium (SFAC)**: Supports agribusiness and startups through its equity grant and credit guarantee schemes. The Equity Grant Scheme provides financial assistance to agricultural startups and agribusiness projects, while the Credit Guarantee Scheme helps them obtain loans from banks and financial institutions.

4. **Initiatives and Grants for Defence-based Startups**

   a. **Innovations for Defence Excellence (iDEX)**: An initiative launched by the Ministry of Defence aims to achieve self-reliance and foster innovation and technology development in defence and aerospace sector. It aims to engage startups, MSMEs, and individual innovators in solving defence and security-related challenges. iDEX provides financial support, mentorship, access to defence establishments for trials, and opportunities for scaling up and showcasing products.
   b. **Technology Development Fund (TDF)**: The TDF scheme is implemented by the Defence Research and Development Organization (DRDO) and provides financial support to industries, including startups, for developing and commercializing defence technologies. The fund supports R&D projects that have the potential for significant impact on defence capabilities.
   c. **Defence Innovation Organization (DIO)**: DIO is an organization under the Ministry of Defence that supports defence startups and fosters innovation in the sector. It provides funding, mentorship, and networking opportunities to startups working on defence-related technologies.
   d. **Defence India Startup Challenge (DISC):** DISC is an initiative that invites startups to propose innovative solutions for specific defence challenges identified by the Indian Armed Forces. Shortlisted startups receive financial support, access to defence facilities for trials, and opportunities for scaling up and deployment of their solutions.
   e. **Defence Investor Cell (DIC)**: The DIC is an initiative by the Ministry of Defence to attract private investment into the defence sector, including investments in defence startups. It aims to create an enabling ecosystem

for defence startups by facilitating interactions between startups, investors, and defence industry stakeholders.

5. **Prime Minister's Employment Generation Programme (PMEGP):** PMEGP works towards providing financial assistance to startups in terms of collateral-free loans at an early stage when they neither have assets nor much revenue to raise traditional loans nor a track record to raise investment.

6. **Atal Incubation Mission (AIM):** It is a flagship program of the NITI Aayog, Government of India. The primary objective is to create a network of world-class Atal Incubation Centers (AICs) in India, to nurture and promote startups and innovative ideas. AICs are provided with financial assistance and operational support by the government and in return, they provide a conducive ecosystem for early-stage startups, offering them access to infrastructure, mentoring, funding, networking opportunities, and other support services.

7. **TIDE by MeitY:** TIDE (Technology Incubation & Development of Entrepreneurs), is an initiative by the Ministry of Electronics and Information Technology (MeitY) to support technology-based startups and entrepreneurs in the country. Under the TIDE program, technology incubation centers set up in academic institutions, research organizations, and other eligible organizations serve as a platform for startups to access infrastructure, mentoring, networking opportunities, funding support, and necessary resources. TIDE provides financial assistance to these incubation centers to establish and operate the facilities. It also supports startups in their initial stages by providing them with grants, seed funding, and access to market opportunities. The focus areas of TIDE include emerging technologies: Internet of Things (IoT), Artificial Intelligence (AI), Robotics, Augmented Reality/Virtual Reality (AR/VR), and other cutting-edge domains.

8. **Startup India Seed Fund Scheme:** It is essential to provide seed funding to startups with innovative ideas to conduct proof of concept trials. DPIIT has created Startup India Seed Fund Scheme (SISFS) with an outlay of INR 945 Crore to provide financial assistance to startups for Proof of Concept, prototype development, product trials, market-entry, and commercialization. It provides easy availability of capital for entrepreneurs at the early stages of the growth of an enterprise.

9. **State Government Schemes:** Different state governments also have special schemes and incentives for startups. Given below are some of the schemes and incentives by Government of Punjab:

Fiscal Benefits and Incentives for Incubators by Govt. of Punjab

Incentives	Extent of Incentive
Capital Subsidy	i) Govt. Host Institutes: Provided a capital grant of 100% of FCI subject to max INR 1 Cr for setting up of Incubator ii) Private Host Institutes and Stand-alone Incubators: Provided capital grant of 50% of FCI; maximum INR 50 lakhs for setting up Incubator.
Recurring Expense	All approved Incubators shall get the support for recurring reimbursement expenses as Operational Subsidy assistance up to the limit of INR 3 lakh per year for a period of 5 years
Mentoring & Training	For issues such as fundraising, scaling, recruitment and product interface, incubators shall be provided mentoring assistance support up to a limit of INR 3 lakh per year for a period of 5 years
Startup Competition	Institutes of National Importance, State Universities & Central Universities, established Incubators in these institutions supported with up to Rs.5 lakh per event.

Fiscal Benefits and Incentives for Startups by Govt. of Punjab

Incentives	Extent of Incentive
Interest Subsidy	Eligible Startups provided interest subsidy of 8% per annum for 5 years on the rate of interest paid on loans obtained from scheduled banks/financial institutions maximum limit of INR 5 lakh per annum
Lease Rental Subsidy	Reimbursement of 25% of lease rental subsidy to eligible Startups, operating from Incubators/IT Parks/Industrial Clusters/notified location for a period of 1-year subject to the ceiling of INR 3 lakh per annum.
Seed Funding	A Seed Grant up to INR 3 Lakh for validation of the idea, prototype development, assistance towards travelling costs and carrying out field/ market research/ skill training/, marketing & activities to set up Startup, etc. Seed funding routed through State/Centre recognized Incubators.
Scale up Funding	Corpus fund of INR 100 Cr dedicatedly for category I funding to meet the funding requirement for the scalability of Startups as follows: (a) Initial corpus of INR 100 Cr to be invested over a period of 5 years as the Alternative Investment Fund (AIF). (b) The Fund would not invest directly into startups but participate with capital commitment in SEBI registered Category 1 AIF, Venture Funds. (c) SIDBI would be professional fund manager for managing this Fund of Fund & would empower their empanelled VCs to fund Punjab-based Startups. (d) 10% contribution to the total corpus of the VC Fund, subject to the condition that the VC invests twice the amount contributed by the State Government in the Startups based in Punjab. The returns from the fund shall be remitted back to the FoF. These returns, along with Capital gains, shall be used to continue to fund Venture Funds.

Startups in Punjab are entitled to following incentives for MSMEs

Startups shall be entitled to the following incentives provided to MSMEs as per the Industrial and Business Development Policy 2017 of the Government of Punjab:

Nature of Incentive	Extent of Incentive
Investment subsidy by way of intra-State sale	Reimbursement of 100% of net SGST for 7 years from the date of commercial production with a cap of 100% of FCI.
Interest Subsidy on term loan in Border Districts and Kandi Area	Interest, subsidy @ 5% pa only in Border Districts and Kandi Area subject to a maximum of Rs.10 lakh per year for 3 years
Interest Subsidy on term loan to SC Entrepreneur/ Women Entrepreneur	Interest, subsidy @ 5% pa only to SC Entrepreneur/ Women Entrepreneur subject to a maximum of Rs.10 lakh per year for 3 years
Interest subsidy under Credit Linked Capital Subsidy Scheme, (CLCSS) of Ministry of MSME, GOI	Interest subsidy of 5% is subject to maximum 5 lakh per year for 3 years and shall not exceed the amount of net SGST paid during the relevant year to eligible units.
Reimbursement of guarantee fee under Collateral Free, Credit Guarantee Trust for MSME (CGTMSE) Scheme	100%, of guarantee fee to be reimbursed to micro and small enterprises subject to a maximum of Rs.1 lac
Financial assistance to SMEs for 'Emerge' exchange platform set up by NSE	To list on 'Emerge' exchange platform set up by NSE, state will provide the following incentives: - 10% of the cost of Public Issue expenses, subject to a maximum of Rs.2.50 lakh for registration of the National Stock Exchange. - Direct subscription up to 10% of the Public Issue to be provided out of corpus to be created jointly with SIDBI, Nationalized banks & the State Government subject to a maximum of Rs. 10 lakhs.
Access to Infrastructure	
Exemption from Electricity Duty	100% exemption for 7 years
Exemption/Reimbursement from Stamp Duty	100% exemption/reimbursement from stamp duty to purchase or lease of land and building
Access to Technology	
Assistance for Technology Acquisition	50% of cost subject to maximum Rs.25 lakh for technology from recognized National Institute

Additional support to the ZED scheme of GOI.	Reimbursement of 50% of expenses subject to a maximum of Rs. 5 lakh incurred on plant and machinery/testing equipment for obtaining at least silver category status under ZED scheme.
Reimbursement of expenses incurred for Energy/ Water/Safety Audit	75%, subject to maximum of Rs. 2 lakh for energy audit and maximum of Rs. 1 lac each for water and Safety Audit
Assistance for Environmental Compliance	50%, financial support subject to max of Rs.25 lakh for setting up of effluent treatment plant and for installation of Air Pollution Control Devices

Access to Market

Reimbursement of expenses incurred for patent registration	75% of expenses subject to 10 lakh for domestic patent and 20 lakh for international patent
Support for Performance and Credit Rating Scheme of Ministry of MSME	Reimbursement of 25% of the fee subject to a maximum of 10 thousands
Reimbursement of quality certifications expenses	100%, subject to a maximum of Rs. 10 lakh
Design Clinic Scheme	Reimbursement of contribution of Rs. 1 lac per program for design awareness program by National Institute of Design, Ahmedabad
Vendor Development	Program Assistance of INR 5 Cr to MSME for assisting the industry in organizing Vendor Development Programs, Buyer–Seller meets, Reverse Buyer-Seller meets.
Marketing Support	Assistance for showcasing products at local, national and international events: 1. @50% of total rent limiting to Rs. 10 lakh for participation of minimum 5 units in Punjab Pavilion in International Trade Fairs abroad 2. @25% of total rent limiting to Rs. 3 lakh for Domestic Conferences and Trade Fairs.
Freight, Assistance to Export Oriented Units	1% of FOB value or actual freight paid from the place of Manufacture to place of shipment, whichever less, maximum Rs.20 Lac per annum
Annual State Awards to MSME, SC, Women and Exporters	Annual award of Rs.3 lakh per unit for excellence in productivity, quality, export for each category.

Punjab Govt Policies to Support Startups

Name of Scheme	Name of Department	Details of Scheme/Support availed	Downloadable Links
IP Support and Facilitation	Punjab State Council for Science & Technology	Startups are being facilitated for filing of IP and Trademark Search	PSCST Notification
Entrepreneurship among Students	Department of Higher Education	Punjab State Entrepreneurship Scheme for the Universities, Colleges and Polytechnics	Higher Ed - Entrepreneurship among Students
Entrepreneurship among Students	Department of Technical Education	For State Technical Universities, Punjab State Technical Education Board & Industrial Training	Technical Ed - Entrepreneurship among Students
Purchase preference to Startups	Department of Industries & Commerce	Purchase Preference to Startups in Public Procurement (Preference to Make in Punjab) Order, 2019	Industries - Public procurement relaxations
Purchase preference to Startups	Department of Food & Civil Supplies	Purchase preference to Startups for the procurement of 30/50 kg HDPE/PP Bags	Food, Civil - Purchase preference
PUNJAB RIGHT TO BUSINESS ACT, 2020	Department of Legal and Legislative Affairs	To provide ease of doing business for newly incorporated MSME through self-declaration, exemptions, speedier approvals and inspections	Self-Declarations for SMEs - Act No. 1 of 2020 Punjab
PUNJAB BUREAU OF INVESTMENT PROMOTION (AMENDMENT) ACT, 2021	Department of Legal and Legislative Affairs	To promote the ease of doing business in the State of Punjab by way of making the process of issuance of regulatory clearances time-bound	Regulatory Clearance Timebound - 2268 dated 06.04.2021
THE PUNJAB ANTI RED TAPE ACT, 2021	Department of Legal and Legislative Affairs	To eliminate Red Tape to reduce cost and burden of compliances through simplified, trust-based procedures	Punjab Anti Red Tape Act, 2021 - 14-Leg-2021 dated 6.4.21

Startup Incubation Ecosystem

"Ideation is important for innovation. But it is only the first step! Incubation must follow and so must acceleration for the circle of innovation to reach completion, or else, you risk expiration."— **Peter-Cole C. Onele**

Startup incubation refers to a process or program designed to support and nurture the development of early-stage startups or business ideas. It typically involves a combination of mentorship, guidance, infrastructure, access to networks, and sometimes financial support.

What are Incubators?

Startup incubators are usually non-profit organizations run by both public and private entities. They are often associated with universities, business schools, private institutes, and government organizations. Business Incubators are the institution that assists entrepreneurs in developing their business and solving problems associated with them, especially in the initial stages, by providing an array of business and technical services, office space, initial seed funds, lab facilities, advisory, network, and linkages. Big brands like **Dropbox** and **Airbnb** were launched through incubator programs.

Business incubators play a vital role at very early stage of business conceptualization, and prototype development, and market validation. But they are not ideal for startups who have crossed the prototype stage and have raised some sort of funding. Business incubator usually plays the following roles:

I – Innovation & Entrepreneurship
N – Networks & Collaboration
C – Competitiveness
U – Understanding the roles (Public/ Private sector)
B – Buy-in
A – Access to Resources
T – Technologies
O – Outreach
R – Review: Monitoring & Evaluation

Startup Accelerators

Startup accelerators are programs designed to help early-stage startup companies grow and succeed. They provide entrepreneurs with resources, mentorship, funding, and a structured environment to rapidly develop their businesses. They typically operate within fixed timeframes, often ranging from three to six months, during which selected startups participate in a focused and intensive program. The key difference between startup incubator and accelerator are as follows:

Incubators v/s Accelerators

Startup Incubators	Startup Accelerators
- Assist ventures with both long-term and short-term growth. - Allow companies to grow at their own pace. - Are generally non-profit organisations. - May not be able to offer access to equity funds. - Don't promise extensive growth to ventures. - Provide services such as Office space, mentorship, networking opportunities, and business development support.	- Assist ventures for short-term growth and that too for a small duration. - Companies are under pressure to grow quickly. - Are usually for-profit organizations. - Offer access to funds and are also known as angel investors. - Promise substantial growth to ventures. - Provide services such as Mentorship, networking opportunities, access to funding, training, and education

Types of Startup Incubators

Not-for Profit Incubators

1. **Government-Supported Incubators**
   Governments sometime themselves establish incubators and provide funds to operate it. For instance:
   - **T-Hub:** The country's major incubator, T-Hub, established by the Telangana government, has incubated 346 startups till 2023. Pegged as a startup engine, T-Hub has played a crucial role in bringing entrepreneurs, venture capitalists, and mentors onto a single platform.

2. **Academic Incubators**
   Governments sometimes provide financial assistance to public or private educational institutions to set up or operate an incubator. For instance:
   - **NSRCEL:** This is one of the most well-known and oldest business incubators in India that is open to all entrepreneurs across sectors, domains, and industries. This incubator provides an ecosystem for development activities and also empowers entrepreneurs through academic research.
   - **CIIE:** One of India's leading innovation centres, IIM Ahmedabad's Centre for Innovation Incubation and Entrepreneurship (CIIE) CIIE provides significant seed-fund and incubation support to aspiring entrepreneurs in IT, cleantech, healthcare and education space.
   - **Centre for Innovation and Entrepreneurship (CIE)**: Another big tech incubator from IIIT Hyderabad, CIE, has incubated 250 startups in the last few years and is now focusing on deep tech startups to strengthen the deep tech startup ecosystem in India.

For Profit Incubators
1. **Private Incubators:**
   These incubators assist high-potential businesses (such as technology-intensive startups) and then reap benefits by selling shares. For instance:
   - **Khosla Labs:** Vinod Khosla and Srikanth Nadhamuni founded Bengaluru- based Khosla Labs, a startup incubator that focuses on startups working on financial inclusion and retail solutions.
   - **Wadhwani Centre for Entrepreneurship Development:** Set up in 2008, this initiative aims at bolstering the tech entrepreneurship in India and is headquartered in ISB Hyderabad.
2. **Corporate Incubators**:
   Corporate incubators target internal and external projects related to the activities of the company. Examples of corporate incubators are as follows:
   - **10,000 Startups:** Hosted by NASSCOM, this initiative aims to incubate, fund, and support 10,000 technology startups in India.
   - **SAP Labs India:** In 2016, SAP Labs India launched its Startup Accelerator Program to drive entrepreneurship and tech development in India.

How Private Incubators make Money?
For-profit incubators usually demand equity in the early-stage startup for their services. They have various other ways of making money, including:
- **Participation fees:** such incubators usually charge a recurring fee from participating startups to cover their costs. Even though it doesn't generate much revenue, the price helps incubators sustain themselves and the startups they support.
- **Support multiple startups**: another important thing to keep in mind is that incubators take in a cohort of early-stage startups with unlimited potential to grow. So, even if a small fraction of them succeeds in getting traction or enough market value, the incubator will get a significant return on its investment.
- **Multiple sources of revenue**: incubators, non-profit or for-profit, have numerous revenue streams coming from different sources. They don't depend on just incubation services for their profits. For example, incubators develop a lot of connections and relationships that help them generate revenue by selling their services, providing consultation, tilting the market in their favour, etc.
- **Royalties from IP commercialization or licensing:** apart from equity, some incubators also demand a percentage of earnings from startups they incubate. But, it is not very easy to earn through royalties as it involves loads of legal arrangements and cash investments. Therefore, this is not the most used revenue source for many incubators.

Top Incubators worldwide

These are the top 15 startup incubators and accelerators worldwide:
- Chinaccelerator
- Startup Wise Guys
- Buildit Accelerator
- Startup Reykjavik
- Axel Springer Accelerator
- Hatchery
- StartupYard
- AWS Activate
- Techstars, USA
- Highline Beta
- Y Combinator, USA
- Venture Catalysts
- Ignite
- Startupbootcamp
- 500 Startups

Incubators in India

India comes in the third place for the startup incubator after the US and China. There are a total of 326 incubation centres in India. Some incubators have a sectoral focus, and some are sector/industry agnostic.

Top 10 Incubators in India

Name of Incubator	location	Focus sector	Contact authority	Email	Mb
Venture catalysts	Mumbai, Delhi-NC, Kolkata, Bengaluru	Consumer internet, AI, IoT, healthcare, fintech, e-commerce,	Apoorva Sharma, Co-founder & President	info@venturecatalysts.in accounts@venturecatalysts.in	80801 73434
WE hub	Hyderabad	Women startups in tech, healthcare, education, sustainability, social impact	Meet Deepthi Ravula	info-wehub@telangana.gov.in	90592 64664
AdvantEdge Founders	Gurugram	Technology, e-commerce, consumer products and services.	Kunal Khattar, Nitin Garg	incubator@advantedge.vc	

Name	Location	Focus	Contact Person	Email	Phone
10000 Startups	Bengaluru	Software development, AI, machine learning, IoT	Mayank Kumar	startups@nasscom.in mkumar@nasscom.in	01204990111
Villgro	Chennai, Bengaluru and Mumbai.	Social enterprises, healthcare, agriculture, education, energy, livelihoods	Paul Basil, Founder & CEO	info@villgro.org	8041631523
Auto Nebula Capital Advisers	Gurugram	Automotive startups: mobility solutions, EVs, autonomous vehicle	Sanjay Puri Founder & Chairman	info@autonebula.com	98198 33740
Marwari catalysts	Ahmedabad, Gujarat	Technology, consumer products, healthcare, fintech, and e-commerce.	Sushil sharma	office@marwaricatalysts.com	96722 24441
Huddle	Bengaluru	Technology, digital media.	Sanil Sachar, Founding Partner	hello@huddle.work	
ITLC, IIT, Hyderabad	Hyderabad	AI, machine learning, robotics, biotechnology nanotechnology, clean energy	Prof. S Suryakumar Faculty In Charge	contact@itic.iith.ac.in	93983 23668
CIIE	Ahmedabad	Technology, healthcare, education, energy, agriculture, social impact.	Kunal Upadhyay	info@ciie.co	7971524201

Atal Innovation Mission (AIM):

AIM supports the establishment of new incubation centres called Atal incubation centres that nurture innovative start-up businesses in their pursuit to become scalable enterprises. The AICs aspire to create world-class incubation facilities across various parts of India with suitable physical infrastructure in terms of independent and operating facilities, coupled with the availability of sectoral experts for mentoring the startups, business planning support, access to seed capital, industry partners, and other relevant components required for encouraging innovative startups.

Currently, HEIs, R&D institutes, the corporate sector's alternative investment funds (AIF) registered with SEBI, business accelerators, groups of individuals, and individuals are eligible to apply for the AIM programme. AIM provides a grant-in-aid of up to Rs.10 crores for a maximum period of 5 years to AICs and 3 years to the EICs (Established Incubation centres) for scale-up to cover capital and operational expenditures required to establish the AIC.

Select Atal Incubation Centers

- AIC @36INC Society
- AIC Aartech Solonics Pvt. Ltd.
- AIC AAU Incubator
- AIC ADT Baramati Foundation
- AIC Ambedkar University Delhi Foundation
- AIC AMTZ MediValley Incubation Council
- AIC AU Incubation Foundation
- AIC BAMU Foundation
- AIC BANASTHALI VIDYAPITH FOUNDATION
- AIC BIMTECH
- AIC BV Foundation
- AIC Catalyst
- AIC CCRI Foundation for Entrepreneurship Development
- AIC Centre for Cellular & Molecular Biology
- AIC CODISSIA Defence Innovation and Atal Incubation Centre
- AIC CV Raman College of Engineering Foundation
- AIC DSU Innovation Foundation
- AIC EMPI Incubation Foundation
- AIC Foundation for Innovation and Social Entrepreneurship
- AIC GIM Foundation
- AIC GISC Foundation
- AIC Great Lakes Balachandran Incubator
- AIC GUSEC
- AIC IIIT KOTTAYAM FOUNDATION
- AIC IIITH FOUNDATION

- AIC IISER PUNE SEED FOUNDATION
- AIC IIT DELHI SONIPAT INNOVATION FOUNDATION
- AIC ISB Association
- AIC ISE Foundation
- AIC Jammu and Kashmir EDI
- AIC Jawaharlal Nehru University Foundation For Innovation
- AIC JKLU (Atal incubation center- JK Lakshmipat University
- AIC Jyothy Institute of Technology Foundation (AIC-JITF)
- AIC LMCP Foundation
- AIC Mahamana Foundation for Innovation and Entrepreneurship - IM-BHU
- AIC MCU Samvaad Bharati Foundation
- AIC-MIT ADT Incubator Forum
- AIC MUJ Incubation Foundation
- AIC Nalanda Institute of Technology Foundation
- AIC NCore Developmental Impact Foundation
- AIC NIFT TEA Incubation Centre for Textiles and Apparels
- AIC NITTE Incubation Centre
- AIC NMIMS Incubation Centre
- AIC Pinnacle Entrepreneurship Forum
- AIC Pondicherry Engineering College Foundation
- AIC Prestige Inspire Foundation
- AIC RAISE BUSINESS INCUBATOR
- AIC Rambhau Mhalgi Prabodhini Foundation
- AIC RNTU Foundation
- AIC Sangam Innovation Foundation
- AIC SELCO Foundation
- AIC Shiksha Infotech Foundation
- AIC Shiv Nadar Research Foundation
- AIC SKU Confederation
- AIC SMU Technology Business Incubation Foundation
- AIC SRS-ICAR-NDRI Foundation
- AIC STPINEXT INITIATIVES
- AIC SURATi iLAB FOUNDATION
- AIC T Hub foundations

For a detailed list of Incubator across India, startup founders visit the following link to identify the AIC, which could be best aligned to their needs:
https://aim.gov.in/selected-atal.php

National Science & Technology Entrepreneurship Development Board (NSTEDB)

The DST, Government of India, established the NSTEDB as an institutional mechanism to help promote knowledge driven and technology-intensive enterprises through Science, Technology & Innovation (ST&I) interventions.
The board paid out ₹200 Crore ($26.2 Million) in 2022-23, and about ₹1000 Crore ($131 Million) had been out paid since the inception of the board. The programs were redesigned and relaunched in 2016 under NIDHI umbrella, NSTEDB's flagship programme for nurturing ideas and innovations into successful startups by further strengthening the Incubators through TBI program in realising the Startup India dream along with the augmented funding, fabrication facilities, prototyping grants and fellowships.

NIDHI Programme at Technology Business Incubators (TBI)

While NSTEDB is the funding agency, the NIDHI programmes are implemented through Technology Business Incubators (TBIs) available around the country.
TBIs are incubation centers that provide infrastructure, mentorship, networking opportunities, and other support services to technology-based startups. TBIs have seen significant growth in India over the years. They are typically associated with academic institutions, research organizations, or industry bodies. TBIs have gained prominence across India, particularly in major cities and technology hubs such as Bangalore, Mumbai, Pune, Chennai, Hyderabad, and Delhi. These regions have a higher concentration of TBIs due to the presence of renowned educational institutions and vibrant startup ecosystems.
Detailed list of TBI across India is available by clicking the following link. Startup founders can identify, which of these TBIs could be best aligned to their needs: https://www.indiascienceandtechnology.gov.in/listingpage/consolidated-list-tbis

All the NIDHI-Startup Funds are disbursed to eligible startups only through eligible NSTEDB-linked incubators across India through following initiative:
- **NIDHI-TBI**
- **NIDHI-SSS**
- **NIDHI- PRAYAS**: It provides support to validate and prototype innovative ideas. It offers financial assistance to innovators to build proof-of-concept and prototype models of their ideas and technologies.
- **NIDHI-ACCELERATOR**
- **NIDHI-CoE**
- **NIDHI-EIR**

Science and Technology Entrepreneurs Parks (STEP)

STEP is an initiative by the DST in India. These parks provide a platform for nurturing innovation, technology transfer, and entrepreneurship. They offer facilities, services, and resources to startups and early-stage technology-based ventures. STEP initiatives are spread across various states in India, with a focus on creating regional hubs for innovation and entrepreneurship. The parks are often located in close proximity to academic institutions, research centers, or industrial clusters.

STEP programme was initiated to provide a re-orientation in the approach to innovation and entrepreneurship involving education, training, research, finance, management, and the government. A STEP creates the necessary climate for innovation, information exchange, sharing of experience and facilities, and opening new avenues for students, teachers, researchers, and industrial managers to grow in a trans-disciplinary culture, each understanding and depending on the other's inputs for starting a successful economic venture. STEPs are hardware intensive with an emphasis on common facilities, services, and relevant equipment.

The major objectives of STEP are to forge linkages among academic and R&D institutions on the one hand and the industry on the other and promote innovative enterprise through S&T persons. STEPs offer the following facilities:

- Testing and calibration facilities, precision tool room/central workshop, prototype development, business facilitation, computing, data bank, library and documentation, communication, seminar hall/conference room, common facilities such as phone, telex, fax, photocopying. It offers services like testing and calibration, and consultancy.
- Training, technical support services, business facilitation services, database and documentation services, quality assurance services, and utility services.

The department has so far catalysed 15 STEPs in different parts of the country, which have promoted nearly 788 units generating an annual turnover of around Rs. 130 crores and employment for 5000 persons. More than 100 new products and technologies have been developed by the STEPs / STEP promoted entrepreneurs. In addition, over 11000 persons have been trained through various skill development programmes conducted by STEPs. STEPs are autonomous bodies registered as societies under the Societies Registration Act.

STEP is promoted around a host institution that could launch, sustain, and help the STEP grow. The host institution should aim at optimum usage of its facility by STEP. Each STEP is expected to carve out a niche for itself regarding the types of products to be developed based on the availability of facilities and expertise in the host institution and the industrial climate of the region. Each project envisages active involvement and participation of agencies such as the host institution, the ultimate user of the facilities, financial institutions, government agencies, and STEP management.

List of STEPs in Institutions

Amity Innovation Incubator
E-3 Block, Ist Floor, Sector 125,
Amity University Campus, Noida
Ph: 0120-4659000/4392243, Email: info@aii.amity.edu

Society for Development of Composites
Composites Technology Park
205, Bande Mutt, Kengeri Satellite Township,
Bangalore -560060
Phone: +91 080 6599 7605, 65581005, 28482771
Email: drgopalan2003@yahoo.com

Technopark – Technology Business Incubator
Trivandrum 695 581
Ph: +91-471-2700222, E-Mail: response@technopark.org

Society for Innovation and Entrepreneurship
Indian Institute of Technology-Bombay
Powai, Mumbai 400 076
Phone: (+91 22) 2576 7072/ 7016, Email: sine@sineiitb.org

Vellore Institute of Technology (VITTBI)
Vellore – 632014
Phone: +91 0416 2202020, Email: outreach.vlr@vit.ac.in

Technology Business Incubator –
University of Madras
Taramani campus, Chepauk, Chennai 600113.
Tel: 044-24540038/9840597373
Email: tbi_unom@yahoo.com, tbi@unom.ac.in

Rural Technology & Business Incubator
Indian Institute of Technology Madras
Chennai 600036
Tel: 044-66469872
Email: suma@rtbi.in, rtbioffice@tenet.res.in

Technology Business Incubator
Bannari Amman Institute of Technology
Sathyamangalam – 638 401.
Phone :- 04295-226321, Email: bit-tbi@bitsathy.ac.in

Periyar Technology Business Incubator
Periyar Maniammai College of Technology for Women, Periyar Nagar,
Vallam-613 403, Thanjavur
Phone:9500997938
E-mail: info@periyartbi.org; ap_aruna@yahoo.co.in

JSSATE – Science and Technology Entrepreneurs' Park
J.S.S. Academy of Technical Education,
C-20/1, Sector-62, Noida-201301, (U.P).
Phone: 08447508727, Email: info@jssstepnoida.org

Krishna Path Incubation Society Krishna Institute of Engineering & Technology 13 KM Stone, Ghaziabad – Meerut Road, Ghaziabad Tel: 09873816176, Email: tbikiet@gmail.com
Entrepreneurship Development Center, NCL Innovation Park, National Chemical Laboratory, Pune-411008 Phone: +91-20-2590-2984/85/86 Email: v.premnath@ncl.res.in,
SJCE – STEP S.J. College of Engineering, Mysore – 570 006 Phone: 0821- 2548286/85, E-mail: enquire@jssstuniv.in
Centre for Innovation Incubation & Entrepreneurship (CIIE) Indian Institute of Management, Vastrapur Ahmedabad 380015 Phone: 079-66324201,079-71524201, Email: write@ciie.co
NITK – Science & Technology Entrepreneurs Park National Institute of Technology – Karnataka, Surathkal - 575025 P.O. Srinivasa Nagar D.K. District. Phone: 0824 2475490, 2475490 E-mail: step@nitk.edu.in
Basaveshwar Engineering College Science & Technology Entrepreneurs Park (BEC-STEP), STEP Road, Behind BTDA Campus, Bagalkot – 587102 Phone: 9740406516, 9448534067, E-mail: mmbecstep@yahoo.com
Science and Technology Park University of Pune, Pune – 411007 Phone: 20 25699206/996000063 E-mail: stp@scitechpark.org.in
Science & Technology Entrepreneurs Park – Thapar Thapar University, Patiala -147001 Punjab Phone: 7025235498. E-mail: manager_step@thapar.edu
TREC-STEP, NIT Campus Tiruchirappalli 620015 Phone: 04312500085, Email: edufeveroutreach@gmail.com
PSG-STEP PSG College of Technology, Peelamedu Coimbatore 641004 Tamil nadu Phone: 04222572177,2572477, Email: acs@psgtech.ac.in
STEP – Indian Institute of Technology, Kharagpur – 721 302. Phone: 03222-281091, 278618, E-mail: mdstep@hijli.iitkgp.ernet.in,
STEP – Guru Nanak College of Engineering, Ludhiana – 141 006 Phone: 7837100954, 9781746007, E-mail: step.gne@gmail.com

NewGen Innovation and Entrepreneurship Development Centre (NewGen IEDC)

The NewGen IEDC scheme promotes innovation and entrepreneurship among students by setting up entrepreneurship development centers in academic institutions. It provides financial support, training programs, mentorship, and resources to encourage students to develop innovative ideas and start ventures.

Incubators at Delhi

Incubator	Address	Focus	Authority	Email	Telephone
Startup Tunnel	A-18, FIEE Complex, Okhla Indl Area, Ph-II, New Delhi	Multi-sectoral (Early-stage startups)	Mr. Anand Kapoor	info@startup-tunnel.com	011-49424040
JSS Technology Incubation Center (TIC)	C-20/1, Sector-62, Noida	Technology and Engineering	Dr. Sanjay Yadav	director@jssstunoida.org	0120-2401293
T-Hub	DLF Cyber City, Phase 3, Sector 24, Gurugram	Technology, Healthcare, Smart Cities	Mr. Ravi Narayan	info@t-hub.co	040-23101452
Atal Incubation Centre (AIC)	Rajiv Gandhi Education City, Kundli, Sonipat		Mr. Deepak Bagla	deepak.bagla@aicrgec.org	011-22717595

Incubators in the State of Punjab & Chandigarh

Name	Location	Focus/ Sector Agnostic	Contact Authority	Email	Tel.
Punjab State E-Governance Society Incubation Center	Mohali	Information Technology and E-Governance	Mr. Rahul Bhandari	rahul.bhandari@punjab.gov.in	01722237052
TBI- IISER	Mohali	Scientific research and innovation	Satyendra Choudhary CEO	ceotbi@iisermohali.ac.in,	01722240266
Chitkara University Innovation Incubator	Rajpura	Student startups	Dr. Adarsh Aggarwal, Dr. Neeraj, Incubation Manager	adarsh.kumar@chitkara.edu.in neeraj.kumar@chitkarauniversity.edu.in	

Venture Lab, Thapar Institute of Engineering & Technology	Patiala		Dr. Karminder, Chief Coordinator Dr. Mandeep Singh, Coordinator Mr. Rahul Sharma, Manager	manager_step@thapar.edu	9799777370
Punjab Agri-Business Incubator (PABI)	Ludhiana	Agriculture and Agri-Business	Dr. S.S. Singh	pabi@pau.edu pabi.ludhiana@pau.edu	01612401960 0161-2414019
PAU	Ludhiana	Food Industry	Dr Poonam Aggarwal Sachdev	hodfst@pau.edu	01612407309
PCTE Group of Institutes Baddowal	Ludhiana			info@pcte.edu.in	01612888500
STPI	Mohali	AI/Data Analytics, IoT & AVG in Agriculture, Healthcare, Finance, Education & Logistics	Ajay. P. Shrivastava	nitin.agrawal@stpi.in, ajay.shrivastava@stpi.in	0172 223 6215
Punjab Biotechnology Incubator	Mohali	Agri, Food, Environment, Biotechnology and Life Sciences and Allied Sectors	Dr. Ajit Dua, EO. Dr Simranpreet Kaur, Scientist, Dr. S.S. Marwaha	ceo.dst.sasn@punjab.gov.in ajit.dua325@punjab.gov.in pmc.pbti.dst@punjab.gov.in	0172 502 0893
Baba Farid Group of Institutions	Bathinda	innovation and entrepreneurship	Dr. Manish Gupta, Mrs. Iqbalpreet Kaur Sidhu Incubation Manager	deanrd@babafaridgroup.com, soe@babafaridgroup.edu.in	9501117069
INST	Mohali	Nanoscience & Nanotech	Dr. Kiran Shankar Hazra	director@inst.ac.in	0172 221 0075
LPU Startup School	Jalandhar		Dr. Suarabh Lakhpal	saurabh.lakhpal@lpu.co.in info@lpu.co.in startupschool@lpu.co.in	01824-517000 01824-404404

Name	Location	Focus	Contact Person	Email	Phone
Innovation & Entrepreneurship Development Campus	Fatehgarh Sahib		HoD	manpreet.arora@bbsbec.ac.in	
Wotta Work Spac	Mohali		Mr. Navneet Brar	navneetbrar@gmail.com	09501340429
MBCIE Incubation Centre	Ludhiana		Dr. Prem Kumar	info@mbcie.org	90419-90400 01613500624
Entrepreneurship Development & Innovation Institute (EDII)	Amritsar	Technology, Manufacturing, Agriculture, and Services	Dr. R.P. Saini	director.teri@dauniv.ac.in	+91-183-2400812
Punjab Technical University (PTU) Incubation center	Jalandhar	Technology and Engineering	Er. Navdeepak Sandhu Deputy Director (CR&A) Mr. Mrigender Bedi, Assistant Director (CR&A)	navdeepak.sandhu@ptu.ac.in, msbedi@ptu.ac.in directoriiic@ptu.ac.in	9478098040 9478098076 01822-662521
Indian School of Business (ISB) Mohali Campus	Mohali	Healthcare, Agritech, Manufacturing, Infrastructure, New Venture in Family Business, Acceleration, Research			0172 459 0000
Chandigarh University Technology Business Incubator (CUTBI)	SCO 223, Sector 36, Chandigarh	Technology and Engineering	Dr. S.S. Walia	directorcutbi@cumail.in	99159-99244
Government Medical College and Hospital Innovation Centre	Government Hospital, Sec 32, Chandigarh	Healthcare and Medical Technology	Dr. G.D. Puri	gmc-principal@nic.in	0172-260102

How Business Incubation Works

The process of business incubation typically involves several stages:
1. **Application**: Startups apply to a business incubator program by submitting an application and business plan. Some incubators have selective application criteria, while others may have a broader range of eligibility criteria.
2. **Screening**: The incubator reviews the application and business plan to determine if the startup is a good fit for the program. The screening process may involve an interview or presentation by the startup.
3. **Incubation**: Once accepted into the program, the startup works with the incubator to develop and execute its business plan. The incubator provides the startup with access to resources, mentorship, and other support services to help them achieve their goals.
4. **Graduation**: Once the startup has achieved its goals and is ready to operate independently, it graduates from the program. Graduation typically involves leaving the incubator's physical space and resources but may still involve ongoing mentorship and networking opportunities.

Costs and Revenue of the Incubators:

COSTS	REVENUE
Infrastructure	Incubation fees
Staffing	Sponsorships –grants
Services and resources	Events
Operational	Equity stake
	Alumni support

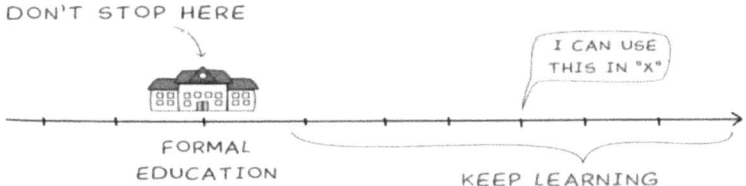

GIFT City Gujarat

"The bottom line is that it's much more difficult to find out what they're investing in once they're offshore," - **Thomas Gober, a financial fraud examiner**.

Gift City (Gujarat International Finance Tec-City) a special economic zone and an international financial services center located near Gandhinagar in Gujarat, India the first operational greenfield project of the Indian Government. It is designed to be a global financial hub rivalling premier international financial zones such as La Defense, London Dockyards, Shinjuku, Lujiazui etc. with an aim to bring in international investment and boost employment opportunities.

The project spread over 886 acres would house multi-national banks, fintech entities, two international stock exchanges as well as India's first international bullion exchange. With 67% of the total area being utilized for commercial activities and rest being taken up for residential and social projects, this project is expected to make a significant contribution to the Indian economy. It has been designed to provide a favourable business environment for various sectors, including startups. The salient features of this project lie in the incentives being offered to institutions set to operate from its two zones classified as the SEZ and Non-SEZ area. GIFT SEZ India's first International Financial Services Centre (IFSC) under Special Economic Zone Act, 2005 ("SEZ Act 2005"), which was notified in 2013 was approved as SEZ in 2017, as a deemed foreign territory. It is to India, similar to what Hong Kong is to China, but not like Dubai or Singapore. It gives corporates freedom to operate as in a foreign country, but the individuals pay taxes under domestic Income Tax laws.

A. **Special Economic Zone (SEZ)**
   The focus is to welcome international companies by providing tax exemptions, duty-free imports and exports along with streamlined and lucid regulatory procedures. Amassing 261 acres of the total 886, it serves as the focus of the GIFT city. It's further bifurcated into SEZ PA (Processing Area) and SEZ NPA (Non-Processing Area).
   a. **SEZ PA**: The heart of it being the IFSC (International Financial Services Centre), which offers state-of-the-art infrastructure, tax and other benefits:
      - Stamp duty & registration/conversion fee exemption
      - Construction subsidy of Rs. 300 per Sq. Ft. of built-up area for vertical IT/ITeS Parks
      - Reimbursement of PF contribution by employer
      - Lease Rental Subsidy – Rs. 3 to Rs. 8 per Sq. Ft. per month
      - The fiscal incentive support under CAPEX-OPEX model to IT/ITeS units can be found in detail on the official site of GIFT City; therein details on the Employment Generation Incentive, Interest Assistance, Atmanirbhar Gujarat Rojgar Sahay and Electricity Duty Incentive can also be found in greater depth on the website.

b. **SEZ NPA –** This area is intended to be utilized for the upkeep of businesses operating in the SEZ PA.
B. **Non-SEZ area (also known as the Domestic Tariff area or the DTA):** Institutions set to operate in this area will cater to the domestic milieu and will come under the bailiwick of Indian laws and regulations. However, to entice and bolster the local leaders, tax incentives have been rolled out generously.

Benefits of Gift City for Startups

Here are some ways in which Gift City can be helpful to startups:
1. **Infrastructure and Connectivity**: Gift City offers state-of-the-art infrastructure and connectivity, including high-speed internet, reliable power supply, and modern office spaces. Certified TIER IV Green Data centre by Tata Communications with a capacity of 900 Racks. These facilities would enable startups to establish their operations in a conducive environment with access to necessary facilities and resources. C-4 (City Command & Control Centre) would use IoT (Internet of Things) to monitor and manage city infrastructure.
2. **Regulatory Benefits**: Startups operating in Gift City can benefit from various regulatory advantages. These include relaxed foreign investment regulations, simplified company registration procedures, and tax incentives. The regulatory framework in Gift City is designed to promote ease of doing business and attract investment.
3. **Access to Capital**: Gift City aims to be a vibrant financial services hub, attracting global banks, financial institutions, and investment firms. This provides startups with increased opportunities for fundraising, venture capital investments, and access to a diverse range of financial services. The project shall open India to foreign investments in a manner that has not been done so far. The recent SVB failure has allowed for a feasible investing opportunity in the GIFT City with around $200 million already being diverted and hopes for more are high.
4. **International Exposure**: Gift City aims to position itself as a global financial center, attracting international businesses and fostering collaborations. Startups in Gift City can benefit from exposure to global markets, networking opportunities with international firms, and access to a diverse talent pool. Bringing international & local institutions on playfield set for fair competition.
5. **Regulatory Sandbox**: Gift City has established a regulatory sandbox that allows startups to test their innovative financial products and services in a controlled environment. This enables startups to experiment and refine their offerings before launching them in the market, reducing regulatory barriers and promoting innovation.
6. **Supportive Ecosystem**: Gift City has developed a supportive ecosystem comprising incubators, accelerators, mentorship programs, and industry associations. Startups can benefit from these resources to gain guidance, mentorship, and networking opportunities, which can accelerate their growth and increase their chances of success. Collectively, it can provide additional fillip to export of goods and services.

Gift City offers a business-friendly ecosystem with favourable regulatory policies, robust infrastructure, access to capital, and international exposure. These factors can provide startups with a competitive edge and create an environment conducive to their growth and success.

Benefits for Startups:

a. GIFT City IFSC acts as an international bank, regulated by RBI, SEBI, PFRDA and IRDAI
b. Startups can bring funds to India without having to convert the same in INR and losing out on currency conversion (i.e., keeping the USD amount intact as it is) and can repatriate and transfer those funds back to the US.
c. There is no tax or filing obligation for the startups with GIFT City account.
d. Indian startups may start housing their operations within GIFT City, rather than Mauritius and Singapore as the government's notification has not exempted investments from countries like Singapore, the Netherlands, Mauritius, and UAE from the angel tax levy. Foreign capital inflow into Indian startups has been growing from these countries in recent times.
e. Multiple Indian startups affected/feeling threat on account of the collapse of Silicon Valley Bank (SVB) in US have started opening accounts with banks having IFSC Banking Unit (IBU) in GIFT City. About $200 million of the $1 billion funds held by Indian startups in Silicon Valley Bank (SVB) were transferred to GIFT City, after the collapse of SVB.
f. Fund management is another financial service that is hosted in GIFT City. Based on the category of license held by the Fund Management Entity (FME), it can launch any of the following schemes at the IFSC that can be useful for startups.
    Venture Capital Scheme
    Restricted Schemes (Non-Retail Schemes) offered under a private placement.
    Retail Schemes of a minimum size over $ 5 million.
    Special Situation Funds
g. To promote innovation of ideas and solutions in financial services market, IFSC also introduced dedicated FinTech sandboxes. DPIIT recognised FinTech startups and other entities can operate in the regulatory sandbox of GIFT City. The sandbox provides a live environment with a limited set of real customers for a limited timeframe. The sandboxes offered to FinTech entities are:

    - IFSCA FinTech Regulatory Sandbox
    - IFSCA FinTech Innovation Sandbox
    - Inter- Operable Regulatory Sandbox
    - Overseas Regulatory Referral mechanism

h. **Tax benefits of GIFT City:** To attract businesses to GIFT City, the Government of India has introduced following direct and indirect tax benefits:

i. **Direct Tax**

- 100 per cent tax exemption for 10 consecutive years out of 15 years.
- Minimum Alternate Tax (MAT) at 9% of book profits of company setup as a unit in IFSC. No MAT if the company opts for new tax regime.
- Dividend received by a non-resident or a foreign company from an IFSC unit will be taxable at a rate of 10 per cent.
- Tax-neutral relocation of offshore funds to GIFT City for fund transfer taking place before 31 March 2025.

ii. **Indirect Tax**

- No GST on services exchanged in IFSC, received by a unit in IFSC or services provided from GIFT City to India.
- State subsidies on lease rental, provident fund contributions, and electricity charged.
- Exemption for investors on Securities Transaction Tax, Commodities Transaction Tax, and stamp duty in respect of transactions carried out on IFSC exchanges.

Administration and Management of GIFT City

The government of Gujarat formed "Gujarat International Finance Tec-City Company Limited (GIFTCL)" to develop and implement GIFT City through its venture Gujarat Urban Development Company Limited (GUDCL). For the purpose of implementation of the SEZ, GIFT Company Limited has set up an SPV (Special Purpose Vehicle) (100% subsidiary of GIFTCL) namely GIFT SEZ Ltd, designated as the developer organization of the SEZ. GIFTCL has also set up 5 subsidiary companies for the implementation of specialized infrastructure including power, water, ICT (Information & Communication Technology), district cooling, and solid waste management.

GIFT City: Current Status

- Since, February 2014, when allotment letters were presented to State Bank of India, US-based World Trade Centre, Tata Communications, I-Plex and Global Group for investing Rs 1,000 crore in the project. GIFT City had 200 companies, India International Bullion Exchange inaugurated in 2022, two international stock exchanges, Aircraft leasing firms, alternative investment fund, banks, broker dealers, clearing corporations, insurance and reinsurance companies, qualified jewellers, ship leasing firms, and IT services among others operating from there by employing 20,000 individuals till June 2023 in companies like JPMorgan Chase & Co., Deutsche Bank AG, Bank of America, and HSBC Holdings Plc.
- GIFT City has a committed investment of Rs.14,500 crore, which is based on the sale of development rights in the project where land is given on a 99-year

lease to investors. The total developable area is 44 million square feet (existing), of which 24 million square feet has already been allotted by June 2023. Around 50 % of land under GIFT Company's ownership has been allotted for development. Since the beginning of construction of first building "Gift One" in 2010, four million square feet (16 buildings) have already been built by July 2023 while 27 additional buildings accounting for roughly 9-10 million square feet were under construction, which are expected to be ready by 2026. The remaining 10 million square feet is under planning.

- In a first cross-border initiative in connecting India and Singapore's capital markets, international investors can now trade through Singapore Exchange (SGX Group) in Nifty from GIFT City from July 3, 2023. SGX Group will provide international access to USD-denominated Nifty contracts, renamed GIFT Nifty, as well as other SGX derivatives products.
- In October 2022 average daily turnover on the two stock exchanges in the GIFT city climbed to $14.6 billion, from $3.4 billion in 2020. Cumulative derivative transactions by banks jumped to $466 billion in 2022, from $22 billion, and cumulative banking transactions rose to $303 billion, from $45 billion in 2020.
- In June 2023, Google announced setting up Global Fintech Operation Centre at GIFT City. The investment comes from the Google's $10 Bn India Digitisation Fund, which has been deployed to invest in tech, telecom and startups in India.
- Australia-based Deakin and Wollongong Universities announced setting up campuses at GIFT City and the beginning of operations from June 2024.
- Presenting the Union Budget 2022-23, Finance Minister Nirmala Sitharaman announced the setting up of an International Arbitration Centre at GIFT city.
- Around 4,500 residential units are currently being built in GIFT City and till July 2023 most of the residential projects were under construction and were yet to be occupied.
- In a first major expansion since GIFT city was conceptualised in 2007 by Government of Gujarat and approved and approved by Government of India in 2008, GIFT city will expand by roughly 2,300 acres. This will expand the project area to more than thrice its existing size, from 1,065 acres to approximately 3,365 acres. The expanded area will not be under the ownership of GIFT Company Ltd but would be developed by private developers in line with GIFT city.

GIFT City: Challenges

The following aspects are holding it back from becoming a buzzing global urban hub:
- Subdued quality of social life for executives and employees because of lack of infrastructure for social, health, educational and recreational activities
- Lack of incentives for C-suite executives to relocate to GIFT city. Under the SEZ Act, there are benefits given to entities, but there is no scheme for individuals. Indians individual earning in foreign exchange from multinational

operations have to pay very high taxes creating reluctance to shift to GIFT City.
- ❖ The restrictions on foreign exchange movement from GIFT-IFSC to abroad for those employed here and earning in dollars.
- ❖ Prohibition regarding buying and consuming alcohol.

What is Startup Finance?

"Never take your eyes off the cash flow because it's the lifeblood of business."—
Sir Richard Branson, business magnate, investor, & author

Entrepreneurial finance refers to the specific area of finance that focuses on the financial decisions and strategies involved in starting, managing, and growing a startup. It encompasses the financial activities and considerations unique to entrepreneurs and startup companies, which involve the process of financial planning, budgeting, forecasting, fundraising, managing financial resources, and risk management, funding from investors, banks, and financial institutions.

It involves an understanding of various financial instruments used to raise capital, such as equity, debt, and hybrid securities, as well as understanding the trade-offs between different types of financing and selecting the most appropriate option for a given business situation. By mastering the principles of entrepreneurial finance, entrepreneurs can optimize their financial strategies and increase the likelihood of success for their businesses. It involves various aspects, including:

1. **Financial Planning**: This involves creating a financial roadmap for the business, including estimating startup costs, projecting future revenues and expenses, and determining the financial viability of the venture.
   Use of Financial Planning for Ventures
   - Good representation essential *(sense checking)*
   - Budgeting *(planning)*
   - Operations management *(cost control)*
   - Reporting *(accountability to shareholders)*
   - Performance-based management *(doing the right things)*
   - Valuation *(getting investors in / selling the company)*
2. **Capital Acquisition**: It deals with raising funds to finance the business venture. Entrepreneurs may seek capital from different sources, such as personal savings, friends and family, through crowdfunding platforms, then from incubators and subsequently from angel investors, then private equity investors for viability gap funding before approaching venture capitalists and finally launching an IPO.
3. **Financial Management**: Entrepreneurs need to effectively manage their financial resources to ensure the venture's success. This includes budgeting, cash flow management, financial reporting, and monitoring key financial metrics: Cost of Capital, and Capital Structure.
4. **Risk Assessment and Management**: Entrepreneurs face various financial risks, such as market uncertainty, competition, and cash flow fluctuations. Understanding and managing these risks is crucial for sustainable growth and long-term success.
5. **Valuation and Exit Strategies**: Entrepreneurs often need to assess the value of their venture for investment purposes or a potential exit.

How is Startup Finance different from Small Business or Corporate Finance?

Entrepreneurial finance, small business finance, and corporate finance are three distinct areas of finance that differ in their focus and application. Here are the key differences between these three fields.

	Startup Finance	**Small Business Finance**	**Corporate Finance**
Scope and Objectives	It focuses on financial aspects of starting, growing, and managing new ventures or startups. The primary objective is to secure funding and resources to launch and scale innovative business.	Financial management of SMEs. The focus is on day-to-day operations, cash flow management, working capital, and growth strategies tailored to the specific needs of small businesses.	Financial management of large organizations. The key objectives: maximizing shareholder value, managing capital structure, investment decisions, and assessing financial health of a company.
Sources of Financing	Entrepreneurs often rely on personal savings, bootstrapping, angel investors, venture capital, crowdfunding, or government grants to fund their startups. They typically face higher risk and limited access to traditional financing.	Small businesses may obtain financing through traditional bank loans, lines of credit, trade credit, equipment leasing, or alternative financing options. They have better track record and collateral to secure funding compared to startups	Established corporations have access to a wide range of financing options: bank loans, bonds, public equity offerings, private placements, retained earnings, and have relationships with financial institutions
Risk and Return Profile	They are risky ventures, with a higher likelihood of failure. Investors seek high returns for taking on risk, as successful startups can offer high profitability and growth potential.	They have lower risk compared to startups but face uncertainties. Investors expect moderate returns, often with a focus on stable cash flows and sustainable growth.	Corporations offer a stable risk profile, with predictable cash flows and a proven business model. Investors seek lower but more consistent returns over time
Decision-Making Processes	Rapid decision-making due to the dynamic and uncertain nature of their environment. Financial decisions are closely linked to strategic choices: product development, market-entry, and scaling plans.	Decision-making involves a mix of operational and financial considerations. It includes managing cash flow, budgeting, controlling costs, and evaluating investment opportunities based on available resources.	Decision-making involves board members, and executives. Focuses on optimizing the allocation of resources, evaluating capital projects, and ensuring financial transparency and compliance.

While there may be overlaps and similarities between these areas, understanding distinctions can help entrepreneurs apply the most relevant financial strategies.

Financial Skills an Entrepreneur Needs

"The accrual method would show the company to be bigger and more profitable than it would appear using the cash method." — **Steven Rogers**

Understanding of finance-related skills is essential for an entrepreneur for managing the financial aspects of their business effectively. Here are some key finance-related skills that entrepreneurs should possess or develop:

1. **Financial Literacy**: It's crucial to understand financial concepts, such as revenue, expenses, profit and loss, cash flow, balance sheets, and financial statements. This knowledge about Return on Investment (RoI), Return on Capital Employed (ROCE) forms the foundation for making informed financial decisions.
2. **Budgeting and Financial Planning**: Being able to create and manage budgets is essential for allocating resources effectively, controlling costs, and forecasting future financial needs. Developing financial projections and planning for different scenarios can help guide your business's growth strategy. Knowing how to budget and spend money wisely is critical to the success of a business in both the short and long term.
3. **Cash Flow Management**: Understanding and managing cash flow is vital for the survival and growth of any business. Entrepreneurs need to monitor their cash inflows and outflows, ensure sufficient working capital, and implement strategies to optimize cash flow, such as managing receivables and payables.
4. **Financial Analysis**: The ability to analyze financial data and make informed decisions based on it is crucial. Entrepreneurs should be able to interpret financial statements, perform ratio analysis, evaluate investment opportunities, and assess the financial health and performance of their businesses.
5. **Funding and Financing**: When starting a company, entrepreneurs dedicate the majority of their time to securing the funding to make their vision a reality. This involves approaching investors and seeking loans that can allow them to launch operations and acquire resources. Funding may be provided by friends, family, venture capitalists, angel investors, banks, and other sources. Entrepreneurs should be aware of the different funding options available to them and be able to assess which options are most suitable for their business. This includes understanding the pros and cons of equity financing, debt financing, grants, and other sources of capital. Seeking out money in creative places must be second nature to build and maintain a successful business. Having the skills to communicate the company's vision is key to any growth-stage business.
6. **Project Finance**: Along with understanding credit, responsible borrowing is necessary so debt can be manageable once growth begins. Startup founders need to be aware about the Payback period.
7. **Risk Management**: Entrepreneurs need to identify and manage financial risks to protect their business. This involves assessing and mitigating risks associated with market volatility, competition, regulatory changes, and financial

uncertainties. Risk management strategies, such as insurance and contingency planning, are essential.
8. **Negotiation, Relationship Building and Communication Skills**: Finance-related skills extend beyond number-crunching. Entrepreneurs need to negotiate with investors, lenders, suppliers, and other stakeholders to secure favourable financial terms. Building strong relationships and effective communication skills are key to successful financial negotiations.
9. **Financial Decision-Making**: Entrepreneurs must make sound financial decisions based on data, analysis, and strategic goals. This includes evaluating investment opportunities, deciding on pricing strategies, assessing the cost-effectiveness of marketing campaigns, and making capital allocation decisions.
10. **Financial Software and Tools**: Proficiency in using financial software and tools can streamline financial processes and improve efficiency. Familiarity with accounting software, spreadsheet applications, financial modelling tools, and online banking platforms can help entrepreneurs manage financial tasks effectively.
11. **Continuous Learning and Adaptability**: The finance landscape is constantly evolving, and entrepreneurs need to stay updated on new financial trends, regulations, and industry-specific knowledge. Being open to learning, adapting to changing financial circumstances, and seeking professional advice when needed are important traits. Entrepreneurs must be flexible, savvy, and fast-moving in order to acquire the financing needed to allow them to focus on scaling operations, hiring employees, and propelling their business forward.

Benefits of Financial Skills
- Helps in not only helping startup founders to convince investors to provide funding but also to transform that funding into tangible growth.
- Understanding how a credit rating will determine loan eligibility is a huge skill to have, especially when starting a business, as it may be one of the few sources of funding available in the early stages.

While it's not necessary for entrepreneurs to be financial experts in every aspect, having a solid foundation in these finance-related skills will enable them to make informed decisions, manage financial resources effectively, and navigate the financial challenges of running a business. It is also important to consider seeking professional advice from accountants, financial advisors, or consultants to complement your own skills and expertise.

Startup Journey

> A lot of people have ideas, but there are few who decide to do something about them now. Not tomorrow. Not next week. But today. The true entrepreneur is a doer, not a dreamer." **–Nolan Bushnell, Entrepreneur**

Startups typically go through various stages as they evolve and grow. Each of these stages have different financial implications (discussed in detail in subsequent chapter), requiring very different financial interventions. While the exact terminology and duration of these stages may vary, the common stages of startups can be broadly described as the 4S's of Business:

1. **Survival Stage**: In the survival stage, startups are focused on establishing a viable business model and achieving product-market fit. They face numerous challenges and uncertainties, including securing initial funding, developing a minimum viable product (MVP), and acquiring their first customers. The primary goal of this stage is to survive by validating the business concept and gaining early traction.
   Characteristics of Survival Stage:
   a. Maximum work done by the entrepreneur.
   b. Founders are the most valuable employee(s) of the company.
   c. The founder is involved in core operations till the venture reaches the next stage.
   d. Pivoting: A startup usually changes its business strategy, product, or services based on market conditions.

2. **Struggle Stage**: The struggle stage is characterized by intense competition, operational challenges, and the need to refine the business model. Startups in this stage face hurdles in scaling their operations, acquiring a larger customer base, and generating consistent revenue. They may also encounter funding difficulties and operational inefficiencies. This stage requires persistence, adaptability, and the ability to overcome obstacles.
   Characteristics of Struggle Stage:
   a. Business model emerges, and there is clarity regarding the scope of the business.
   b. The product gets settled after initial pivoting.
   c. Refinement starts happening in the processes.
   d. Traction: Quantitative evidence of market demand. A proof that someone wants the product. It communicates momentum in market adoption.
   e. Repeat customers: Business starts seeing some repeat orders.
   f. Loyalist: Loyal customers start spreading the word of mouth.
   g. Word of mouth/mouse marketing starts building up both offline as well as on online platforms.

3. **Stability Stage**: Startups that successfully navigate the struggle stage reach the stability stage. In this phase, the business has achieved a level of stability and sustainability. They have refined their product or service, established a loyal customer base, and generated consistent revenue. Their focus shifts towards improving operational efficiency, optimizing processes, and enhancing customer experience. The goal in this stage is to solidify the business's position and create a foundation for further growth.

   Characteristics of Stability Stage:
   a. Focus is on acquiring new customers.
   b. Fundraising becomes critical for expansion.
   c. Team building to hire professionals to lead the verticals.
   d. Putting in place a Board of advisors for getting to the next stage.

4. **Scaling Stage**: The scaling stage is characterized by rapid growth and expansion. Startups in this stage have validated their business model, demonstrated scalability, and have the potential to capture a significant market share. They focus on accelerating growth, entering new markets, and scaling operations. This stage involves securing additional funding, building a high-performing team, and implementing strategies to capture a larger market share while maintaining profitability.
   Characteristics of Scaling Stage:
   a. Increasing revenue without a substantial increase in resources requirement.
   b. Wealth / Value Creation for shareholders
   c. The focus is to automate everything that could be automated while the business is scaling up to increase the pace as well as to reduce the costs.

The transition between these stages is not always linear, and startups may face challenges or opportunities that require revisiting previous stages. Additionally, the duration of each stage can vary significantly depending on the industry, market conditions, and the startup's specific circumstances.

Successful startups navigate these stages by continuously learning, adapting their strategies, and leveraging their strengths to overcome challenges. Each stage presents unique opportunities and risks, and startups must make critical financial decisions and allocate resources effectively to progress toward sustainable growth.

OUTGROWING

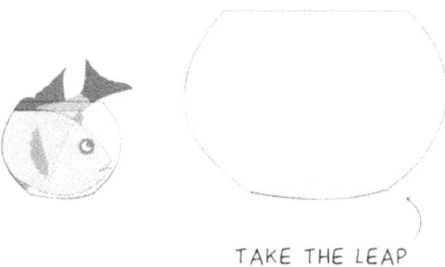

TAKE THE LEAP

Startup Stages and Financial Implications

"The rewarding thing isn't merely to start a company or to take it public. It's like when you're a parent. Although the birth experience is a miracle, what's truly rewarding is living with your child and helping him grow up." — **Steve Jobs**

Startups go through different stages, and each has its own financial implications. Entrepreneurs have access to various types of sources to fund their ventures at different stages. Generally, early-stage startups are not aware of the forum that they need to approach at which stage with respect to their funding requirements.

Stages of Startup and Source of Finance

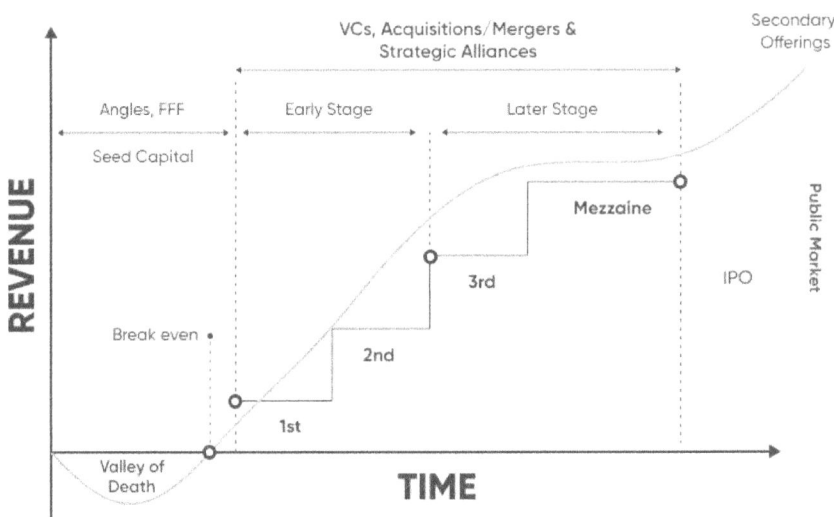

Here are some common types of finance available to entrepreneurs at different stages:

A. **Idea stage:** An idea is potential solution to a problem or a pain that either nobody else is solving or not solving efficiently or effectively. At this stage, the finances usually come from the following sources:
   a. **Personal Savings**: Many entrepreneurs initially finance their startups using personal savings. This involves using their own money, whether it's from savings accounts, investments, or other personal assets.
   b. **Financial bootstrapping**: Financial bootstrapping is self-funded businesses by personal savings, including borrowed or invested funds from family or friends, as well as income from initial sales. Bootstrapped business ventures

do not rely on traditional financing methods, such as funding from investors, crowdfunding, or bank loans. Founder(s) usually invests their own money and resources and uses them to propel the business forward with the following approaches to keep the business lean:
- Joint utilization
- Owner financing
- Sweat equity: a contribution toward a business venture, which is not monetary and comes in the form of mental effort, and time.
- Delayed payments: Delayed payments to suppliers and advances from customers for their orders help financially sustain the operations.
- Minimization of inventory: Reducing inventory to bare minimum frees up the working capital.

c. **Friends and Family**: During initial stage of a startup, entrepreneurs may seek financial support from friends and family members who believe in their business idea. They contribute finance in lieu of equity investments, soft refundable loans usually without interest, or even gifts.

This stage refers to largely self-funded businesses by personal savings, borrowed or invested funds from family or friends, and income from initial sales.

B. **Co-founder Stage:** It is the stage when the idea conceived by the founder is liked by another person(s) who also thinks that the problem exists and needs to be solved, then he/she/they become co-founders.

It is the most crucial stage as most of the disputes occur at this stage, and startups get closed even when they have a scalable business model and a good turnover. This is because most of them don't make a co-founder agreement in which all the terms and conditions are written and agreed upon. For example, a person initially invested in the startup with a 50% share but left after some time, and another person worked in that startup and made it profitable, but the person who left the business at the start still holds 50% shares, so in such cases co-founder agreement is important in which all the details are written like what will be the roles and responsibilities of each founder, what if a founder leaves the startup in a mid-way, their funding proportion, their equity shares, etc. Therefore, during the co-founder stage, startup founders need a founders' agreement ("Agreement"), a contract that is executed between all the co-founders of a company. The Agreement sets forth the ownership, rights, responsibilities, dispute resolution, and other terms to be executed between the founders and the company.

Co-founder Agreement:

This agreement saves from making a company on the first day of the idea as it is a valid document that shows the idea validation and gives proof of the startup. A founders' agreement is a contract that is executed between all the co-founders of a company. The Agreement sets forth the ownership, rights, responsibilities, dispute resolution, and other terms to be executed between the founders and the company. The co-founder agreement usually comprises the following clauses:

- What is the startup doing or expected to do?
- What is the product or service it is offering or likely to offer?
- What will be the capital contribution to be made by different founders?
- How much funds provided by each founder?
- Who will fulfill additional requirements of funds, if required at a later stage?
- Equity distribution ratio amongst co-founders.
- Incorporation and ownership.
- Restrictions and required approvals clearly stated.
- Duties of different co-founders.
- Provisions regarding resignation and removal of a founder, and consequent implications.
- Non-compete clause for co-founders after they exit.

A sample Co-founder Agreement Template is in the Appendix section.

C. **Incubation Round:** At this stage, a startup is like a seed buried in the ground. Though invisible to the world yet requiring basic resources and nurturing for the radicle to emerge from the seed. Incubation at an incubator can facilitate in reducing costs, provision of mentoring, networking as well as access to funds. The cofounders usually approach incubators to raise seed funds or seed grants to meet the growing expenses. There are also incubation centers supported by the government that provide guidance and funds to startups in the initial stage. Most of the incubators based at educational institutions have been selected by the central as well as state governments for disbursing government grants to startups under various schemes.

D. **Accelerator Stage:** As the venture matures, it might be useful to move from an incubator to an accelerator as they provide better opportunities to connect with angel investors for raising funding, which the incubators are usually not able to provide.

E. **Concessional Bank Loans for Startups:** Government has launched several collateral-free concessional loan schemes that a startup can apply for at this stage as the business has enough credentials to submit a loan application. These are discussed in detail later in the book in a dedicated chapter.

F. **Crowdfunding:** Crowdfunding is a method of raising funds for a venture by obtaining small contributions from a large number of people, typically via an online platform. It involves pooling together small amounts of money from a large group of individuals, often referred to as the "crowd," to collectively support an enterprise.

G. **High Net Worth Individuals (HNIs) (up to Rs. 1 cr per investor per startup)**: These are a class of individuals having an investible surplus of more than Rs.5 crore. Such investors are categorised as High net worth (HNW) investors looking to make investments in the private market with budding startups that interest them and align with their passions. HNIs invest in these startups as they provide them with an opportunity to create a diverse portfolio with the potential for big returns. With more opportunities to invest directly in startups shaking up their industries, more investors are looking to fund the businesses they see making seismic impacts in their markets.

This form of investment requires **Shareholder agreement.** A shareholder agreement is an arrangement that defines the relationship between shareholders and the company. This agreement safeguards the rights and obligations of the majority and minority shareholders and ensures all shareholders are treated fairly as per pre-determined terms and conditions.

H. **Pre-Seed Funding** (Ranges from INR 1 crore to INR 3 crores): Investors often get an equity stake of around 10% in exchange for the capital invested as seed funding in a very early stage of the startup building.

I. **Seed/Angel Funding** (Ranging from INR 1 cr to INR 25 crores): Angel investors are wealthy private individuals or a network of individuals who invest a part of their wealth in innovative companies and provide early-stage capital to startups in exchange for equity ownership to help them grow expeditiously within the city or state. These investors often have industry experience and can provide mentorship and guidance in addition to funding. They usually prefer to invest in startups that have got traction as proof of concept. The investment size depends on the startup's potential, industry, and the investor's preferences. Some angel investors in India also participate in syndicates or angel networks, which allow them to pool funds for larger investments.

J. **Bank Loans**: At this stage of the entrepreneurial journey, banks are willing to provide term loan, working capital loan, and overdraft facility against a business or personal collateral or track record.

K. **Pre-series/Bridge Round: Viability gap funding (Ranges Rs.5 - Rs.10 cr.)**
Before being eligible for VC funding, startups might look for a bridge round or a viability gap funding round to have the resources for laying the foundation for scaling up the enterprise. This is a short-term arrangement as funds provided by angel investors are no longer sufficient to meet the requirements for scaling up the operations, and VCs might take some more time to consider the enterprise for funding.

Micro VCs fill a critical gap between the angel ecosystem and the early-stage VC market. They are small, nimble, and focused teams that help founders get their nascent ventures off the ground before they are ready for a full series round. Thematic micro-VCs have also increased in India: **Pentathlon** for SaaS, and **Lumikai** for gaming. Family offices of corporate promoters, and first-time funds remained active in India over 2022, participating in more than 300 deals, in line with 2021. Micro VCs number grew in India to more than 80. Several launched larger funds: $55 million Artha Select Fund by **Artha Capital**, and the $25 million **Auxano Fund**. Early-stage VCs love collaborating with micro-VCs as

they have already examined those deals in detail and have richer information pertaining to them.
L. **Venture Capital (VC) Funding:** Venture capital is a method in which investors fund a fast-growing company for equity with the intention of selling their stake at the IPO or Pre IPO stage. VCs are private equity investors who take on high risks, take an active role in guiding the company, and expect high profitability when investing in new ventures. There are multiple series of VC funding as described below:
   a. **Series A Funding (Ranges between Rs.25cr - 100cr or more)**: Series A deals maintained an average deal size of $11 million in 2022. It typically occurs after the angel round and viability gap funding stage. Series A funding is usually sought when the startup has achieved certain milestones, such as product development, market validation, and initial customer traction, maybe in the number of users, revenue, KPI, or any other, and is ready to lift themselves. Startups at this stage are expected to have a validated business model, market traction, and potential for growth. At this stage, the startup aims to secure funding for scaling operations and expanding market reach.
   b. **Series B Funding: (Ranges between Rs.100 cr - 200 cr or more)**: It is generally secured when the startup has made significant progress in terms of growth and market presence. By this stage, the startup has a proven business model, revenue streams, a proven track record, strong growth potential, and a clear plan for scaling its operations. The startups already have a large customer base and are ready to scale up for expansion purposes, so they require funding. Series B funding is often used to support aggressive expansion plans, enter new markets, and further develop the product or service offerings. This funding is often done by the same investors who led the previous round of funding, with investors choosing to reinvest.
   c. **Series C Funding** (**Ranges between Rs.200 crs - 500 crs.**): It is typically sought when a startup has achieved substantial growth and aims to scale its operations even further. At this stage, the startup may have successfully captured a significant market share, demonstrated consistent revenue growth, and gained a competitive edge. Thus, it is a stage wherein the startups have proven themselves and are well-established with a successful leading business. Series C funding is primarily focused on expanding the company's market dominance, investing in R&D, acquiring complementary businesses, and preparing for potential IPO or acquisition. Startups may require funding to target the international market.
   d. **Beyond Series C** (**Range from INR 100 crores to several hundred crores or more**): Funding amounts in subsequent rounds can vary significantly based on the startup's growth trajectory, market dominance, and potential.

M. **Mergers and Buyouts**: Buyouts exchange ownership of the company with another party in order to build its value. Buyouts have been discussed in detail in a separate chapter later in the book.

N. Private Equity (PE) or Pre-IPO Round: Private Equity Funds are a group of investors who make a direct investment in an established but not yet publicly listed company. PEs invest in a wide range of industries and verticals and not just scaling tech like the way VCs and Angels do. This round might give an exit to early-stage investors who have made significant gains on their investment but don't want to risk their exit till IPO.

These funding ranges are indicative and can vary based on the specific circumstances and investor appetite in the Indian startup ecosystem. Startups are advised to research and engage with potential investors to understand their investment criteria and funding expectations accurately. In India, the amounts that startups can expect from seed funding, angel investors, and venture capitalists in various rounds of funding can vary significantly based on factors such as the startup's industry, growth potential, market conditions, and the specific terms negotiated. These figures are indicative and are subject to change and may vary depending on the specific circumstances.

Geographic Spread of Startup Funding in India

Different cities are at different stages with respect to the development and maturing of the entrepreneurial ecosystem prevalent over there. The city wise breakup of funding raised by startups in India in 2021 is presented below. This illustration can provide insight to startups with respect to directing their efforts for raising startup funding.

City wise Startup Funding 2021

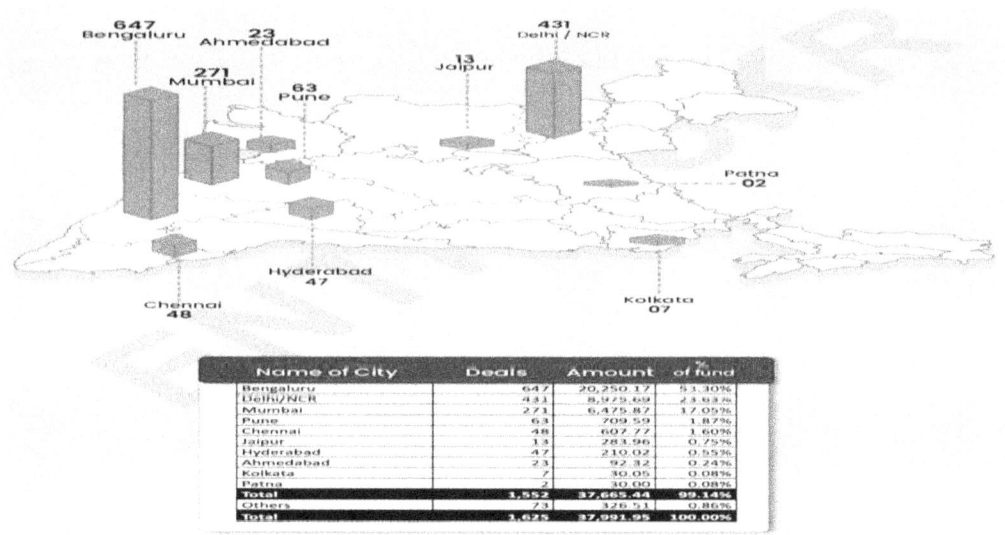

Name of City	Deals	Amount	% of fund
Bengaluru	647	20,250.17	53.30%
Delhi/NCR	431	8,979.69	23.63%
Mumbai	271	6,475.87	17.05%
Pune	63	709.59	1.87%
Chennai	48	607.77	1.60%
Jaipur	13	283.96	0.75%
Hyderabad	47	210.02	0.55%
Ahmedabad	23	92.32	0.24%
Kolkata	7	30.05	0.08%
Patna	2	30.00	0.08%
Total	**1,552**	**37,665.44**	**99.14%**
Others	73	326.51	0.86%
Total	**1,675**	**37,991.95**	**100.00%**

Source: Fintrackr Media Reports

O. Initial Public Offering (IPO): One of the major objectives of a startup is to get to the Initial Public Offering (IPO) stage, which is a process through which a privately held company offers its shares to the public for the first time through a stock exchange, allowing individuals and institutional investors to purchase ownership stakes in the company. It is a significant milestone for a company as it transitions from being privately owned to becoming a publicly traded entity. This is the stage that offers an opportunity for the early investors to take an exit and make a return on their investment in the startup.

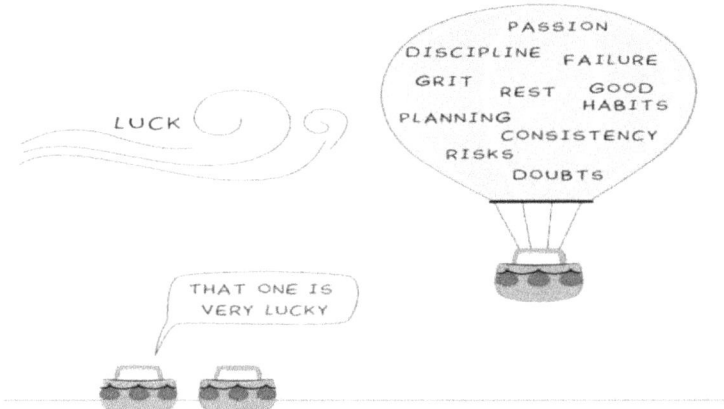

Business Model Canvas

"A small business is an amazing way to serve and leave an impact on the world you live in."
– Nicole Snow, Wall Street Journal and USA Today bestselling author

The journey of a startup can start from a sketch made on a restaurant napkin. Amazon's entire business model was sketched on a single sheet of paper illustrating the strategy that would drive the business.

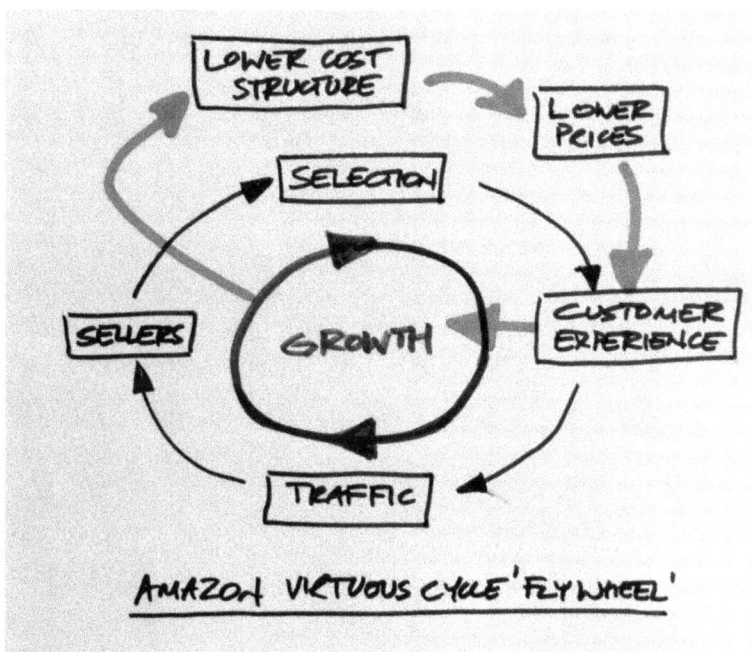

The Business Model Canvas is a tool that facilitates providing a visual representation of a startup founder's business model. It offers a concise and comprehensive overview of how a business would create, deliver, and capture value. Thus, it helps the startup founder to illustrate and validate his/her business idea on various parameters. It also helps the startup founder by enabling a structured clarity regarding various aspects of the proposed business idea.

The canvas consists of nine key building blocks that capture the essential elements of a business. These building blocks are:

Blank Business Model Canvas Template

Key Partners	Key Activities	Value Proposition	Customer Relationship	Customer Segments
	Key Resources		Channels	
Cost Structure				Revenue Streams

1. **Value Proposition**: "The key reason for a customer to buy your product." It's a short description of the unique value that the business offers to its customers that too **without any vague descriptions and jargon**. It can be read in less than 5 seconds and still clearly coneys, i.e., what the product is all about. It articulates how the unique combination of product features, services, or solutions:
   ❖ addresses a particular customer need.
   ❖ how it solves customers' problem(s),
   ❖ what benefits it creates for the market to be targeted.
   ❖ what additional value it brings for the potential customers.

   Thus, in a nutshell, value proposition tells prospects why they should do business with you rather than your competitors. A few truly great examples of value propositions from leading startups are as follows:
   ❖ Uber – The Smartest Way to Get Around
   ❖ Slack – Be More Productive at Work with Less Effort
   ❖ Digit – Save Money Without Thinking About It

   Though the startup can have short and simple official tagline, it's advisable to have different value propositions for different customer segment focused on covering different customer needs.

   This is one of the most important steps in the startup journey because if this is not in place, other things might not help. So, in order to learn how to develop a sound value propositions the team can perform the following activities by inviting people who are in direct contact with customers or people from your target market:

- ❖ **Step- I: Pains -** Ask audience to describe every bad experience the audience goes through before, during, and after completing the task, when your product is not there.
- ❖ **Step-II: Define your Products and Services**. List all features the value proposition is built around.
- ❖ **Step- II: Customer Jobs - Jointly map** all big and small tasks the product will help the customers to accomplish with your product.
- ❖ **Step-IV: Gains** Describe every good experience a customer will have during and after completing the task, by using your product outlining how exactly the product's features are eliminating pains and generating gains.
- ❖ **Step-V: Value Proposition:** Develop a crisp and concise description of your product benefits highlighting the major gain or summarizing different gains.

2. **Customer Segments**: Identifies the specific groups of customers or market segments that the business aims to serve. It helps define and profile the target audience in order to understand their needs and characteristics.

   For modern day tech-based businesses, Technographic segmentation, which defines what devices, mobile apps, and desktop programs different set of customers most frequently use is also very important along with demographic and psychographic segmentation. This helps startups know how clients with different devices would experience your product and company can tailor or customise its content specifically to targeted customers' needs. As technology has become a significant driver of occupations and lifestyles, understanding this dimension is vital for understanding the target audience.

   In case of freemium models, it is important to develop the profiles of free users and paying customers. For instance, half of the freemium online gaming companies' revenue comes from only 0.19 percent of mobile gamers. Therefore, knowing the motivations of free users and then bucketing the paying customers into different sub-categories of those bringing the highest/moderate/low value is significantly important.

3. **Channels**: Describe "How a company aims at delivering value proposition to its customer segments." It outlines the distribution and communication channels through which the business interacts with customers and delivers its value proposition. It includes both physical and digital channels and also comprises brand awareness creation as well as providing post-purchase customer support. Osterwalder and Pigneur highlighted the following five phases of channels development:
   a. **Raising awareness** of potential users about your product through a wide range of channels: Blogging, social media, content marketing, generating word of mouth.
   b. **Help customers evaluate your Value proposition.** Try-before-you-buy technique, guide them through a product to ensure they received the

desired value or realized its potentials. Case studies and reviews could also be used to help customers understand the value.

c. **Facilitate Purchase:** How to buy your product online, or from App Store or through another platform. Need to ensure that users feel comfortable and confident during the payment process and believe it to be safe and agree with the terms and conditions.

d. **Product delivery:** Ensure that your customer gets update on delivery or can track the delivery in case it is a tangible product, or in case of the app/software that it has been installed correctly and operates in a manner in which it is expected to do.

e. **Post-purchase support: Developing** the refund/cancellation policy. How do customers contact and to whom when they experience a problem or have a question? What is the onboarding process? Chatbots, simulation, or videos can be used as one of the post-purchase channels. Customer feedback surveys can be sent, or online reviews can be tracked as well as comments on questions (Quora), customer complaint, or feedback website can be analysed, and personal recommendations can be created based on the user activity.

4. **Customer Relationships**: Defines the types of relationships the business establishes and maintains with its customers. It covers aspects such as customer acquisition, retention, and support. There are the following five possible cases of customer relationships:

    - **Personal assistance.** Startups can make the contact channels diverse and accessible so that customer can contact at any time prior to or after the purchase via e-mail, phone, or chatbot.
    - **Self-service.** Providing systems like IVR or tracking links to the B2C customers.
    - **Automated service.** Providing AI-powered recommendations such as movies (Netflix) and playlists (Spotify), or auto generated emails and reminders. This service imitates human interaction and keep customers engaged.
    - **Communities.** Companies can create a community around a product/brand where users can exchange knowledge for better understanding customers' journey. For instance, Oracle community with half a million active participants helps customers find advice among fellow users.
    - **Co-creation.** Companies match content creators and content consumers. YouTube, Quora, Twitter, etc. creating customer relationships using this is as model.

5. **Key Activities**: Identifies the core activities and operations that are essential for the business to deliver its value proposition. It includes activities such as production, marketing, distribution, and customer service. For tech led companies, key activities van be categorised into three main categories:

    - Production.

- Problem-solving
- Platform

6. **Key Resources**: They play a direct role in creating and delivering the value proposition to customer segments and supporting customer relationships. Thus, they represent the assets, and capabilities required to operate the business effectively. They can be broadly categorised into the following five resources:
    - Physical resources (equipment, facilities)
    - Intellectual property
    - Human resources, and
    - Financial
    - Strategic partnerships.

   For different types of businesses, the core resource varies. For a software business, core resources are human and intellectual resources comprising algorithm, software, patents, copyrights, licenses, and customer knowledge; and human resources comprising software engineers, marketing specialists are valuable assets.

7. **Key Partnerships**: Describes the external entities or organizations that the business collaborates with to leverage resources, reduce costs, or enhance value creation. It can include suppliers, strategic alliances, or distribution partners.

   Strategy alliances of startup with non-competing organization to leverage each other's resources can be vital for both conserving resources as well as building scale. This also help in developing reliable and long-term relationships.

8. **Revenue Streams**: Specifies how the business generates revenue from its customers. It identifies the pricing mechanisms, revenue models, and sources of income for the products or services offered. Startups need to develop their Revenue Model, which comprises a strategy that goes into identifying and managing its different Revenue streams.

    - **Advertising:** Free to use platforms such as YouTube, Twitter, Google, and Facebook, free-to-download apps and services have survived and grown on advertising revenue.
    - **Affiliate Marketing:** Startups can earn commissions by referring other products and services that could be beneficial to their users or routing traffic to other websites.
    - **Subscriptions.** This model is good for Software as a Service (SaaS), Platform as a Service (PaaS), or Infrastructure as a Service (IaaS) businesses. It also good for on-demand streaming services, such as Netflix, Spotify, or online publications, like The Economic Times.
    - **Sponsorship.** Startups can request individuals or organisations to support their efforts through sponsorships.

- **Freemium**. By attracting an audience to the basic set of features a startup can convert some of them into paying customers (another Customer Segment) and offering them premium features.
- **Fee-based:** Startups can charge a fee per service or a fee for a period time for which the service can be accessed by the users.

9. **Cost Structure**: Outlines the costs and expenses incurred by the business to deliver value, maintain customer relationships, and buying resources to operate its business model. It includes both fixed and variable costs, such as production costs, marketing expenses, personnel costs, and infrastructure expenses. For a product development software company:
    a. **Operational expenses**:
        - **R&D costs:** According to MarketRealist, 10 to 20 % of costs in the software industry go for R&D, only 5 % of the total amount goes into innovation, and the rest goes to testing.
        - **Sales and marketing activities**: About 25 % of revenue is spent on marketing and sales.
        - **Customer Success Management** (Support costs): Customer retention and handling customer requests takes a big chunk of expenses.
    b. **Capital costs**:
        - Acquiring physical resources such as buildings and computers
        - Upgrading physical resources, such as buildings and computers.
    c. **Overhead costs**:
    d. **Staff costs**
        - Resources spent on hiring, training, and retaining employees.

The Business Model Canvas is a flexible and dynamic tool that allows entrepreneurs and managers to visualize, analyze, and iterate on their business models. It enables a holistic understanding of how different elements of a business interact and how they contribute to its overall value creation and sustainability.

The canvas is often used in conjunction with other strategic tools and frameworks to support business planning, innovation, and decision-making processes. It can be easily adapted and modified as the business evolves, making it a practical tool for startups and established companies alike.

Business Model and Key details of select Startups

Startup	Offering	Business Model	Partnership	Revenue
Swiggy	Food delivery platform	hyper-local food delivery	- Restaurant - delivery partners	- 15%-25% on bill amount - Premium membership to restaurants - Membership to customers - Offers on payment methods
Paytm	Payment Wallet	Marketplace: Payment services, Recharge, booking, Bill Payments, Buy & Sell Paytm Mall: a mobile-centric marketplace		- Payment services, - commission from Recharge and Fee, Bill Payments, - Booking, - Paytm Mall
Ola	Mobile application for Cab rental	Cab service to customers	- customer order cab - driver to receive requests	- Commission on trips
Oyo	Mobile application for booking for stay and rental	Aggregation and franchise	- Hotels	- Commission from booking - Selling Franchise to hotels - Oyo townhouse - Oyo Studio Stays - Oyo commercial - Oyo wizard
Flipkart	e-commerce platform	Business to Consumer	- Buyers - Sellers	- Commission from sellers - Sale of private labels - Convenience charges paid by for fast delivery. - Advertisements - payment service
Byju's	Online learning service	Freemium	-	- Subscription - Classroom sessions

Revenue and Cost Drivers

"Revenue is vanity, profit is sanity, but cash is king."

Before starting an enterprise, it is important for the startup founders to have a basic understanding of the potential revenue and cost drivers for their forthcoming enterprise. This information would help them understand the key metrics they can use to measure their performance and major cost heads. This understanding would form the basis of budgeting they are expected to undertake before formally taking a plunge to launch their enterprise. For startup founders, understanding is essential for the following reasons:

- **Business Planning**: Knowledge of revenue and cost drivers helps founders in creating a solid business plan. By understanding what factors contribute to revenue generation and cost incurrence, founders can set realistic targets, allocate resources effectively, and develop strategies to optimize profitability.
- **Financial Projections**: Revenue and cost drivers form the foundation of financial projections for startups. Founders need to estimate future revenues and costs to assess the financial feasibility and potential profitability of their business. Accurate projections assist in making informed decisions, securing funding, and attracting investors.
- **Resource Allocation**: Identifying revenue and cost drivers enables founders to allocate resources efficiently. By understanding which activities or products generate the most revenue and which incur the highest costs, founders can prioritize investments, optimize operations, and focus on areas with the greatest potential for growth and profitability.
- **Pricing and Revenue Optimization**: Revenue drivers provide insights into pricing strategies and revenue optimization. Founders can evaluate the value proposition of their products or services, determine optimal pricing levels, and identify ways to increase customer acquisition, retention, and monetization. Understanding revenue drivers helps founders make data-driven pricing decisions to maximize revenue and market share.
- **Cost Management**: Knowledge of cost drivers is crucial for effective cost management. Founders can identify and monitor the key cost components of their business, understand cost structures, and implement cost reduction strategies where necessary. By analyzing cost drivers, founders can optimize operational efficiency, control expenses, and improve overall profitability.
- **Performance Monitoring:** Revenue and cost drivers act as key performance indicators (KPIs) for tracking business performance. By regularly monitoring these drivers, founders can assess the effectiveness of their business strategies, identify trends, and make timely adjustments to achieve desired outcomes. Revenue and cost drivers provide insights into the financial health and sustainability of the startup.
- **Investor Communication:** When seeking funding or engaging with potential investors, founders must be able to articulate the revenue and cost drivers of

their business. Investors want to understand the growth potential, scalability, and profitability of the startup. Demonstrating a deep understanding of revenue and cost drivers instils confidence in investors and enhances the chances of securing funding.

Revenue and cost drivers are fundamental elements that shape the financial performance and success of a startup. Founders who possess a clear understanding of these drivers are better equipped to make informed decisions, plan strategically, optimize operations, attract investment, and drive sustainable growth for their startups. A brief overview of revenue and cost drivers is as follows:

Revenue Drivers
1) Number of customers
2) Transactions per customer
3) Average transaction size
4) Average value service contract
5) Average value from consumables per base sale
6) Frequency of add-on sales per installed base sale
7) Milestone payments
8) Royalty percentage on net sales
9) Frequency of customer upgrades

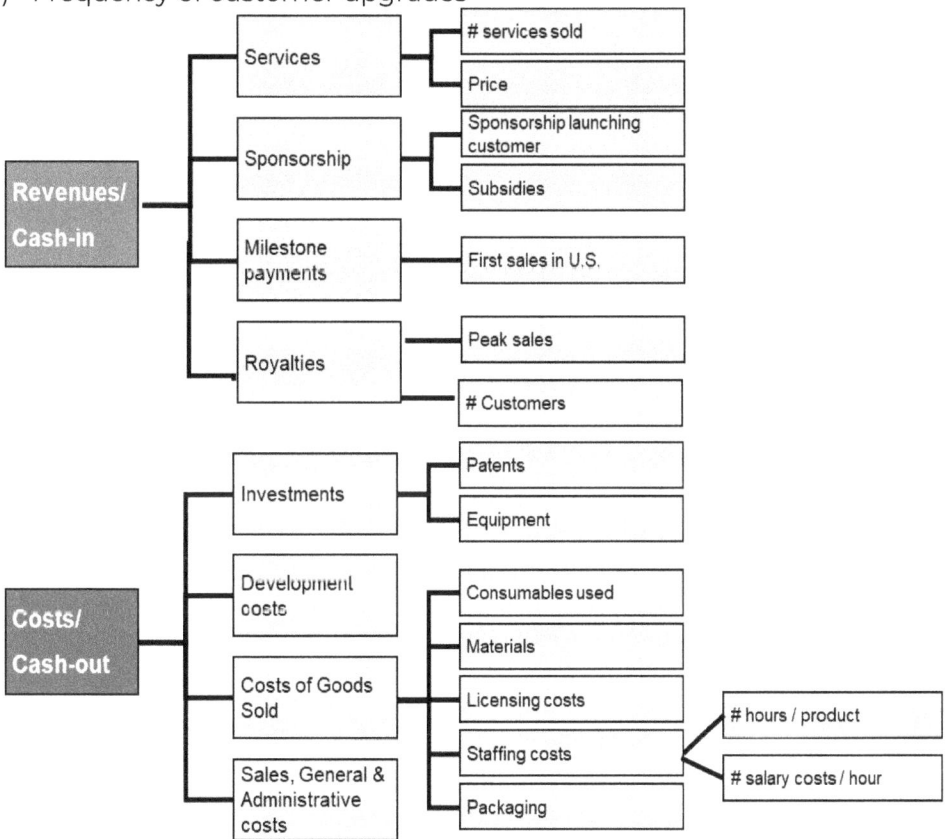

Cost Drivers for Product Businesses
1) Manufacturing
2) Materials cost
3) Labour costs
4) After sales services
5) Marketing (Exhibition, Demo, Display, Sample)
6) Toxicity screening
7) Infrastructure
8) Maintenance

Cost Drivers for Service Businesses
1) Salaries based on skills
2) Marketing
3) Toxicity screening
4) Infrastructure
5) Maintenance
6) Capacity utilisation

Budgeting

"The secret of getting ahead is getting started. The secret of getting started is breaking your complex overwhelming tasks into smaller manageable tasks, and then starting on the first one." **–Mark Twain, American Humorist, and Author**

Budgeting is a crucial aspect both at the time of planning a startup as well as later while managing a startup, as it helps founders allocate resources effectively and make informed financial decisions. Here are some key steps and considerations for a startup founder for doing budgeting before launching a startup:

1. **Identify your business goals:** Clearly define your short-term and long-term objectives. Understanding your goals will help you determine where to allocate your financial resources.
2. **Estimate startup costs:** Calculate the initial costs required to get your business off the ground. This includes expenses such as market research, product development, legal fees, branding, equipment, technology, office space, and initial marketing efforts.
   Cost items to be included in the budget
   - Personnel
     - Salaries: CEO, CXO, Executive/Technician
     - Social benefits: CEO, CXO, Executive/Technician
     - Insurances: CEO, CXO
   - **Infrastructure**
     - Building
     - IT & Communication
     - Furniture
     - Software
   - **Legal**
     - Notary, Lawyer, Advisors, Patent costs
   - **Operational**
     - Raising money, Representation & Travel
     - IT equipment & Software licenses
     - Inventory & Consumables
     - Outsourcing & Production
     - Research studies & Testing
     - Authorization & Fees
     - Marketing
     - Sales
3. **Create a cash flow projection:** Develop a cash flow forecast that outlines your expected revenue and expenses over a specific period, typically monthly or quarterly. This projection will help you understand when your business might face cash shortages or have excess funds.
4. **Track and categorize expenses:** Establish a system to track your startup's expenses. Categorize them into different groups like payroll, marketing,

operations, technology, and administrative costs. This will provide clarity on where your money is being spent and allow you to identify areas where you can cut costs or optimize spending.
5. **Prioritize essential expenses:** Differentiate between essential and non-essential expenses. Focus on allocating resources to areas critical for business operations and growth while minimizing non-essential expenditures.
6. **Plan for contingencies:** Set aside funds for unexpected expenses or emergencies. Having a financial buffer can help your startup navigate unforeseen challenges without disrupting operations.

Budgeting is an ongoing process, and it's important to adapt and refine your budget over a period of time at a fixed frequency, i.e., once in a quarter, or once in six months as the startup grows and evolves.

Why is it important to make cash flow projections before starting a startup?

Creating cash flow projections before starting a startup is crucial for the following reasons:

1. **Financial Planning**: Cash flow projections help you estimate the expected inflows and outflows of cash for your startup. By analyzing your projected cash flows, you can identify potential funding gaps and plan your financial resources accordingly. It allows you to determine how much capital you need to start and sustain your business until it becomes self-sufficient.
2. **Budgeting and Resource Allocation**: Cash flow projections enable you to develop a budget for your startup's operations. You can allocate resources to different areas of your business, such as marketing, product development, hiring, and infrastructure, based on the projected cash flow. This helps you make informed decisions on how to allocate limited resources effectively.
3. **Managing Expenses and Burn Rate**: Cash flow projections allow you to estimate your startup's burn rate, which is the rate at which you can spend money before generating sufficient revenue. By understanding your burn rate, you can closely monitor your expenses and make adjustments if necessary to ensure that your cash reserves can last as planned.
4. **Identifying Cash Flow Challenges**: Cash flow projections help you identify potential cash flow challenges in advance. For example, you may identify periods where cash outflows exceed inflows, indicating a need for additional funding or adjustments to your business strategy. Anticipating these challenges allows you to proactively seek funding, negotiate payment terms with suppliers, or make operational changes to maintain a healthy cash flow.
5. **Investor Confidence**: Cash flow projections are essential when seeking funding from investors or lenders. Investors want to understand your startup's financial viability and how their investment will generate returns. Providing realistic cash flow projections demonstrates your financial acumen, business planning, and commitment to managing the financial aspects of your startup effectively.

6. **Business Decision-Making**: Cash flow projections serve as a valuable tool for making strategic business decisions. They help you assess the financial implications of different scenarios, such as pricing changes, scaling operations, entering new markets, or introducing new products. By analyzing the impact on cash flow, you can make informed decisions that align with your financial goals and the long-term sustainability of your startup.

Thus, having a clear picture of cash flow projections is an essential tool for financial planning, and budgeting before launching your startup. It can also be illustrated graphically for a quick understanding of all the stakeholders involved in strategic and financial decision-making.

Revenues, Costs, and Net Cash Position Projections

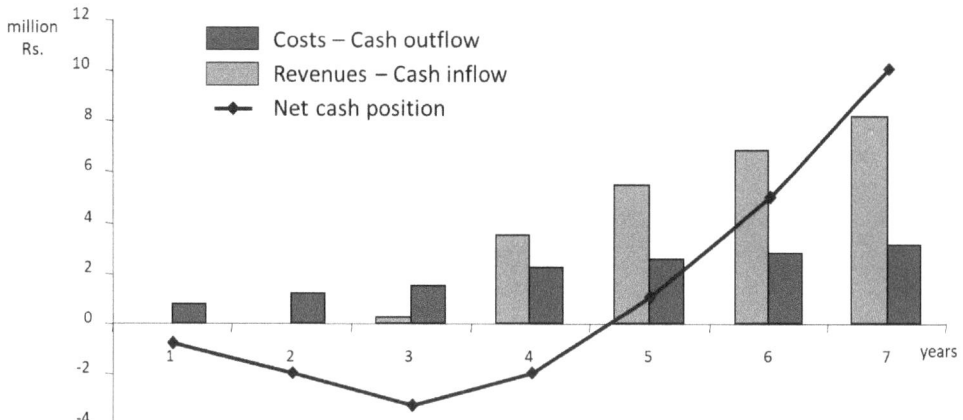

Financial Reserves before Starting a Startup

"Any time is a good time to start a company."– **Ron Conway, Noted Startup Investor, SV Angel**

Planning financial reserves is an important aspect of preparing for the uncertainties and challenges that may arise during the early stages of starting an enterprise. Here are some steps to consider when planning financial reserves as an entrepreneur before launching your enterprise:

1. **Assess Start-up Costs**: Begin by estimating the initial costs required to launch your enterprise. This includes expenses such as equipment, inventory, licenses/permits, marketing, legal fees, and any necessary renovations or setup costs. Create a detailed budget to determine the total amount needed to start your business.
2. **Identify Operating Expenses**: Calculate your projected monthly operating expenses, which include ongoing costs such as rent, utilities, salaries/wages, insurance, marketing/advertising, and supplies. Determine how many months' worth of expenses you should have in reserve to cover your business's initial period until it becomes self-sustaining.
3. **Evaluate Cash Flow**: Analyze your projected cash inflows and outflows to understand your business's cash flow dynamics. Identify potential cash flow gaps and periods when expenses may exceed revenues. Having a reserve can help bridge these gaps and provide a buffer during slow periods or unexpected events.
4. **Consider Contingencies**: Anticipate unexpected expenses or unforeseen circumstances that could impact your business. This could include equipment breakdowns, legal disputes, changes in regulations, or economic downturns. Factor in a contingency amount in your financial reserves to address these situations.
5. **Determine an Adequate Reserve Amount**: There is no fixed rule for how much financial reserve an entrepreneur should have before starting an enterprise, as it depends on various factors such as the industry, business model, and risk profile. However, a common recommendation is to have at least three to six months' worth of operating expenses as a reserve. This provides a cushion to cover initial start-up challenges and helps you sustain the business during the early stages.
6. **Expenses to meet family requirements:** Before plunging full-time into entrepreneurship, the founder should try to have financial reserves equivalent to 6 months of his/her family expenses.
7. **Seek Professional Advice**: Consider consulting with a mentor who can provide guidance specific to your business and industry. They can help you assess your financial needs, estimate appropriate reserve amounts, and provide insights based on their experience.

Financial reserves are not meant to be idle funds, but a safety net for your business's stability and growth. As you develop your business plan, it's crucial to factor in these reserves as part of your overall financial strategy.

Organization Structures: Financial Implications

"The way to get started is to quit talking and start doing." **–Walt Disney, Co-Founder, Disney**

Characteristics of basic types of Startup Entities

- **Partnership Firm:** 2-100 members, unlimited liability, registration is optional but advisable.
- **Limited Liability Partnership (LLP):** Minimum 2 and maximum undefined members, liability is as per the agreement, and registration is compulsory.
- **Private Ltd Company:** Minimum 2 and maximum 50 members, liability limited, registration compulsory.
- **One Person Company (OPC):** OPC is registered as a private company and ends with Pvt Ltd, has perpetual succession (nominee for succession mentioned in a memorandum with consent, not minor) nominee should be nominee in only one OPC, a conversion allowed à residency limit reduced to 120 from 180 days in the previous year. Now NRI also allowed to incorporate OPC.

Different forms of organizational structures have varying financial implications. Here are the financial implications of commonly used organizational structures:

Types of Organization Structure	Ease of Formation	Liability	Tax Implications	Access to Capital
Sole Proprietorship	The simplest form of business structure, requiring minimal legal formalities and costs to establish	Owner has unlimited personal liability for business debts & obligations. Personal asset may be at risk if business failure or legal liabilities	Income from the business is taxed as personal income of owner. The owner reports business income on their personal tax return	May face challenges in raising capital as they rely primarily on personal funds, loans, or reinvested profits
Partnership	Relatively easy to form, requiring a partnership agreement clearly outlining rights, responsibilities,	All partners have unlimited liability for business debts and obligations.	Profits & losses to partners who report them on their tax returns. Partners are individually	May face challenges in attracting external investors due to the shared liability and

	profit sharing, and dispute resolution mechanisms	Each partner personally liable for the actions and debts of other partners	responsible for paying taxes on their share of partnership income	potential conflicts among partners
One Person Company Pvt Limited Company	Requires filing Memorandum and Articles of Association with Registrar of Companies (RoC). Compared to public limited companies, the administrative requirements are less burdensome	limited liability protection, separating owners' personal assets from business liabilities, debts, and legal obligations		More flexibility in raising capital compared to sole proprietorship or partnership. They can issue shares to investors and attract external funding.
Public Limited Company	Face more stringent legal and regulatory requirements than other structures. Need to maintain financial records, hold board-level and general body meetings	Limited liability protection to shareholders, separating personal assets from business liabilities. Shareholders are not personally responsible for corporation's debts.	Subject to corporate income tax on their profits. Shareholders are subject to individual taxes on dividends they receive, resulting in potential double taxation	Greater access to capital compared to other structures. They can issue shares to raise funds or issue bonds to borrow money from investors or financial institutions

Hence, startup founders need to have an understanding which organization structure would best suit their long-term strategic needs at the time of the registration of their organization.

Cost of Capital

> "Recycling capital can be a very profitable activity."
> — **Hendrith Vanlon Smith Jr, CEO of Mayflower-Plymouth**

Cost of capital is the minimum rate of return that a business can expect to earn on its investments. In other words, the cost of capital is the minimum required rate of earnings or the cut-off rate for capital expenditures. It is the minimum required rate of return on the invested funds so that the firm can pay the cost of funds obtained for investment. as per the expectation of various suppliers of capital (long-term). It is the minimum rate of return, which ensures that the market value of shares of the company does not fall.

The cost of capital is a critical concept in finance and plays a significant role in decision-making. Key reasons why knowledge of cost of capital is important:

1. **Investment Decisions**: The cost of capital is used as a benchmark to evaluate the feasibility of investment projects. It helps determine whether the expected returns from a project are sufficient to cover the cost of capital. By comparing the expected returns with the cost of capital, businesses can make informed decisions about whether to proceed with an investment or choose alternative projects.
2. **Capital Budgeting**: When assessing different investment opportunities, businesses use the cost of capital to calculate financial metrics such as Net Present Value (NPV) and Internal Rate of Return (IRR). These metrics consider the time value of money and help determine the value and profitability of an investment. The cost of capital serves as the discount rate in these calculations, reflecting the required return on invested capital.
3. **Capital Structure Decisions**: The cost of capital also affects decisions related to capital structure, which involves determining the mix of debt and equity financing. By comparing the cost of different sources of capital, such as debt and equity, businesses can determine the optimal capital structure that minimizes the overall cost of capital. This decision impacts the company's risk profile, financial stability, and cost of raising funds.
4. **Valuation of Businesses**: The cost of capital is an essential component in business valuation models, such as discounted cash flow (DCF) analysis. By discounting future cash flows at the appropriate cost of capital, the present value of the business can be determined. The cost of capital reflects the required return expected by investors and helps estimate the value of the company's underlying assets and cash flows.
5. **Performance Evaluation**: It is used as a benchmark for evaluating the performance of a business or investment. If a project or business generates returns that exceed the cost of capital, it is considered value-creating. On the other hand, if the returns are below the cost of capital, it indicates value destruction. By monitoring and comparing actual returns with the cost of

capital, businesses can assess their performance and identify areas for improvement.
6. **Risk Assessment**: It reflects the risk associated with an investment or business. Riskier investments generally require a higher expected return and, therefore, have a higher cost of capital. By considering the cost of capital, businesses can assess the risk-reward trade-off and make decisions that align with their risk tolerance and strategic objectives.

The cost of capital is crucial for evaluating investment opportunities, making capital structure decisions, and assessing risk. It serves as a key factor in financial decision-making and helps businesses allocate capital efficiently, maximize shareholder wealth, and achieve their financial goals.

Sources of Capital

A Company can obtain capital from different sources viz.,
- Shareholders: both equity and preference share capital,
- Borrowing from public
- Financial institutions,
- Banks
- Grants
- CCD and Convertible Notes
- Revenue ploughed back as retained earnings.

Each source of capital involves certain costs and carries different levels of risk, which is compensated to them. This cost is that rate which must be paid to obtain the funds.

Components of Cost of Capital

- K_d = Cost of debt.
- K_p = Cost of preference shares.
- K_e = Cost of equity shares.
- K_{re} = Cost of retained earnings.
- K_o = Weighted Average Cost of Capital

The component costs are combined according to the weight of each component of capital to obtain the Weighted average costs of capital.

Weighted Average Cost of Capital (WACC)

It is a financial metric that represents the average rate of return a company needs to generate to cover its financing costs. It takes into account the proportion of debt and equity in the company's capital structure. Here's a step-by-step process to calculate the WACC:

1. **Determine the Capital Structure**: Start by identifying the company's capital structure, which includes the proportion of debt and equity used to finance its operations. This information can be obtained from the company's balance sheet and financial statements.
2. **Assign Weights to Debt and Equity**: Assign appropriate weights to the proportion of debt and equity in the capital structure. These weights represent the percentage of total capital contributed by each source. For example, if the company's capital structure consists of 70% debt and 30% equity, the weights would be 0.70 and 0.30, respectively.
3. **Determine the Cost of Debt**: Calculate the cost of debt, which is the average interest rate the company pays on its outstanding debt. This can be determined by considering the current interest rates on the company's debt instruments or by analyzing the yield to maturity of its bonds.
4. **Determine the Cost of Equity**: Calculate the cost of equity, which represents the rate of return required by equity investors to compensate for the risk associated with investing in the company. This can be determined using various methods, such as the Capital Asset Pricing Model (CAPM), Dividend Discount Model (DDM), or other valuation techniques.
5. **Calculate the Weighted Average Cost of Capital (WACC)**: Use the following formula to calculate the WACC:
   WACC = (Weight of Debt * Cost of Debt) + (Weight of Equity * Cost of Equity)
   Multiply the weight of debt by the cost of debt and add it to the product of the weight of equity and the cost of equity. The result will give you the WACC as a percentage.
6. **Interpret the WACC**: The calculated WACC represents the minimum rate of return the company needs to generate to meet its financial obligations and satisfy its investors. It can be used as a benchmark for evaluating potential investment projects or determining the cost of capital for valuation purposes.

The WACC is an estimate and may vary based on factors such as market conditions, the company's risk profile, and the availability of different sources of financing. It's important to periodically review and adjust the WACC calculation as the company's capital structure and market conditions change.

Capital Structure

"It doesn't matter whether a company is big or small. Capital structure matters. It always has and always will."

Determining the optimal mix of debt and equity for a company, also known as the capital structure, involves evaluating various factors and striking a balance between risk and return. Capital Structure refers to the mix of sources from where the long-term funds required in a business may be raised, i.e., what should be the proportions of Equity share capital, Preference share capital, Internal sources, Debentures, and other sources of funds in the total amount of capital.

How to determine Debt and Equity mix

While there is no one-size-fits-all approach, here are some key considerations for determining the debt-equity mix:
1. **Assess the company's financial position**: Evaluate the company's current financial situation, including its profitability, cash flow, and asset base. Understand the company's borrowing capacity, ability to service debt, and the cost of borrowing.
2. **Analyze risk profile**: Assess the risk profile of the company, including industry dynamics, market conditions, and competitive position. Evaluate the company's sensitivity to economic fluctuations, cash flow volatility, and potential risks specific to the industry it operates in.
3. **Cost of capital**: Understand the cost of debt and equity for the company. Consider factors such as interest rates, market conditions, credit ratings, and investor expectations. Determine the cost of raising funds through debt and equity instruments.
4. **Debt capacity**: Determine the company's debt capacity by analyzing factors such as cash flow generation, asset base, debt service coverage ratio, and financial ratios. Assess the company's ability to manage and repay debt obligations.
5. **Risk tolerance**: Evaluate the company's risk tolerance level, which may vary depending on its stage of growth, industry, management's risk appetite, and investor preferences. Consider the impact of leverage on the company's stability and flexibility.
6. **Financial flexibility**: Assess the company's need for financial flexibility. Consider factors such as capital expenditure requirements, working capital needs, growth opportunities, and potential contingencies. Determine the importance of maintaining liquidity and the ability to adapt to changing market conditions.
7. **Regulatory and contractual obligations**: Consider any regulatory requirements or contractual obligations that may impact the capital structure decisions. Certain industries or jurisdictions may have specific restrictions or guidelines on debt-to-equity ratios or other financial metrics.

8. **Market conditions and investor preferences**: Take into account market conditions and investor preferences for the company's securities. Evaluate the company's access to debt and equity markets, investor demand for its securities, and the overall cost of capital in the market.
9. **Seek professional advice**: It is advisable to consult with financial advisors, investment bankers, or other professionals who specialize in corporate finance and capital structure decisions. They can provide insights, and financial modelling expertise and assist in analyzing the optimal mix of debt and equity for the company.
10. **Continuous monitoring and adjustment**: Once the initial capital structure is determined, it's important to continuously monitor and evaluate its effectiveness. Regularly review the company's financial performance, market conditions, and refinancing opportunities. Adjust the capital structure as needed to align with changing circumstances and optimize the company's overall financial position.

Finding the optimal debt-equity mix is a dynamic process and may evolve over time as the company's circumstances change. It requires a careful balance between risk, cost, flexibility, and the company's growth objectives.

Difference between Common stock and Preferential equity (Preferred) stock

The key distinctions between common stock and preferential equity stock in terms of rights and privileges associated with each type of stock are as follows:

- ❖ **Ownership and voting rights**:
  - ➢ **Common Stock**: Common stock represents ownership in a company and typically grants shareholders voting rights in corporate matters. Common shareholders have the right to elect the board of directors and vote on important company decisions.
  - ➢ **Preferred Stock**: Preferred stock also represents ownership in a company but generally does not provide voting rights. Preferred shareholders usually do not have the same voting power as common shareholders, although there may be exceptions in certain circumstances.
- ❖ **Dividends:**
  - ➢ **Common Stock**: Common shareholders may receive dividends, but the payment of dividends is typically at the discretion of the company's management and is contingent on the company's profitability and available funds.
  - ➢ **Preferred Stock**: Preferred shareholders often have a preferential right to receive dividends before common shareholders. The dividend rate for preferred stock is usually fixed or determined as a percentage of the stock's par value. Preferred shareholders are entitled to receive dividends before any dividends are distributed to common shareholders.
- ❖ **Liquidation preference:**
  - ➢ **Common Stock**: In the event of liquidation or bankruptcy, common shareholders are entitled to the remaining assets after all debts, obligations, and preferred stockholder claims have been satisfied.

- ➢ **Preferred Stock**: Preferred shareholders have a higher claim on the company's assets in the event of liquidation. They generally have a predetermined liquidation preference, which means they are entitled to receive their investment amount or a specific multiple of their investment before common shareholders receive any distribution.
- ❖ **Risk and returns:**
  - ➢ **Common Stock**: Common shareholders bear greater risk compared to preferred shareholders. They have the potential for higher returns through capital appreciation and may benefit if the company's value increases over time.
  - ➢ **Preferred Stock**: Preferred shareholders have a more stable and predictable income stream. They receive fixed dividends, which are generally paid at regular intervals. However, they typically do not participate in the same level of capital appreciation as common shareholders.

The specific rights and features of common and preferred stock can vary based on the company's bylaws and the terms set forth in the stock issuance. These differences are general guidelines, and the actual rights and privileges associated with each type of stock can be customized by the issuing company. Both common stock and preferred stock play a crucial role in capital structure and provide different options for companies to raise funds and attract investors with varying risk preferences and objectives.

Convertible Debentures and Non-convertible Debentures

Convertible debentures and non-convertible debentures are two types of debt instruments that companies can issue to raise capital. The key difference between them lies in their convertibility into equity shares. Here's a comparison:

- ❖ **Convertibility**:
  - ➢ **Convertible Debentures:** Convertible debentures have an option or feature that allows the debenture holders to convert their debt into equity shares of the issuing company. The conversion may occur at a predetermined price, ratio, or formula, and it is typically exercised at the option of the debenture holder.
  - ➢ **Non-Convertible Debentures**: Non-convertible debentures do not offer the option of conversion into equity shares. They remain as debt throughout their tenure and are redeemed by the issuer at maturity, along with any accrued interest.
- ❖ **Returns and Interest**:
  - ➢ **Convertible Debentures**: Convertible debentures may offer potential upside through equity participation if the debenture holders choose to convert their holdings into equity shares. They may also pay periodic interest to the debenture holders until conversion.
  - ➢ **Non-Convertible Debentures**: Non-convertible debentures provide fixed returns to the debenture holders in the form of regular interest payments

throughout the tenure of the debenture. The interest rate and payment terms are specified at the time of issuance and remain constant until maturity.

- ❖ **Risk and Flexibility**:
  - ➢ **Convertible Debentures**: Convertible debentures provide the debenture holders with the flexibility to convert their investment into equity shares when they believe it is favourable, allowing them to potentially participate in the company's growth. However, if the conversion option is not exercised, the debenture holders may face the risk of their investment being subject to the creditworthiness and performance of the issuer.
  - ➢ **Non-Convertible Debentures**: Non-convertible debentures are considered less risky compared to convertible debentures because they offer a fixed income stream and repayment of principal at maturity. Investors of non-convertible debentures are not exposed to the fluctuation of the issuer's share price.
- ❖ **Investor Base:**
  - ➢ **Convertible Debentures**: Convertible debentures tend to attract investors who are interested in the potential upside of equity participation along with the stability of fixed income. Investors with higher risk tolerance and a belief in the future prospects of the issuing company may find convertible debentures appealing.
  - ➢ **Non-Convertible Debentures**: Non-convertible debentures are often favoured by investors seeking stable fixed-income returns without exposure to equity market risks. They are suitable for risk-averse investors who prioritize regular interest payments and capital preservation.

The specific terms and conditions of convertible and non-convertible debentures can vary based on the issuing company, market conditions, and regulatory requirements. Investors should carefully review the offering documents and consult with financial professionals to understand the features and risks associated with these debt instruments before making any investment decisions.

Difference between Compulsory Convertible Debentures and Convertible Notes (SAFE Notes)

Comparison between Compulsory Convertible Debentures (CCDs) and Convertible Notes (CNs), the financial instruments that can be used by companies to raise capital are as follows:

- ❖ **Nature:**
  - ➢ **CCDs**: CCDs are debt instruments issued by a company that are mandatorily convertible into equity shares at a predetermined date or event, typically at the option of the issuer.
  - ➢ **CNs**: Convertible notes are debt instruments that can be converted into equity shares at a later date or event, usually at the option of the holder.

- ❖ **Conversion**:
  - ➢ **CCDs:** CCDs have a mandatory conversion feature, meaning they must convert into equity shares at a specified time or event, such as the occurrence of a particular milestone or upon a specific date. The conversion terms are predetermined and binding.
  - ➢ **CNs**: Convertible notes provide the holder with the option to convert the debt into equity shares at a later stage, usually upon a subsequent financing round or a specified trigger event. The conversion terms are negotiated and agreed upon at the time of issuance.
- ❖ **Conversion Price**:
  - ➢ **CCDs**: The conversion price for CCDs is predetermined and fixed at the time of issuance. It may be based on a formula, a discount to the future equity price, or a combination of factors.
  - ➢ **CNs:** The conversion price for convertible notes is typically determined based on the valuation of the company at the subsequent financing round or trigger event. It may include a discount or a cap to provide the noteholder with a potential benefit.
- ❖ **Interest and Redemption:**
  - ➢ **CCDs**: CCDs usually carry an interest component that is payable periodically until conversion. They have a fixed maturity or redemption date, at which point the debenture is mandatorily converted into equity shares.
  - ➢ **CNs**: Convertible notes may or may not carry an interest component. They generally have a maturity date but can be repaid in cash instead of converting into equity if the conversion option is not exercised.
- ❖ **Regulatory Considerations:**
  - ➢ **CCDs**: CCDs are regulated by the Companies Act and applicable securities laws in the respective jurisdictions where they are issued.
  - ➢ **CNs:** Convertible notes are commonly used in startup and early-stage financing and are subject to applicable securities regulations and agreements between the parties involved.

Both CCDs and CNs offer companies a means to raise funds while providing investors with the potential for equity participation. The choice between the two depends on factors such as the company's capital structure, stage of growth, investor preferences, and regulatory requirements. It is advisable to consult legal and financial professionals when considering the issuance of either instrument to ensure compliance with applicable laws and optimize the financing structure.

Optimum Capital Structure

The capital structure is said to be the optimum capital structure when the firm has selected such a combination of equity and debt so that the wealth of the firm is maximum. At this capital structure, the cost of capital is minimum, and the market price per share is maximum. In theory, one can use optimum capital structure, but in practice, appropriate capital structure is a more realistic term than the former.

Guidelines for Optimum Capital Structure

Optimum capital structure guidelines refer to the ideal mix of debt and equity financing that a company should aim for to achieve an efficient and sustainable financial structure. While there is no one-size-fits-all approach, here are general guidelines for determining optimum capital structure for a company:

1. **Balance risk and return:** Optimal capital structure should strike a balance between risk and return. A higher proportion of debt can increase financial risk due to interest obligations & potential default, but it may offer tax advantages and a lower cost of capital. Equity financing dilutes ownership but provides more flexibility and reduces financial risk. Consider the risk tolerance of your company, industry norms, and the potential RoI when deciding the ideal mix.
2. **Industry considerations:** Different industries have varying capital structure requirements. Some industries with stable cash flows and predictable earnings may tolerate higher debt levels, while others with more volatile revenue streams may opt for lower debt and higher equity to mitigate risk. Analyze industry benchmarks and the financial characteristics of your specific sector to inform your capital structure decisions.
3. **Growth stage and business lifecycle**: The growth stage and business life cycle of a company can influence its capital structure needs. Startups and early-stage companies may rely more on equity financing to fuel growth, while more mature companies with established cash flows may have a higher debt component. Consider the growth trajectory and lifecycle stage of your business to determine the appropriate balance.
4. **Cash flow and profitability**: Assess your company's cash flow generation and profitability. Companies with strong and consistent cash flows may be more capable of servicing debt and can afford to have a higher debt component in their capital structure. Conversely, companies with uncertain cash flows or negative profitability may need to rely more on equity financing.
5. **Financial flexibility and strategic objectives:** Consider your company's strategic objectives and the need for financial flexibility. Equity financing can provide more flexibility in adapting to changing market conditions and pursuing growth opportunities. Debt financing may limit flexibility but can provide leverage for investment or expansion. Evaluate your long-term goals and the capital structure that aligns with your strategic vision.
6. **Cost of capital**: Compare the cost of debt and equity financing options. Debt generally has a lower cost of capital due to tax advantages and lower required returns. Evaluate the interest rates, expected returns, and associated costs of each financing source to determine the most cost-effective capital structure.
7. **Risk appetite and stakeholders' preferences**: Take into account the risk appetite of your shareholders, investors, and lenders. Some stakeholders may prefer a more conservative capital structure with lower leverage, while others may be more open to taking on higher levels of debt. Align your capital structure decisions with the preferences and risk profiles of your stakeholders.

Capital structure decisions should be based on a comprehensive analysis of your company's financial position, risk profile, and strategic objectives. Consulting with financial experts in corporate finance can provide valuable insights in this regard.

Financial Leverage

Equity is the cushion that protects financial institutions from unexpected changes in the value of their assets. The greater the leverage, the smaller the losses required to wipe out a company's equity, leaving it without enough money to repay the people who hold its debt. **- Alex Berenson**

The dictionary meaning of the term 'Leverage' refers to "an increased means of accomplishing some purpose." Leverage allows us to accomplish certain things which are otherwise not possible, viz, lifting heavy objects with the help of leverage. In financial management, the term 'leverage' is used to describe the firm's ability to use fixed-cost assets to increase the return to its owners, i.e., equity shareholders.

Guidelines regarding Financial Leverage

Financial leverage refers to the use of borrowed funds (debt) to finance investments or operations in order to magnify the potential returns to equity shareholders. While leveraging can enhance returns, it also increases financial risk. Here are some guidelines regarding financial leverage:

1. **Understand the concept of leverage**: Financial leverage involves using borrowed funds to invest in assets or projects that are expected to generate a return higher than the cost of borrowing. Leverage can amplify profits when returns are positive, but it can also magnify losses when returns are negative.
2. **Evaluate risk tolerance**: Assess your risk tolerance and the risk appetite of your stakeholders. Higher levels of leverage expose a company to greater financial risk, including the risk of insolvency if cash flows are insufficient to cover interest payments. Consider the stability of your cash flows, industry dynamics, and the potential impact of economic downturns when determining the appropriate level of leverage.
3. **Debt capacity and coverage ratios**: Evaluate your company's debt capacity, which is the amount of debt it can reasonably sustain given its cash flow, profitability, and collateral. Assess debt coverage ratios such as interest coverage ratio (ICR) and debt service coverage ratio (DSCR) to ensure that your company's cash flows are sufficient to cover interest payments and debt obligations.
4. **Cost of debt and equity**: Compare the costs of debt and equity financing options. Debt typically has a lower cost of capital due to tax advantages and lower required returns. Consider the interest rates, fees, and associated costs of debt financing relative to the potential returns to determine the cost-effectiveness of leverage.
5. **Balance debt and equity**: Strive for a balanced capital structure that optimizes the benefits of leverage while maintaining financial stability. Avoid excessive leverage that could jeopardize your company's solvency and

creditworthiness. Consider industry benchmarks and risk profiles of similar companies when determining the appropriate mix of debt and equity.
6. **Cash flow management**: Maintain a strong focus on cash flow management. Ensure that your company's cash flows are sufficient to cover debt service obligations and provide a cushion to withstand any unforeseen challenges. Effective cash flow management can help mitigate the risks associated with leverage.
7. **Monitor covenants and obligations**: Understand the terms and conditions of your debt agreements, including any financial covenants or restrictions. Stay compliant with these obligations to maintain a healthy relationship with lenders and avoid potential default risks.
8. **Scenario analysis and stress testing**: Conduct scenario analysis and stress testing to evaluate the impact of adverse events on your company's financial position. Consider how changes in interest rates, market conditions, or business performance could affect your ability to meet debt obligations. This analysis can help you assess the robustness of your capital structure. Seek professional advice: Consider consulting with financial advisors, accountants, or experts in corporate finance who can provide guidance on the appropriate level of financial leverage for your specific circumstances. They can help you analyze risk-return trade-offs, evaluate financing options, and optimize your capital structure.

Remember that the optimal level of financial leverage can vary depending on factors such as industry dynamics, business model, growth stage, and risk appetite. It's important to carefully assess your company's financial position, cash flow generation, and risk tolerance when making decisions regarding financial leverage.

Incubator Grant Schemes

There is a moment of conception and a moment of birth, but between them there is a long period of gestation. **-Jonas Salk**

The MEITY Grant in India for startups refers to the grant provided by the Ministry of Electronics and Information Technology (MEITY) to support and promote the growth of startups in the technology and innovation sectors. MEITY is a government ministry responsible for formulating policies, promoting digital initiatives, and fostering entrepreneurship in the electronics and information technology industries.

The MEITY Grant aims to provide financial assistance to startups in various stages of their journey, from ideation to market entry and scaling up. The grant is typically awarded through competitive selection processes or application-based programs. It is intended to support startups in developing innovative products, technologies, and solutions that align with the government's vision of digital transformation and technological advancement.

The specific focus areas and eligibility criteria for MEITY Grants may vary based on the programs or initiatives launched by the ministry at different times. However, some common areas of support include:

1. **Research and Development (R&D)**: MEITY Grants may be available to startups engaged in cutting-edge research and development activities, encouraging innovation and the creation of intellectual property.
2. **Incubation and Acceleration:** The grant supports startup incubators and accelerators that provide the necessary infrastructure, mentorship, and resources to foster the growth of startups.
3. **Proof of Concept (POC) and Prototype Development:** MEITY Grants may assist startups in developing proof of concept or building prototypes for their innovative ideas or technologies.
4. **Market Entry and Commercialization**: The grants may provide financial support to startups in entering the market, launching their products, and achieving commercial success.

To apply for MEITY Grants or to gather more information, it is advisable to visit the official website of the TBIs and STEPs that have been approved by the Ministry of Electronics and Information Technology for examining the applications and disbursing the grant to successful applicants. The application processes, eligibility criteria, and deadlines for MEITY Grants are typically outlined in the respective programs or notifications released by the ministry.

Incubator Seed Funding Schemes

Phases of the creative process: **Preparation**-gathering impressions, **Incubation**-letting go of certainties, **Immersion/Illumination**-creative intervention/risk, and **Revision**-conscious structuring and editing of creative material.
Gail Sheehy

Seed funding provided by the government refers to financial support given to early-stage startups or entrepreneurial ventures to help them kickstart their business operations and achieve initial milestones. Here are some common forms of government seed funding:

1. **Grants**: Governments may offer grants specifically designed for startups and entrepreneurs. These grants are non-repayable funds provided to support business development, product innovation, research, or market expansion.
2. **Equity Investments**: Governments may invest in startups in exchange for equity ownership. This can be done through dedicated government investment funds or venture capital arms established by the government.
3. **Subsidies**: Governments may provide subsidies to startups to reduce costs associated with specific business activities. These subsidies could cover expenses related to research and development, marketing, export promotion, or hiring skilled employees.
4. **Loan Programs:** Governments may offer low-interest or interest-free loans to startups. These loans can be used for business development, technology adoption, infrastructure development, or working capital requirements. Startup loans are often designed to be more flexible and accessible compared to traditional bank loans.
5. **Incubator and Accelerator Support**: Governments may fund or operate incubators and accelerators that provide seed funding as part of their support programs. These programs typically include mentorship, infrastructure, networking opportunities, and financial assistance for startups.

The availability and terms of government seed funding programs vary across countries and regions. It is recommended to explore the specific government agencies, ministries, or economic development organizations in your country to learn about the seed funding programs available and their application processes.

Startup India Seed Fund Scheme (SISFS)

The SISFS is an initiative by the Government of India to provide financial assistance to early-stage startups for proof of concept, prototype development, product trials, market-entry, and scaling up. It offers up to Rs..20 lakhs as seed funding to eligible startups through incubators recognized by the Department for Promotion of Industry and Internal Trade (DPIIT). This INR 945 Cr Startup India Seed fund Scheme was launched in 2021 to aid the setting up and growth of new startups.

Need for Startup India Seed Fund Scheme

Easy availability of capital is essential for entrepreneurs at the early stages of the growth of an enterprise.
Funding from angel investors and venture capital firms becomes available to startups only after the proof of concept has been provided. Similarly, banks provide loans only to asset-backed applicants.
It is essential to provide seed funding to startups with innovative ideas to conduct proof of concept trials.

Objective of the Scheme

Startup India Seed Fund Scheme (SISFS) aims to provide financial assistance to startups for proof of concept, prototype development, product trials, market entry and commercialization.
This would enable these startups to graduate to a level where they will be able to raise investments from angel investors or venture capitalists or seek loans from commercial banks or financial institutions. Government seed funding programs vary across countries and may have different names and eligibility criteria.

How Startup India Seed Fund Operates

The Seed Fund will be disbursed to eligible startups through eligible incubators across India

Nodal Department	DPIIT: Department for Promotion of Industry and Internal Trade
Experts Advisory Committee (EAC)	Government Representatives & Industry Experts
Incubators	Govt assisted/Not-Govt assisted Incubators Operational for at least 2-3 years
Eligibility for Startups	DPIIT-recognised Startups Incorporated less than 2 years ago

Features of the startup India seed fund scheme

1. Year-round 'Call for Applications' for Incubators and Startups
2. Sector-agnostic
3. No mandatory physical incubation
4. PAN-India startup program
5. Startups can apply to 3 incubators simultaneously

Incubator Soft Loan Schemes

> Ideas, like young wine, should be put in storage and taken up again only after they have been allowed to ferment and to ripen.
> **Richard Strauss**

Technology Business Incubator (TBI) Scheme: TBIs provide incubation facilities and financial support to startups in the technology sector. Under this scheme, selected startups can avail loans or financial assistance for product development, mentoring, marketing, and other business-related activities.

Convertible Notes

Convertible notes are a popular source of funding for startups, especially in the early stages of their development. A convertible note is a debt instrument that can be converted into equity (ownership shares) at a later stage, typically during a subsequent funding round or when certain predefined conditions are met. Here are some key points to understand about convertible notes:

1. **Structure**: Convertible notes are typically structured as loans that carry an interest rate and a maturity date. Instead of receiving immediate repayment, the investors have the option to convert the loan into equity at a later date.
2. **Conversion**: The conversion of the note into equity is triggered by a specific event, such as a subsequent equity financing round. The terms of conversion, such as the conversion price or conversion rate, are determined during the negotiation of the convertible note agreement.
3. **Interest and Repayment**: Convertible notes may accrue interest over the term of the loan. However, instead of paying interest in cash, it is often added to the principal amount and converted into equity upon conversion. Repayment of the principal amount is typically triggered only if a conversion event does not occur.
4. **Valuation**: Valuation of the startup is usually not determined at the time of issuing the convertible note. The conversion rate is usually set based on the valuation established during a future funding round or a predetermined valuation cap or discount specified in the convertible note agreement.
5. **Benefits for Startups**: Convertible notes offer several benefits to startups. They provide a relatively quick and simple way to raise funds without the need for immediate valuation negotiations. Startups can secure funding at an early stage when it may be challenging to determine a fair valuation. Convertible notes also delay the dilution of existing shareholders until a later stage when the startup's valuation is better established.
6. **Risks for Investors**: While convertible notes can be advantageous for startups, they also carry risks for investors. If the conversion event does not occur, the investor may not receive a return on their investment, and the debt may need to be repaid at maturity. Additionally, if the subsequent equity

financing round values the company at a lower price than anticipated, the investor may experience dilution of their ownership stake.

The specific terms and conditions of convertible notes can vary depending on the negotiation between the startup and the investor. It is advisable for startups and investors to seek legal counsel and carefully consider the terms of the convertible note agreement before proceeding with this form of funding.

Compulsorily Convertible Debentures (CCDs)

Convertible debentures are debt instruments that carry a fixed interest rate and have the option to convert into equity shares of the issuing company at a later date or upon the occurrence of a specific event, such as a subsequent funding round or a predefined milestone.

1. **Debt Instrument**: CCDs are essentially loans taken by the company, where the investors lend money to the startup in exchange for the debentures. The startup pays regular interest on the debentures to the investors until conversion.
2. **Conversion into Equity**: The conversion of CCDs into equity shares is generally triggered by a specific event, such as a subsequent funding round or meeting predetermined conditions. The terms and conditions of conversion, including the conversion price or conversion ratio, are typically predetermined and specified in the CCD agreement.
3. **Conversion Event**: The conversion of CCDs into equity shares is triggered by a specific event, such as a subsequent equity financing round or the occurrence of certain milestones or conditions specified in the debenture agreement.
4. **Interest and Repayment**: CCDs carry a fixed interest rate, and the startup is required to make regular interest payments to the debenture holders. However, unlike traditional debt instruments, CCDs are usually compulsorily converted into equity shares, and repayment of the principal amount does not typically occur unless a conversion event does not take place. If the conversion event does not occur, the startup is typically obligated to repay the debenture amount at maturity.
5. **Interest and Repayment**: CCDs accrue interest over the tenure of the debenture, and the interest is usually paid periodically or added to the principal amount. If the conversion event occurs, the outstanding CCDs are converted into equity shares, and the debt is effectively retired.
6. **Valuation and Terms**: The valuation of the startup is often not determined at the time of issuing CCDs. The conversion price or conversion ratio is usually determined during a subsequent funding round or based on the valuation established during a subsequent funding round or a predetermined valuation cap or discount specified in the debenture agreement.
7. **Benefits for Startups**: CCDs offer startups a way to raise funds while providing flexibility in managing debt repayment. They allow startups to attract investors who may be interested in converting their investment into equity, potentially reducing the cash outflow and preserving the company's

cash position. CCDs can also help delay the valuation negotiation process until a subsequent funding round.
8. **Risks for Investors**: While CCDs can be advantageous for startups, they also carry risks for investors. If the conversion event does not occur, the investor may not receive a return on their investment, and the debenture may need to be repaid at maturity. Additionally, if the subsequent equity financing round values the company at a lower price than anticipated, the investor may experience dilution of their ownership stake.

The specific terms and conditions of CCDs can vary depending on the negotiation between the startup and the investor. Startups and investors are advised to seek legal counsel and carefully review the debenture agreement to understand the rights, obligations, and risks associated with CCDs as a funding source.

Types of Business Loans

A bank is a place that will lend you money if you can prove that you don't need it.
– Bob Hope

Business loans are designed to meet the financial needs of businesses. They can vary based on the specific requirements of the business and the purpose of the loan. Here are some common types of business loans:

1. **Startup Loans**: Startup loans are specifically tailored for new businesses with limited operating history. They can provide capital for initial setup costs, inventory, marketing, or hiring employees. Lenders may require personal guarantees and collateral to mitigate the risk. (Discussed in detail in the subsequent chapter)
2. **Term Loans:** Term loans provide a lump sum of money upfront, which is repaid over a fixed period with regular instalments. They are often used for business expansion, purchasing machinery, or financing long-term projects.
3. **Equipment Loans:** These loans are specifically designed to finance the purchase of equipment or machinery for the business. The equipment itself serves as collateral, and the loan term is typically based on the expected lifespan of the equipment.
4. **Working Capital Loan**: It is a loan availed to fund the day-to-day operations of a business, ranging from payment of employees' wages to covering accounts payable.
5. **Overdraft**: It provides access to a specified amount of funds that can be drawn upon as needed. It offers flexibility, allowing businesses to manage cash flow fluctuations and cover short-term expenses. Interest is usually charged only on the amount borrowed.
6. **Invoice Financing**: Also known as accounts receivable financing, this type of loan allows businesses to borrow against their outstanding invoices. Lenders provide a percentage of the invoice amount upfront and collect the payment directly from the customers. It helps businesses improve cash flow while waiting for invoices to be paid.
7. **Loan against Property (LAP)**: These loans are used for purchasing, refinancing, or developing commercial properties such as office buildings, retail spaces, or industrial facilities. They are secured by the property and typically have longer repayment terms.
8. **Personal Loans:** Personal loans are often used by business founders to meet their working capital requirements.
9. **Credit Card Loans:** In extreme cases, startup founders resort to taking credit or withdrawing cash from their credit card accounts so as to meet their immediate and urgent needs.

The availability and terms of business loans can vary depending on the lender, the business's financial health, creditworthiness, and the specific requirements of the loan.

Requirements for getting Term Loan

The requirements for a term loan may vary depending on the lender and the specific terms of the loan. However, here are some common requirements that businesses typically need to fulfil when applying for a term loan:

1. **Business Registration:** The business should be a legally registered entity, such as a sole proprietorship, partnership, private limited company, or limited liability partnership (LLP). The registration documents, such as the Certificate of Incorporation or Partnership Deed, will be required.
2. **Business Vintage**: Lenders generally prefer businesses to have a minimum operational history of at least 3 years. However, some lenders may consider providing term loans to businesses with a shorter operational history.
3. **Financial Documents**: Businesses are usually required to provide financial documents to demonstrate their financial health and repayment capacity. These documents typically include audited financial statements such as the Profit and Loss Statement, Balance Sheet, and Cash Flow Statement for the past 2-3 years.
4. **Bank Statements**: Lenders often request bank statements for the business accounts for the past 6-12 months. These statements help assess the cash flow, transaction history, and repayment behaviour of the business.
5. **Turnover and Profitability**: Lenders consider the business's turnover and profitability to evaluate its financial performance and repayment capacity. Documents such as Goods and Services Tax (GST) returns, income tax returns, or sales invoices may be required to verify the business's revenue generation and profitability.
6. **Creditworthiness**: The credit history and creditworthiness of the business and its promoters play a crucial role in the loan approval process. Lenders typically check the credit score, credit report, and repayment track record to assess the borrower's creditworthiness.
7. **Collateral or Security:** Depending on the loan amount and the lender's policies, term loans may require collateral or security. This could include assets such as property, machinery, inventory, or accounts receivable. However, some lenders also provide unsecured term loans based on the borrower's creditworthiness.
8. **Business Plan**: Lenders may request a comprehensive business plan that outlines the purpose of the loan, the utilization of funds, and the projected financial performance of the business.

These requirements can vary among lenders, and additional documentation or conditions may be requested based on the lender's policies and the specific circumstances of the business.

Requirements to get Working Capital Loan

The specific requirements for a working capital loan may vary slightly depending on the lender. However, here are some common requirements that businesses typically need to fulfil when applying for a working capital loan:

1. **Business Registration**: The business should be a legally registered entity, such as a sole proprietorship, partnership, private limited company, or limited liability partnership (LLP). The registration documents, such as the Certificate of Incorporation or Partnership Deed, will be required.
2. **Business Vintage**: Lenders usually require the business to have a minimum operational history of at least 2-3 years. However, some lenders may consider providing loans to newer businesses with a shorter operational history.
3. **Financial Documents**: Businesses are generally required to provide financial documents to demonstrate their financial health and repayment capacity. These documents may include audited financial statements, such as the Profit and Loss Statement, Balance Sheet, and Cash Flow Statement, for the past 2-3 years.
4. **Bank Statements**: Lenders may request bank statements for the business accounts for the past 6-12 months to assess the cash flow and transaction history.
5. **Turnover and Profitability**: Lenders often consider the business's turnover and profitability to evaluate its financial performance. They may require documents such as the Goods and Services Tax (GST) returns, income tax returns, or sales invoices to verify the business's revenue generation and profitability.
6. **Creditworthiness**: The credit history and creditworthiness of the business and its promoters are significant factors considered by lenders. A good credit score and a clean repayment track record enhance the chances of loan approval.
7. **Collateral or Security**: Depending on the loan amount and the lender's policies, some working capital loans may require collateral or security. This could include assets such as property, inventory, or accounts receivable. However, certain lenders also provide unsecured working capital loans based on the borrower's creditworthiness.
8. **Business Plan**: Lenders may request a detailed business plan that outlines the purpose of the loan, the utilization of funds, and the projected financial performance of the business.

These requirements can vary among lenders, and additional documentation or conditions may be requested based on the lender's policies and the specific circumstances of the business.

Concessional Bank Loans for Small Businesses

"Our public sector bank officials avoid making any new lending decisions – because lending always exposes them to some (infinitesimal) risk of being blamed for the loan going wrong."
Abhijit Banerjee

Concessional loan schemes for startups in India are government initiatives aimed at providing financial support to startups and promoting entrepreneurship in the country. These schemes offer loans to startups at lower interest rates and with favourable repayment terms to help them overcome the challenges of accessing affordable capital. Here are some of the notable concessional loan schemes for startups in India:

➢ **Mudra Yojana:** The Pradhan Mantri Mudra Yojana (PMMY) aims to provide financial support to micro and small enterprises, including startups. It offers loans categorized into three categories: Shishu (up to Rs. 50,000), Kishore (from Rs. 50,001 to Rs. 5 lahks), and Tarun (from Rs. 5,00,001 to Rs. 10 lakhs). These loans are available through banks, non-banking financial companies (NBFCs), microfinance institutions, etc.

1. **Shishu loan**
    ➢ It is a category of loans aimed at providing financial support to micro and small enterprises in India. The term "shishu" means child or infant in Hindi, and in the context of the PMMY, it refers to the smallest loan category meant for startups and micro-businesses in their early stages.
    ➢ The loan amount offered under the Shishu category is up to Rs. 50,000, and it is intended for businesses requiring a small amount of capital for initial setup, working capital, purchasing equipment, or meeting other business-related expenses.
    ➢ These loans are collateral-free, meaning borrowers do not need to provide any security or guarantor to avail the loan. The interest rates charged on Shishu loans are usually lower compared to conventional loans, and the repayment period is flexible, typically ranging from 3 to 5 years.
    ➢ To avail Shishu loan, individuals need to approach banks, microfinance institutions, or non-banking financial companies (NBFCs) that are authorized to offer loans under the PMMY. The application process involves submitting the necessary documents, such as identity proof, address proof, business plan, and other relevant information as required by the lending institution.
    ➢ Micro business owners are advised to check with the authorized lenders or visit the official PMMY website for the most up-to-date information on Shishu loans and their application process.

2. **Kishore loan**
    ➢ The term "Kishore" means adolescence or youth in Hindi, and in the context of the PMMY, it refers to the loan category meant for businesses that have grown beyond the startup stage but still require a moderate amount of capital for expansion and growth.
    ➢ Kishore loans provide financial assistance to micro-businesses that need funds to expand their operations, purchase machinery or equipment, increase working capital, or meet other business-related requirements. The loan amount offered under the Kishore category is above Rs. 50,000 and up to Rs. 5 lakhs.
    ➢ Kishore loans are collateral-free, meaning borrowers are not required to provide any security or guarantor to avail the loan. The interest rates charged on Kishore loans are usually competitive, and the repayment period is flexible, typically ranging from 3 to 7 years.
    ➢ To avail Kishore loan, individuals can approach banks, microfinance institutions, or non-banking financial companies (NBFCs) that are authorized to offer loans under the PMMY. The application process involves providing the necessary documents, such as identity proof, address proof, business plan, financial statements, and other relevant information as required by the lending institution.
    ➢ It's important to note that the specific terms and conditions of Kishore loans may vary based on the lending institution and government guidelines. Small business owners are advised to check with authorized lenders or visit the official PMMY website for the most up-to-date information on Kishore loans and their application process.

3. **Tarun loan**
    ➢ The term "Tarun" means young or energetic in Hindi, and in the context of the PMMY, it refers to the loan category meant for businesses that have grown beyond the initial stages and require a higher amount of capital for expansion, diversification, or scaling up their operations.
    ➢ Tarun loans are designed to meet the financial requirements of established micro-businesses that need funds for various purposes such as purchasing equipment, expanding infrastructure, marketing, working capital, or any other business-related needs. The loan amount offered under the Tarun category is above Rs. 5 lakhs and up to Rs. 10 lakhs.
    ➢ Tarun loans are collateral-free, meaning borrowers are not required to provide any security or guarantor to avail the loan. The interest rates charged on Tarun loans are usually competitive, and the repayment period is flexible, typically ranging from 3 to 7 years.
    ➢ To avail Tarun loan, individuals can approach banks, microfinance institutions, or non-banking financial companies (NBFCs) that are authorized to offer loans under the PMMY. The application process involves providing the necessary documents, such as identity proof,

address proof, business plan, financial statements, and other relevant information as required by the lending institution.
- It's important to note that the specific terms and conditions of Tarun loans may vary based on the lending institution and government guidelines. Entrepreneurs are advised to check with authorized lenders or visit the official PMMY website for the most up-to-date information on Tarun loans and their application process.

- **Credit Guarantee Fund Scheme for Startups (CGFS):** The Government has established the Credit Guarantee Scheme for Startups to provide credit guarantees to loans extended to DPIIT-recognised startups by Scheduled Commercial Banks, Non-Banking Financial Companies (NBFCs), and Venture Debt Funds (VDFs) under SEBI registered Alternative Investment Funds. CGSS is aimed at providing credit guarantees up to a specified limit against loans extended by Member Institutions (MIs) to finance eligible borrowers, viz. DPIIT recognised startups. Launched by the Small Industries Development Bank of India (SIDBI), CGFS provides collateral-free loans to startups in technology-driven sectors. The scheme offers a credit guarantee cover for up to 85% of the loan amount, with a maximum loan limit of Rs.2 crore.

- **Stand-Up India Scheme:** This scheme primarily focuses on providing financial assistance to women and SC/ST entrepreneurs. Under this scheme, startups can avail loans ranging from Rs. 10 lakhs to Rs. 1 crore for setting up new enterprises. The loan is available through scheduled commercial banks, and the repayment period can extend up to 7 years.

It's important to note that these schemes may have specific eligibility criteria, documentation requirements, and application procedures. Startup founders are advised to visit the official websites of the respective schemes or contact the relevant government authorities for detailed information and application processes.

Feasibility Report for a Bank Loan

"A well-constructed numerical estimate is worth a thousand words." – **Charles Schultze, former Director of the US Bureau of Budget**

Preparing a feasibility report for a bank loan involves assessing the viability and profitability of a proposed business or project to determine its potential for success. Here are some steps to help you in preparing a feasibility report for a bank loan:

1. **Executive Summary:** Begin the report with an executive summary that provides an overview of the project, its objectives, and the loan amount being sought. Summarize the key findings and recommendations of the report.
2. **Introduction:** Provide a detailed introduction to the project, including its background, purpose, and goals. Describe the industry or market in which the business operates and highlight any unique aspects or competitive advantages.
3. **Market Analysis:** Conduct a thorough market analysis to assess the demand for your product or service. Include information about target customers, market size, growth potential, and competition. Provide data on industry trends, market share, and customer preferences.
4. **Technical and Operational Feasibility:** Outline the technical and operational aspects of the project. Describe the production process, required equipment and technology, location, infrastructure, and any legal or regulatory requirements. Assess the availability and feasibility of resources, including raw materials, labour, and utilities.
5. **Financial Projections:** Present detailed financial projections for the project. Include estimates of revenue, expenses, and cash flow for at least the first three to five years. Calculate key financial ratios such as return on investment (ROI), payback period, and net present value (NPV). Provide assumptions and justifications for the projections.
6. **Risk Assessment:** Identify and analyze the potential risks and challenges associated with the project. This could include market risks, operational risks, financial risks, or regulatory risks. Offer mitigation strategies to address these risks and demonstrate your ability to manage them effectively.
7. **Management and Team:** Highlight the skills, qualifications, and experience of the management team responsible for executing the project. Outline their roles & responsibilities and emphasize their track record and relevant achievements.
8. **Loan Request and Repayment Plan:** State the amount of loan you are seeking and the purpose for which it will be used. Provide a detailed repayment plan, including loan tenure, interest rates, and any collateral or security offered.
9. **Appendices:** Include supporting documents such as market research data, financial statements, project plans, resumes of key team members, and any other relevant information that adds credibility to your feasibility report.

Remember to adhere to the specific requirements and guidelines provided by the bank or lending institution when preparing the feasibility report. It's also recommended to seek professional advice or assistance from financial experts or consultants to ensure the report is comprehensive, accurate, and well-presented.

Credit Rating: Startup Finance

The interest rate you receive, however, is contingent on your credit score. -
Jean Chatzky

Credit rating agencies play a significant role in startup finance by providing credit assessments and ratings for startups and their financial instruments. Here are the key roles credit agencies perform in startup finance:

1. **Credit Assessment and Rating:** Credit agencies assess the creditworthiness of startups by analyzing their financial health, business operations, and credit history. They evaluate various factors such as the startup's revenue, profitability, debt levels, management team, industry dynamics, and market position. Based on their assessment, credit agencies assign credit ratings to the startup, indicating the level of credit risk associated with lending or investing in the startup.
2. **Investor Confidence**: Credit ratings provided by credit agencies help build investor confidence in startups. A higher credit rating indicates a lower credit risk, making the startup's financial instruments more attractive to potential investors. Investors, such as banks, institutional investors, and individual lenders, often rely on credit ratings to assess the creditworthiness of startups before deciding to invest or lend money to them.
3. **Access to Capital**: Credit ratings from reputable credit agencies can enhance a startup's ability to access capital. A favourable credit rating may enable startups to secure loans, issue debt instruments (such as bonds or commercial paper) or attract equity investors more easily. Financial institutions and investors may be more willing to provide capital to startups with higher credit ratings, as it indicates a lower likelihood of default or credit risk.
4. **Cost of Capital:** The credit rating assigned by credit agencies can impact the cost of capital for startups. A higher credit rating may result in lower interest rates on loans or lower yields on debt instruments, making capital more affordable for startups. Conversely, a lower credit rating may lead to higher borrowing costs or the need to offer higher returns to investors to compensate for the perceived higher risk.
5. **Transparency and Market Perception**: Credit agencies provide transparency and information to the market about startups' creditworthiness. Credit ratings are widely recognized and understood by market participants, allowing investors, lenders, and other stakeholders to assess the startup's financial strength and risk profile. The credit rating serves as an independent assessment and helps market participants make informed decisions.
6. **Continual Monitoring**: Credit agencies monitor the creditworthiness of startups on an ongoing basis. They may update credit ratings periodically or issue credit reports to reflect changes in the startup's financial position, business performance, or market conditions. This ongoing monitoring provides

stakeholders with up-to-date information and helps identify any potential changes in credit risk.

It's advisable for startups and investors to consider multiple sources of information and conduct their own due diligence when assessing a startup's creditworthiness. Overall, credit agencies play a crucial role in startup finance by providing independent credit assessments and ratings that influence investor confidence, access to capital, and the cost of capital for startups. Their evaluations and ratings serve as a tool for startups and investors to make informed financial decisions.

Process for a startup to get Credit Rating

The process for a startup to obtain a credit rating from a credit rating agency involves several steps. Here's a general overview of the process:

1. **Research and Selection**: Start by conducting research to identify credit rating agencies that operate in your country or region. Consider factors such as the agency's reputation, credibility, expertise in assessing startups, and their track record of providing accurate and reliable credit ratings. Evaluate their criteria for rating startups and their industry specialization, if any.
2. **Contact the Credit Rating Agencies**: Reach out to the selected credit rating agencies to express your interest in obtaining a credit rating for your startup. You can typically contact them through their official website, email, or phone.
3. **Provide Information**: The credit rating agency will require detailed information about your startup to assess its creditworthiness. This may include financial statements, business plans, historical performance data, future projections, details about your industry, and any other relevant information they request. Ensure that the information provided is accurate, complete, and up to date.
4. **Engagement and Due Diligence**: The credit rating agency will evaluate the provided information and conduct their due diligence. They may ask for clarification or additional details during this process. Their analysts will assess your startup's financial health, risk profile, industry outlook, management capabilities, and other relevant factors.
5. **Credit Rating Assessment**: Based on their analysis, the credit rating agency will assign a credit rating to your startup. The credit rating reflects the agency's opinion on the creditworthiness and ability of your startup to meet its financial obligations. The rating may include a letter or alphanumeric code that represents different levels of credit risk and may be accompanied by an outlook (positive, stable, negative) indicating the agency's view on the future creditworthiness.
6. **Credit Rating Report**: The credit rating agency will provide you with a credit rating report that explains the rationale behind the assigned credit rating. The report will detail the factors considered, strengths and weaknesses identified, and any specific risks or concerns. It is a valuable document that can be shared with potential lenders, investors, and other stakeholders.
7. **Review and Dissemination**: Review the credit rating report thoroughly to understand the agency's assessment. If you believe there are errors or omissions, you may request a review or clarification from the credit rating

agency. You can then choose to disseminate the credit rating to relevant parties, such as lenders, investors, or regulatory bodies, as required.

The specific process and requirements may vary among credit rating agencies. Some agencies may have specific criteria or minimum thresholds for providing ratings to startups. It is advisable to consult with the credit rating agency directly to understand their specific process, documentation requirements, timeline, and associated costs. Obtaining a credit rating from a reputable credit rating agency can provide valuable insights and enhance your startup's credibility in the eyes of potential lenders, investors, and other stakeholders.

Peer 2 Peer Lending

Our primary objective in every mortgage transaction should be to borrow in a way that reduces debt, improves financial stability, and helps us get debt free in as short a time as possible!"
— **Dale Vermillion**

Peer-to-peer (P2P) lending, also known as peer lending or social lending, is a form of lending that connects individual borrowers directly with individual lenders through an online platform. It eliminates traditional intermediaries, such as banks or financial institutions, and allows individuals to lend and borrow money from one another. P2P lending platforms act as facilitators, matching borrowers with lenders based on their specific needs and preferences.

Peer-to-peer lending is often confused with crowdfunding, one could argue that peer 2 peer lending is a subcategory of crowdfunding, but the key difference is that P2P is about loans rather than equity purchase or donation.

Here's how P2P lending generally works:

1. **Borrower Application**: Individuals seeking a loan apply through a P2P lending platform by providing their personal and financial information, including the desired loan amount, purpose, and repayment terms.
2. **Credit Assessment**: The P2P platform assesses the creditworthiness of the borrower by analyzing their credit history, income, employment, and other relevant factors. Some platforms use their own credit scoring models, while others rely on external credit bureaus.
3. **Loan Listing**. If the borrower meets the platform's eligibility criteria, their loan request is listed on the platform. The listing includes details about the borrower, loan amount, interest rate, and other relevant information.
4. **Lender Participation**: Individual lenders, often referred to as investors, review the loan listings on the platform and decide whether to invest in a particular loan. They can evaluate borrower profiles, risk factors, and the potential return on investment.
5. **Fund Disbursement**: Once sufficient lenders commit to funding the loan, the P2P platform disburses the loan amount to the borrower. In some cases, a single lender may fund the entire loan, while in others, multiple lenders contribute smaller amounts to fulfil the loan.
6. **Loan Repayment**: The borrower repays the loan, including interest, in regular instalments over the agreed-upon term. The P2P platform collects the payments from the borrower and distributes them to the lenders.
7. **Platform Fees**: P2P lending platforms typically charge fees to both borrowers and lenders for using their services. These fees can vary depending on the platform and may include origination fees, servicing fees, or transaction fees.

P2P lending offers benefits to both borrowers and lenders. Borrowers may find it more accessible and flexible than traditional lending options, especially if they have limited credit history or face challenges in obtaining loans from banks. They may also benefit from potentially lower interest rates compared to other forms of borrowing. Lenders, on the other hand, have the opportunity to earn interest income by investing in loans and diversify their investment portfolio. It's important to note that P2P lending carries certain risks. Borrowers may face higher interest rates compared to bank lending. An overview of different Peer 2 Peer lending platforms is as follows:

Platforms Facilitating Peer-to-Peer Lending in India

Name of P2P Platform	Interest Rate (p.a.)	Loan Amount	Repayment Tenure	Listing/ Registration Fee
Lendbox	12% onwards	Rs.25,000 to Rs.5 lakh	6 months to 24 months	Rs.500
i2ifunding	12% onwards	Up to Rs. 10 lakhs	3 months to 36 months	Rs.100 plus GST
Faircent	9.99% onwards	Rs.10,000 to Rs.5 lakh	6 months to 36 months	Rs.500
OMLP2P	10.99% onwards	Rs.25,000 to Rs.10 lakh	3 months to 36 months	Rs.100
i-lend	15% onwards	Rs.25,000 to Rs.5 lakh	6 months to 36 months	-
LenDenClub	6.5% onwards	Rs.25,000 to Rs.5 lakh	3 months to 24 months	Rs.750

Regulation of P2P lending varies across countries, and it's advisable for participants to understand the legal and regulatory framework in their jurisdiction. Additionally, individuals considering P2P lending should conduct thorough research on the platforms, understand their terms and conditions, and assess the associated risks before participating.

Crowdfunding

> "If you need to raise funds from donors, you need to study them, respect them, and build everything you do around them." — **Jeff Brooks**

Crowdfunding is a method of raising funds for a venture by obtaining small contributions from a large number of people, typically via an online platform. It involves pooling together small amounts of money from a large group of individuals, often referred to as the "crowd," to collectively support a specific goal or initiative.

Crowd Funding Platforms in India

These are the various crowd platforms through which people support the startup by providing funds in small amounts. These funds are given at post idea stage when startups need funds to develop the product/prototype. These funds can be provided in the form of grants, loans, or equity. In India, there are several crowdfunding platforms that facilitate raising funds for various purposes, including business ventures, social causes, creative projects, and personal needs. Here are some popular crowdfunding platforms in India:

1. **Ketto**: Ketto is one of the largest crowdfunding platforms in India, focusing on social causes, nonprofits, and personal emergencies. It enables individuals and organizations to raise funds for medical expenses, education, disaster relief, NGOs, and more.
2. **Milaap**: Milaap is a crowdfunding platform that supports fundraising for medical treatments, education, disaster relief, and community development projects. It allows individuals, nonprofits, and social enterprises to create campaigns and reach out to a large donor community.
3. **ImpactGuru:** ImpactGuru is a crowdfunding platform specifically dedicated to medical fundraising. It helps individuals and families raise funds for medical treatments, surgeries, and healthcare emergencies.
4. **Wishberry**: Wishberry is a crowdfunding platform that focuses on creative projects, including films, music albums, books, art, and technology innovation. It allows artists, creators, and entrepreneurs to raise funds and engage with their supporters.
5. **FuelADream:** FuelADream is a crowdfunding platform that supports a wide range of projects, including social causes, creative endeavours, startups, and personal goals. It provides tools and resources to individuals and organizations to raise funds and promote their campaigns.
6. **BitGiving**: BitGiving is a crowdfunding platform that caters to various categories, including social causes, creative projects, and startups. It enables individuals and organizations to raise funds and build a community around their initiatives.

7. **Catapooolt**: Catapooolt is a crowdfunding platform that supports fundraising for startups, social ventures, creative projects, and personal causes. It offers different crowdfunding models, including rewards-based crowdfunding and equity crowdfunding.
8. **Rang De**: Rang De is a unique crowdfunding platform that focuses on providing microcredit and low-cost loans to entrepreneurs and individuals from underserved communities in India. It aims to alleviate poverty and promote financial inclusion.

These are just a few examples of crowdfunding platforms in India, and there are many others available as well. It's important to research and evaluate the features, fee structures, success rates, and terms and conditions of different platforms before choosing one that aligns with your specific fundraising needs and goals.

Crowdfunding Process

The process of crowdfunding typically involves the following key elements:

1. **Venture:** A person or startup initiates a crowdfunding campaign to raise funds seeking capital for a specific business idea.
2. **Online Platform:** Crowdfunding campaigns are usually hosted on specialized online platforms, commonly known as crowdfunding platforms or websites. These platforms provide a digital space where project creators can showcase their initiatives, set fundraising goals, and interact with potential backers.
3. **Backers:** Individuals who contribute money to support a crowdfunding campaign are called backers. Backers are typically motivated by an interest in the project or the potential for rewards or returns offered by the campaign.
4. **Funding Models:** Different types of crowdfunding models: donation-based, reward-based, equity-based, and debt-based crowdfunding are as follows:
    - **Donation-based crowdfunding:** Backers contribute money without expecting financial returns. This model is often used for charitable causes or community projects.
    - **Reward-based crowdfunding:** Backers contribute funds in exchange for non-financial rewards or pre-purchasing a product or service offered by the campaign. This model is commonly used by entrepreneurs and product developers.
    - **Equity-based crowdfunding:** Backers invest money in a company or startup in exchange for equity or ownership stake in the business. This model allows individuals to become shareholders and potentially benefit from the future success of the venture.
    - **Debt-based crowdfunding:** Backers lend money to individuals or businesses, expecting repayment of the principal amount plus interest over time. This model functions similarly to a loan.
5. **Campaign Duration and Goals:** Crowdfunding campaigns typically have a defined timeline during which the project creator aims to reach their funding goal. The funding goal represents the amount of money required to bring the project to fruition. If the campaign does not reach its funding goal within the specified timeframe, the funds are usually returned to the backers.

Crowdfunding has gained popularity as a means to access capital, engage with a supportive community, validate ideas, and democratize fundraising. It provides an alternative avenue for entrepreneurs and individuals to seek financial support and bring their projects to life, often bypassing traditional funding sources like banks or angel investors.

Regulations regarding crowdfunding in India:

The regulations regarding crowdfunding in India are primarily governed by the Securities and Exchange Board of India (SEBI). SEBI has introduced specific regulations to govern crowdfunding activities in the country. Here are the key regulations related to crowdfunding in India:

1. **SEBI (Alternative Investment Funds) Regulations, 2012:** These regulations define the framework for Alternative Investment Funds (AIFs), which includes certain categories of crowdfunding platforms. Crowdfunding platforms in India can operate as AIFs under specific categories, such as Venture Capital Funds (Category I AIFs) or Angel Funds (Category II AIFs).
2. **SEBI (Listing of Specified Securities on Institutional Trading Platform) Regulations, 2013:** These regulations pertain to crowdfunding platforms that seek to facilitate the listing of specified securities on an institutional trading platform. It provides guidelines for the eligibility criteria, disclosures, and obligations of issuers and platforms involved in such crowdfunding activities.
3. **SEBI (Issue of Capital and Disclosure Requirements) Regulations, 2018:** These regulations govern the issuance and listing of securities by companies in India, including crowdfunding offerings. Startups and other companies seeking to raise funds through crowdfunding must comply with these regulations in terms of disclosures, filing requirements, and investor protection measures.
4. **SEBI (Investment Advisers) Regulations, 2013:** These regulations apply to crowdfunding platforms that provide investment advisory services. Crowdfunding platforms acting as investment advisers must register with SEBI and comply with the regulatory requirements related to their advisory activities.
5. The concept of equity crowdfunding was discussed in a paper by the Securities and Exchange Board of India (SEBI) in 2014. Its provisions are as follows:
    - In the Indian context, QIBs, companies, high net worth individuals and eligible retail investors (ERI) can be allowed to invest in crowdfunding issuances.
    - Minimum annual income of ERIs could be ₹25 lakh and they should have filed tax returns for at least two years. There should be limit of ₹1 lakh for investment in each crowdfunding campaign. The retail investors should not be allowed to invest more than 5 per cent of their net worth in such issues. It will be the job of the platforms to screen the investors and ensure that the investors meet these criteria.
    - The size of each crowdfunding campaign should be limited to ₹10 crore and the issuing company should file all related information regarding the

- management, business and financials along with past legal record with SEBI. This will go a long way towards increasing the credibility of these issuances.
- Financial statements of the issuer should be disclosed on the company website every six months and SEBI should also lay down the net worth and other criteria for entities eligible to launch equity crowdfunding platforms.

The regulations related to crowdfunding may evolve over time, and it is recommended to refer to the latest guidelines issued by SEBI or consult with legal professionals for the most up-to-date information.

Registrar of Companies (RoC): Perspective on Crowdfunding

RoC in March 2023 issued notices against companies that violated the provisions of the Companies Act related to private placement of securities through crowdfunding platform. The RoC took action against firms that raised equity investment through technology platforms that made online pitches to investors, which was deemed to be in violation of the Companies Act. Section 42 of the Companies Act, which prohibits companies from using public advertisements or marketing channels to inform the public about private placement of securities.

The RoC imposed penalties on a Delhi-based company and its directors for allegedly violating the provision of the Companies Act. The company was penalized ₹2 lakh, and each of the two directors was penalized ₹1 lakh. The RoC argued that using technology platforms to reach a large number of investors through online pitches transformed the private placement into an unauthorized public offer. Private placement offers are limited to a maximum of 200 persons under the Companies Act. The RoC stated that it was unable to impose a penalty on the technology platform involved in the default because the Companies Act provision dealing with private placements did not allow for penalties on such platforms. However, the RoC asserted that the platform had facilitated the subject company's violation of the Companies Act. (Source: https://www.livemint.com/news/india/equity-crowd-funding-by-startups-draws-regulator-s-ire-11677863341914.html)

The RoC's actions were driven by the need to protect the interests of investors and ensure the bona fide nature of companies seeking investments. The regulator aims to prevent instances of companies raising capital and subsequently disappearing, especially when targeting small investors outside of stock exchanges. Equity crowdfunding involves solicitation at an early stage, which presents both benefits and risks. The actions taken by the RoC reflect the regulatory focus on ensuring compliance with the Companies Act and safeguarding the interests of investors in the context of private placement of securities through technology platforms.

Crowdfunding Platforms: Key Outcomes

Crowdfunding Platform	Success till December 2019
Catapooolt	Helped 40 projects to raise funds amounting to almost 150,000 USD from over 2000 contributors.
DreamWallets	Have raised about 1 crore in cash and kind
Faircent	With 6,000 potential lenders and 26,000 wantto-be borrowers on its platform, Faircent has disbursed total loans of almost USD 973,000 in the last 24 months
FuelADream	Notable campaigns included a battery-powered e-bike and a canal to irrigate a village's arid farmland

Source: Singh, V. (2020) Crowd funding in India, Studies in Indian Place Names, 40 (60)

Readiness for Funding from Angel Investors

"Life is not always a matter of holding good cards, but sometimes playing a poor hand well." **–Jack London, Author**

Before approaching the angel investors, startup founders should do their homework and prepare sound answers to the questions that they are likely to face during and after their pitching. These are some of the aspects that startup founders must be familiar with before developing their pitch for potential investors.

Product Market Fit (PMF)

PMF often associated with startups and early-stage ventures is a stage at which a product or service meets the needs of its target market effectively, resulting in strong customer demand and satisfaction, leading to repeat orders or generation of word of mouth or word of mouse. It signifies the alignment between the value proposition of a product and the demands of the market it serves.

The concept of Product-Market Fit was popularized by venture capitalist Marc Andreessen, who described it as follows: "Product/market fit means being in a good market with a product that can satisfy that market." The emphasis is on finding the right market, rather than solely focusing on the product.

It is an important milestone for startups and businesses because it indicates that they have found a market segment where their offering resonates and delivers value. It suggests that the product has achieved a level of market acceptance and can attract and retain customers.

Achieving Product-Market Fit is often an iterative process that involves gathering customer feedback, making product improvements, and refining the value proposition. Startups and businesses typically engage in market research, user testing, and continuous validation to understand customer needs, iterate their product or service, and ensure alignment with the target market.

A key mantra for knowing whether a startup has achieved Product-Market fit is assessing the answer to these two questions:

- **What is your customers' willingness to buy your product?**
- **Is there one burning need that you are addressing, and customers are saying "Thank God you are there"?**

If the willingness after becoming aware is decent and the product/service is solving a critical need of a market segment, it can be an indication that it is a starting point of Product-Market fit or the Product-Market fit has arrived. This might require a few iterations and pivoting to happen.

Some indicators of Product-Market Fit include:

1. **Customer Satisfaction**: Customers are highly satisfied with the product or service and find it valuable for addressing their needs or solving their problems.
2. **Retention and Engagement**: Customers continue to use the product or service over time, and there is a low churn rate. They are actively engaged and derive ongoing value from the offering.
3. **Strong Demand**: There is significant and growing demand for the product, leading to increased adoption and usage. This demand may result in organic growth and word-of-mouth referrals.
4. **Market Differentiation**: The product stands out from competitors and offers a unique value proposition that resonates with the target market. It addresses a specific pain point or provides a superior solution compared to existing alternatives.
5. **Sustainable Business Model**: The product has a viable and scalable business model, allowing the company to generate revenue and achieve profitability.

Once a company has achieved Product-Market Fit, the journey does not end here rather, it actually starts, and the startup founder can periodically ask the follow-up question:

- **How can the subsequent customers get more value as the solution becomes better and more nuanced?**

After attaining the PMF the company is better positioned for growth and can focus on scaling operations, expanding the customer base, and capturing a larger market share. For example, Whatsapp a messaging application founded in 2009 by Brian Acton and Jan Koum brought down the cost of overseas communication a big pain point at that time and a key barrier to almost zero. It gained popularity due to its ease of use. From that stage they gradually started adding more value by adding more features, evolving with consumer behaviour, and changing the industry dynamics.

SaaS Businesses: An example of Product-Market Fit

SaaS software that helps companies become more efficient is likely to be valuable. Especially in traditional industries that don't grow much and face constant pressures with changing customer preferences, developing a SaaS product is a winning formula. The benefits from the SaaS software can be in the form of:
- Can your software help acquire customers more efficiently, and reach them faster-better-cheaper?
- Can software help in managing teams, especially on the field, better? Do more with less?
- Can your software deal with customer complaints and requests and provide customer service faster-better-cheaper?

- Can software digitize the workflows that form backbone of the organizations, making them better-faster-cheaper and also generate reports and analysis for better decision-making and monitoring the performance and progress?

At the core of SaaS solution for traditional industries lies a custom-built workflow that can replace a traditional pen and paper-based process and the software become the central nervous system of these organizations. Over time, this workflow platform becomes indispensable, with large parts of the organization relying on it. Eventually, it integrates with itself the other co-dependent sub-systems in the organization. Thus, starting from being a tool, it evolves into a platform embedding payments and customer interface with the organization workflow.

Moat

Before developing a pitch, it's important for a startup founder to understand Moat. In the context of startups, a moat refers to a sustainable competitive advantage that helps a company maintain its market position and fend off competition. The concept of a moat was popularized by renowned investor Warren Buffett, who compared a business to a castle with a moat protecting it from attackers.

In the startup world, having a moat is crucial for long-term success and value creation. It involves building barriers that make it difficult for other companies to replicate or compete effectively with the startup's products or services. These barriers can take various forms and may include:

1. **Technological innovation**: Developing proprietary technology or intellectual property that gives the startup an edge over competitors. This could be in the form of patents, trade secrets, or unique algorithms.
2. **Network effects**: Creating a product or platform that becomes more valuable as more users join or engage with it. Network effects make it challenging for competitors to attract users away from an established platform due to the existing user base and the benefits derived from network participation.
3. **Economies of scale**: Achieving cost advantages by scaling operations and increasing production. Startups that can efficiently produce and distribute their products or services at lower costs have a competitive advantage over newcomers who cannot match their economies of scale.
4. **Branding and reputation**: Building a strong brand image and customer loyalty can create a moat by establishing trust, recognition, and customer preference. Well-known brands often enjoy customer preference and are harder to dislodge from their market position.
5. **Regulatory advantages**: Operating in a regulated industry where obtaining licenses, permits, or compliance with regulations presents barriers to entry. This can protect startups from new entrants who may struggle to navigate regulatory hurdles.
6. **Unique data or information**: Accumulating and leveraging valuable data or insights that are difficult for competitors to acquire or replicate. Startups with access to unique datasets or proprietary information can build products or services that are hard to reproduce.

7. **Switching cost**: The total cost that is likely to be incurred if the supplier has to be changed can be deterrent and provides shield from competitors for early movers.
8. **Taste:** As consumers developed likeness for a particular taste a good number of them usually don't prefer to adopt late entrants, which are likely to have a different taste than the one they have got used to.
9. **Distribution:** It takes a lot of time, money and effort to build a distribution channel. So, the availability of distribution channel can provide significant advantage for a start that has already established a distribution channel over those who have yet to do the same.
10. **Location based advantage:** Especially in industries like retail, and hospitality, location provides a significant advantage as those spaces are limited and not easily replicable.

It's important to note that a moat is not a guarantee of success, and startups must continue to innovate and adapt to changes in the market to remain competitive. Additionally, moats can be eroded over time if competitors find ways to overcome the barriers or if market dynamics shift significantly. Therefore, startups should always be vigilant and continuously strive to strengthen their moats while staying agile and responsive to market changes.

Employee Stock Options (ESOPs)

"Highly engaged employees make the customer experience. Disengaged employees break it."
Timothy R. Clark - Founder and Chairman, TR Clark Associates

An Employee Stock Option (ESOPs) is a financial instrument that grants employees the right to purchase a specific number of company's shares at a predetermined price, known as the exercise or strike price, within a specified period. It is a form of compensation offered by companies to attract and retain talented employees.

Before raising funding startup founders want to have a high-quality team in place that can assure the investors. Therefore, a good number of them issue ESOPs to attract top quality talent from leading organizations in order to impress investors as it demonstrates to investors the employee retention in short to medium term. Here are some key features and considerations related to ESOPs:

1. **Granting of options**: Companies grant stock options to employees as part of their compensation package. The number of options granted and the terms and the associated conditions are determined by the company's stock option plan.
2. **Exercise price**: The exercise price is the predetermined price at which employees can buy the company's stock when exercising their options. The exercise price is usually set at the current market price of the stock on the date of grant or at a discount to the market price.
3. **Vesting period**: Stock options typically have a vesting period, which is the length of time an employee must wait before being able to exercise the options. Vesting encourages employees to remain with the company and aligns their interests with the company's long-term performance.
4. **Expiration date**: Each stock option has an expiration date or the maturity date. It represents the last date on which the employee can exercise the option. If the option is not exercised before the expiration date, it becomes worthless.
5. **Financial gain**: When employees exercise their stock options, they can purchase shares of company stock at the exercise price. If the market price of the stock at that time is higher than the exercise price, employees can sell the shares in the market and realize a financial gain.
6. **Risks and considerations**: ESOPs carry certain risks and considerations. The value of the options depends on the future performance of the company's stock. If the stock price declines or remains below the exercise price, the options may not have any value. Additionally, there may be tax implications associated with the exercise and sale of stock options.

ESOPs are often viewed as a way to align the interests of employees and shareholders, as employees have the opportunity to benefit from the company's success through stock ownership. They provide employees with a potential financial incentive and can play a role in motivating and rewarding employees for their contribution to the company's growth.

Factors to be kept in mind while Issuing ESOPs

When issuing ESOPs, companies should consider several factors to ensure the effective implementation and management of the stock option program. Here are some key factors to keep in mind:

1. **Objectives and strategy**: Clearly define the objectives of the stock option program and align it with the company's overall strategy. Determine whether the primary purpose is to attract and retain talent, incentivize performance, or align employee interests with those of shareholders.
2. **Eligibility and criteria**: Determine which employees are eligible to participate in the stock option program. Consider factors such as job level, tenure, performance, and contribution to the company's success.
3. **Granting terms**: Establish the terms and conditions of the stock options, including the number of options granted to each employee, the exercise price, vesting period, and expiration date. Ensure that the terms are fair, consistent, and compliant with applicable regulations and accounting standards.
4. **Communication and education**: Clearly communicate the stock option program to employees, providing information on how it works, the potential benefits, and the associated risks. Educate employees about the value of stock options, taxation implications, and importance of long-term financial planning.
5. **Valuation and pricing**: Determine the appropriate exercise price for the options. Consider factors such as the current market price of the company's stock, industry benchmarks, and the potential future value of the stock. Ensure that the exercise price is set at a fair and reasonable level.
6. **Compliance and legal considerations**: Adhere to legal and regulatory requirements related to stock option plans. Comply with securities laws, tax regulations, and accounting standards. Consult with legal, tax, and accounting professionals to ensure compliance and mitigate potential risks.
7. **Plan administration**: Establish a robust system for administering the stock option plan, including processes for granting options, tracking vesting periods, managing exercises and expirations, and accurately accounting for the stock-based compensation expense.
8. **Dilution and shareholder approval**: Consider the potential impact of issuing additional shares through the stock option program on existing shareholders' ownership and voting rights. Determine whether shareholder approval is required for issuance of stock options and comply with applicable regulations.
9. **Performance metrics and goals**: Link the stock option program to performance metrics and goals that align with the company's strategic objectives. Consider incorporating performance-based vesting criteria tied to individual, team, or company-wide performance targets.
10. **Regular review and evaluation**: Continuously review and evaluate the effectiveness of the stock option program. Monitor its impact on employee retention, motivation, and overall company performance. Consider making modifications to the program based on feedback and business conditions.

By carefully considering these factors, companies can design and implement ESOPs that effectively motivate and reward employees while aligning their interests with the long-term success of the organization.

ESOP Allocation, Expansion, and Buyback in Indian Startups

There is an increasing trend of ESOP allocation, expansion, and buyback in Indian startups, signaling the maturity of the ecosystem. This indicates the recognition of the importance of rewarding employees creating wealth opportunities for them as startups achieve significant milestones. In 2021, more than three dozen Indian startups facilitated or announced ESOP buyback programs worth around $440 million. This marked eight times increase compared to the previous year, reflecting the growing importance of rewarding employees through liquidity events.

Fintrackr's research shows that companies such as Flipkart, Swiggy, PhonePe, Udaan, ShareChat, Razorpay, CRED, Browserstack, Meesho, Spinny, Zerodha, Unacademy, upGrad announced ESOP buyback program worth more than $440 million. Flipkart ($80.5 million), Browserstack ($50 million), upGrad ($29.5 million), Udaan ($23 million), CRED ($19.3 million), ShareChat ($19.1 million), and PhonePe ($18 million) were the top buyers of ESOPs in the list. According to *Fintrackr*'s data, around a dozen companies including Zerodha, Swiggy, Unacademy, FirstCry, Urban Company and Meesho bought close to $50 million worth of ESOPs from their employees.

If Swiggy and Zerodha turned out to be the biggest fortune creators for their employees in the in 2020 with $9 million worth of buyback each, then Swiggy has also announced that it will buy stock worth $23 million held by their employees in 2022.

According to a report by Longhouse Consulting, Flipkart has created a Rs 17,000 crore ($2.26 billion) ESOP pool whereas Oyo has created a pool of Rs 7,569 crore ($1 billion). Zomato, Paytm and Nykaa have an ESOP pool of Rs 5,639 crore ($750 million), Rs 4,571 crore ($610 million) and Rs 4,280 crore ($570 million), respectively. Byju's has an ESOP pool of Rs 3,092 crore ($412 million). In October 2021 stockbroking platform Zerodha allocated 7,00,000 options worth Rs 100 crore ($13.3 million) under its fresh ESOPs Plan 2021. Earlier, OfBusiness expanded its ESOP pool size to Rs.282 crore or $38.5 million. *Entrackr* had exclusively reported both developments. According to ShareChat, its ESOP pool is currently valued at Rs 1,280 crore or $170 million. Among the 43 startups that achieved unicorn status in 2021, 15 of them, including Spinny, CRED, Urban Company, BharatPe, Meesho, Moglix, UpGrad, and ShareChat, provided ESOP liquidity programs.

Key Metrics for Pitching

"Without a yardstick, there is no measurement, and without measurement, there is no control." **– Pravin Shah**

Every domain has its vocabulary; knowing it and using it makes one a worthy member of that community. On the contrary, not knowing them creates an impression that one is naive and has not yet seasoned to become worthy of higher consideration. Some of the important terms usually used during the pitching process by the startup founders and investors are as follows:

A. **GMV:** Stands for Gross Merchandise Value. It is a metric commonly used in the e-commerce industry to measure the total value of merchandise or goods sold through a platform or marketplace over a specific period. GMV represents the aggregate value of all the transactions that occur on the platform, irrespective of any discounts, returns, or cancellations.
GMV includes the total value of goods sold, including taxes, shipping charges, and any additional fees. It provides a measure of the scale and growth of a platform's business by capturing the total transactional value generated within a given timeframe.
GMV is an essential metric for e-commerce platforms, as it helps assess their market presence, revenue potential, and ability to attract customers and drive transactions. It is often used in performance evaluations, business planning, and investor reporting.
GMV does not directly represent the revenue or profitability of a platform. It is a measure of the transactional volume and value without accounting for costs, expenses, or profit margins associated with the goods sold. Therefore, it is crucial to consider other financial metrics, such as revenue, net profit, and gross profit, to evaluate the financial health and profitability of a business.

B. **TG:** "TG" is an abbreviation for "Target Group" or "Target Market." It refers to the specific group of people or customers that a startup aims to reach, serve, and cater to with its products or services. Identifying the target group is a critical aspect of a startup's marketing and business strategy. By defining a well-defined target group, startups can better understand their potential customers' needs, preferences, and pain points. This enables them to tailor their products or services to meet the specific requirements of their target audience and improve their chances of success in the market. The process of identifying the target group involves market research, customer segmentation, and analysis of consumer behaviour. Startups may consider various factors, such as demographics, psychographics, geographic location, and behaviour patterns, to define their target group accurately. Once the target group is identified, startups can design their marketing campaigns, messaging, and sales strategies to resonate with their intended audience. This focused approach helps in optimizing marketing efforts and resources, resulting in better customer acquisition and brand positioning.

C. **ICP:** Ideal Customer Profile is a detailed description of the characteristics, traits, and attributes of the perfect or ideal customer for a particular product or service. It helps businesses and marketers identify and understand the type of customer who would derive the most value from their offerings and be most likely to make a purchase.

Creating an ICP involves analyzing existing customers, market research, and gathering data to define a specific set of criteria that the ideal customer possesses. These criteria may include demographic information (age, gender, location, etc.), psychographic traits (interests, hobbies, values, lifestyle), pain points, buying behaviour, and other relevant factors that play a role in the decision-making process.

By understanding their Ideal Customer Profile, businesses can better tailor their marketing strategies, product development, and overall approach to attract and retain the most valuable customers. It enables companies to focus their efforts and resources on the audience that is most likely to generate long-term profitability and success.

D. **TAM:** Total Addressable Market TAM represents the total market demand for a particular product or service. It is the entire revenue opportunity available in a market if a company were to capture 100% of the demand without any competition or constraints. TAM provides an estimation of the maximum revenue potential for a product or service in a given market.

E. **SAM:** Serviceable Addressable Market SAM represents the segment of the TAM that a company can realistically address and serve. It considers the specific subset of the market that a company's business model, resources, and capabilities can effectively reach. SAM takes into account factors such as geographic limitations, customer segments, distribution channels, and the company's competitive positioning.

F. **SOM:** Serviceable Obtainable Market SOM represents the portion of the SAM that a company can realistically capture or obtain over a specific period. It considers factors such as the company's marketing efforts, sales capabilities, and competitive landscape. SOM provides an estimation of the market share a company can realistically achieve given its market entry and growth strategies.

G. **Average Order Value (AOV):** AOV quantifies the average spending by a customer per transaction, revealing the financial impact of individual customers.

H. **LTV (Life Time Value) or CLV (Customer Lifetime Value):** It is a metric that quantifies the total predicted value a customer will generate for a business over the entire duration of their relationship with that business. LTV helps businesses understand the long-term revenue potential and profitability associated with acquiring and retaining customers. To calculate LTV, businesses typically consider factors such as:

a. **Average Purchase Value**: The average amount of money a customer spends during each transaction.
b. **Purchase Frequency**: The average number of times a customer makes a purchase within a specific period.
c. **Customer Lifespan:** The average length of time a customer continues to engage with a business.

The formula for calculating LTV is:

LTV = (Average Purchase Value) x (Purchase Frequency) x (Customer Lifespan)

For example, if the average purchase value is Rs.50, the purchase frequency is 4 times per year, and the customer lifespan is 5 years, the LTV would be Rs.50 x 4 x 5 = Rs.1,000.

LTV is an important metric for businesses because it helps them determine how much they can invest in customer acquisition, retention, and marketing efforts. By comparing the LTV of different customer segments or cohorts, businesses can identify their most valuable customers and allocate resources accordingly. It also assists in making informed decisions about pricing strategies, customer loyalty programs, and customer relationship management.

Calculating LTV involves making certain assumptions and predictions, and it may vary based on customer behaviour, market dynamics, and other factors. Therefore, LTV should be used as a guideline and regularly monitored and updated to reflect changing customer trends and business conditions.

I. **Customer Acquisition Cost (CAC)**: It is a metric that quantifies the average cost a business incurs to acquire a new customer. It measures the amount of money a company spends on marketing, sales, and other related activities to attract and convert a prospect into a paying customer.

To calculate CAC, divide the total costs associated with customer acquisition over a specific period by the number of customers acquired during that same period. The formula for calculating CAC is:

CAC = Total Cost of Customer Acquisition / Number of Customers Acquired

The costs included in the calculation of CAC may vary depending on the business and its specific marketing and sales strategies. Common expenses considered in CAC calculations include:

a. **Marketing Costs**: These include expenses related to advertising, digital marketing campaigns, content creation, social media promotion, search engine marketing, and marketing efforts for acquiring new customers.
b. **Sales Costs**: These are expenses associated with sales activities such as sales team salaries, commissions, bonuses, sales tools and software,

customer relationship management (CRM) systems, and any other costs directly related to the sales process.
   c. **Onboarding Costs**: These are costs incurred during the onboarding and initial setup of new customers, including implementation, training, and customer support.
   d. **Overhead Costs**: Certain overhead costs that can be attributed to customer acquisition, such as salaries of marketing and sales managers, rent for office space used by marketing and sales teams, and other related expenses, may be included.

CAC is usually calculated over a specific period, such as a month, quarter, or year. The result is an average cost per customer acquired during that period.

Monitoring and analyzing CAC is crucial for businesses to understand the efficiency and effectiveness of their customer acquisition strategies. By comparing CAC with customer lifetime value (LTV) and other relevant metrics, businesses can assess the profitability and sustainability of their customer acquisition efforts. If the CAC exceeds the LTV, it may indicate an unsustainable customer acquisition strategy, and adjustments may be needed to improve profitability.

CAC is used as a benchmark to evaluate the return on investment (ROI) of marketing and sales campaigns, optimize marketing channels, set pricing strategies, and allocate resources more effectively to acquire customers in a cost-efficient manner.

J. **Gross Margin (GM):** Also known as Gross Profit Margin, is a financial metric that represents the percentage of revenue remaining after deducting the cost of goods sold (COGS). It measures the profitability of a company's core operations and indicates how efficiently a company is generating profit from its production or sale of goods. The formula to calculate Gross Margin is as follows:

Gross Margin = (Revenue - Cost of Goods Sold) / Revenue * 100

In this formula, the revenue represents the total sales or revenue generated by the company, while the cost of goods sold includes the direct costs associated with producing or acquiring the goods that are sold. It typically includes expenses such as raw materials, manufacturing costs, direct labor, and direct overhead.

Gross Margin provides insight into a company's ability to generate profit from its products or services before considering other operating expenses. A higher Gross Margin indicates that a company is generating more revenue relative to its production costs, which is generally desirable as it allows for greater profitability.

Gross Margin is often expressed as a percentage, representing the portion of revenue that remains after accounting for the cost of goods sold. For example, if a company has Rs.1,000,000 in revenue and Rs.700,000 in COGS, the Gross Margin would be calculated as follows:

Gross Margin = (Rs.1,000,000 - Rs.700,000) / Rs.1,000,000 * 100 = 30%

A higher Gross Margin indicates greater profitability, as a larger portion of revenue is retained as gross profit. It is important to compare Gross Margins across industries and with competitors to gain a better understanding of a company's performance and efficiency in generating profits from its core operations.

It's worth noting that Gross Margin does not account for other operating expenses such as selling and marketing expenses, administrative costs, or taxes. Therefore, it provides an indication of profitability at the gross profit level and should be considered alongside other financial metrics for a comprehensive assessment of a company's financial health.

K. **Business Unit Economics:** Also known as **Unit Economics**, refers to the financial analysis of the profitability and sustainability of a specific business unit or product/service offering within a larger company. It involves examining the revenue and cost drivers associated with a particular unit to understand its financial performance and viability.

The primary goal of analyzing business unit economics is to determine whether a specific business unit or product/service is generating sufficient revenue and operating with favourable margins to cover its costs and contribute to the overall profitability of the company. It helps assess the financial health and potential of individual units and provides insights into their long-term viability and scalability. Key components of Business Unit Economics include:

1. **Revenue Generation**: This involves understanding the sources of revenue for the business unit and evaluating the unit's ability to generate sales or attract customers. Revenue drivers may include product sales, subscription fees, advertising revenue, or any other form of income associated with the unit.
2. **Cost Structure**: Analyzing the cost structure of the business unit is crucial to determine its profitability. This includes identifying and quantifying the various costs associated with producing, marketing, and delivering the product/service. Costs may include direct costs of production, overhead expenses, marketing expenses, personnel costs, and other operating expenses.
3. **Profitability Metrics**: Business unit economics involves assessing key financial metrics to evaluate the unit's profitability. These metrics may include gross margin (revenue minus direct costs), operating margin

(revenue minus all operating costs), net profit margin (revenue minus all costs, including taxes and interest), and other relevant profitability ratios.
4. **Customer Acquisition Cost (CAC)**: It refers to the cost associated with acquiring a new customer, including marketing expenses, sales commissions, and any other costs incurred during the customer acquisition process.
5. **Lifetime Value of a Customer (LTV)**: LTV represents the estimated revenue a business can generate from a customer over the entire customer lifecycle.

Analyzing business unit economics is essential for strategic decision-making, resource allocation, and optimizing the profitability of individual business units or product lines. It helps identify areas for improvement, cost optimization opportunities, pricing strategies, and growth potential. By understanding the unit economics, companies can make informed decisions about scaling, investing resources, and prioritizing initiatives within their business operations.

L. **Burn Rate:** Burn rate refers to the rate at which a company or organization depletes its cash reserves or funds over a specific period. It represents the net negative cash flow or the amount of money a company spends each month or year to cover its operating expenses, such as salaries, rent, utilities, marketing, research and development, and other costs.

The burn rate is typically expressed as a monthly or annual figure. It is a crucial metric for startups and early-stage companies, particularly those that have not yet achieved profitability, as it helps assess the sustainability of their financial operations and the runway they have before running out of funds.

A high burn rate indicates that a company is spending money at a rapid pace and depleting its cash reserves quickly. Conversely, a low burn rate suggests that a company is conserving cash and can sustain its operations for a more extended period.

The burn rate is often used in conjunction with the concept of "runway," which represents the length of time a company has before it exhausts its available funds based on its current burn rate. The runway is calculated by dividing the available cash or funds by the burn rate.

Managing the burn rate is crucial for companies, especially startups, as it impacts their financial health and ability to reach key milestones. Startups typically aim to minimize their burn rate while simultaneously working towards achieving positive cash flow or securing additional funding.

The burn rate can be influenced by various factors, including:

1. **Operating Expenses**: The level of operating expenses, including personnel costs, marketing expenses, research and development costs, and other

overhead expenses, contribute to the burn rate. Controlling and managing these expenses can help lower the burn rate.
2. **Growth Strategy**: Companies pursuing aggressive growth strategies may have higher burn rates as they invest heavily in expanding their operations, acquiring customers, or entering new markets. This approach aims to capture market share and achieve economies of scale.
3. **Revenue Generation**: Companies that generate revenue can offset their burn rate to some extent. Increasing revenue through sales, subscriptions, or other sources can help reduce the negative cash flow and extend the runway.
4. **Funding Rounds**: The timing and success of fundraising efforts can have a significant impact on a company's burn rate. Raising additional funds through equity financing or debt financing can provide the necessary capital to sustain operations and extend the runway.

Managing the burn rate requires careful financial planning, monitoring, and decision-making. Startups need to balance their growth objectives with financial sustainability to ensure they have sufficient runway to achieve their milestones, secure profitability, or attract further funding if needed.

M. **Burn multiple P3M**: "P3M" refers to a **period of three months** (i.e., a quarter), thus, it is a measure that assesses the multiple or ratio of cash burn over a three-month period.

N. **Runway:** Runway for startups refers to the length of time a startup can sustain its operations before depleting its available funds. It represents the estimated duration, typically measured in months, that a startup can continue operating and covering its expenses without additional funding or achieving profitability.

The runway is calculated by dividing the available cash or funds by the startup's monthly burn rate, which is the rate at which the company is spending money and depleting its cash reserves. The burn rate is determined by the startup's operating expenses, such as salaries, rent, marketing, research and development, and other costs.

The concept of runway is important for startups because it helps determine their financial sustainability and the time, they have to achieve key milestones or secure additional funding. A longer runway provides more time for the startup to refine its product, acquire customers, generate revenue, and reach a point of self-sufficiency or profitability.

Here's a simplified example to illustrate the calculation of runway:
Available Funds: Rs.500,000
Monthly Burn Rate: Rs.25,000
Runway = Available Funds / Monthly Burn Rate
Runway = Rs.500,000 / Rs.25,000
Runway = 20 months

In this example, the startup has a runway of 20 months, meaning it can continue its operations for 20 months before exhausting its available funds based on its current burn rate. The startup needs to carefully manage its expenses, revenue generation, and fundraising efforts to ensure it can extend or replenish its runway as needed.

Having a longer runway provides several benefits to startups:

1. **Time for Product Development and Iteration**: Startups can use the extended runway to refine their product or service, iterate based on user feedback, and improve the market fit. It allows for more time to test hypotheses, make adjustments, and build a better offering.
2. **Customer Acquisition and Growth**: With a longer runway, startups can invest in customer acquisition, marketing campaigns, and growth initiatives to attract and retain customers. They have more time to build a user base and generate revenue.
3. **Investor Confidence**: Investors are often interested in startups with a longer runway as it indicates a greater buffer for achieving milestones and attracting additional funding. A longer runway can enhance investor confidence in the startup's ability to execute its business plan.
4. **Flexibility and Adaptability**: Startups with a longer runway have more flexibility to adapt to market changes, pivot their strategies, or explore new opportunities without the pressure of immediate financial constraints.

Managing and extending the runway is a critical aspect of startup operations. Startups can achieve this by optimizing their burn rate, controlling expenses, generating revenue, securing funding through equity financing or debt financing, and demonstrating progress towards key milestones that increase their valuation and attract investors.

Ultimately, a longer runway provides startups with the necessary time and resources to navigate the early stages of their journey and increase their chances of long-term success.

O. **Churn Rate**: Also known as customer attrition rate, is a metric that measures the rate at which customers or subscribers cancel or discontinue their relationship with a company's product or service over a specific period. It is an important metric for startups and subscription-based businesses as it reflects the loss of customers and revenue.

Churn rate is expressed as a percentage and is calculated by dividing the number of customers lost during a period by the total number of customers at the beginning of that period. The formula for calculating it is as follows:

Churn Rate = (Number of Customers Lost / Total Number of Customers) x 100

For example, if a startup had 500 customers at the beginning of a month and lost 20 customers during that month, the churn rate would be:

Churn Rate = (20 / 500) x 100 = 4%

A high churn rate indicates that a significant portion of customers is discontinuing their subscriptions or leaving the company's product or service. This can have negative implications for the startup's revenue, growth, and long-term sustainability. On the other hand, a low churn rate suggests that customers are satisfied and staying loyal to the company. Analyzing churn rate helps startups in several ways:

1. **Customer Retention**: Churn rate is a key metric for monitoring customer retention and loyalty. Startups can identify trends and patterns in customer churn, understand the reasons behind it, and take proactive measures to improve customer satisfaction and reduce churn.
2. **Revenue Impact**: Churn rate directly affects a startup's revenue. Losing customers leads to a decline in monthly recurring revenue (MRR) and can hinder the company's growth and profitability. By tracking churn rate, startups can assess the financial impact and take actions to mitigate revenue loss.
3. **Product/Service Improvement**: High churn rates may indicate issues with the product or service that are causing customers to leave. Startups can analyze churn patterns, collect feedback from departing customers, and make improvements to address pain points, enhance user experience, and increase customer satisfaction.
4. **Customer Success and Support**: Monitoring churn rate helps startups identify areas where they can improve customer success initiatives and support services. By understanding the reasons behind customer churn, startups can provide better support, optimize onboarding processes, and enhance customer relationships.
5. **Business Planning and Forecasting**: Churn rate is an important factor for business planning and forecasting, particularly in terms of revenue projections and customer acquisition targets. Startups can use historical churn data to make informed decisions about resource allocation, growth strategies, and customer acquisition efforts.

Reducing churn rate requires a combination of effective customer onboarding, proactive customer support, continuous product improvement, and addressing customer needs and pain points. By focusing on customer retention and reducing churn, startups can build a more sustainable and successful business. Churn rate can vary across industries and business models. What may be considered a high churn rate in one industry could be acceptable in another. Startups should compare their churn rate to industry benchmarks or competitors to gain a better understanding of their performance and identify areas for improvement.

P. MRR: MRR stands for Monthly Recurring Revenue and is a key metric used by startups and subscription-based businesses to measure their monthly revenue from recurring sources. It represents the predictable and recurring revenue generated by the company's subscription-based products or services on a monthly basis.

MRR is particularly relevant for startups that operate on a subscription or recurring revenue model, where customers pay a regular fee for ongoing access to the product or service. It provides insights into the stability and growth potential of the business. There are two main components in calculating MRR:

1. **Number of Subscribers**: MRR is calculated by multiplying the number of subscribers or customers by the average revenue per customer. This includes all active paying customers during a specific period, typically a month.
2. **Average Revenue per Customer:** The average revenue per customer is determined by dividing the total revenue generated from subscriptions by the number of customers.

The formula for calculating MRR is as follows:

MRR = Number of Subscribers x Average Revenue per Customer

MRR helps startups in several ways:
1. **Revenue Measurement:** MRR provides a clear picture of the company's monthly revenue from recurring sources. It allows startups to track their revenue growth, identify trends, and assess the impact of pricing changes or customer churn.
2. **Financial Planning**: MRR is an essential metric for financial planning and forecasting. It provides visibility into the company's future revenue streams and helps in setting realistic revenue targets and budgeting.
3. **Performance Tracking**: Startups can monitor changes in MRR over time to evaluate the success of their customer acquisition and retention efforts. It helps identify growth opportunities, measure the impact of marketing and sales initiatives, and assess the effectiveness of pricing strategies.
4. **Investor Attraction**: MRR is a crucial metric for investors, particularly for startups seeking funding. It demonstrates the potential for predictable and scalable revenue, which can increase the attractiveness of the business to investors and potential acquirers.
5. **Churn Analysis**: MRR enables startups to analyze customer churn, which is the rate at which customers cancel their subscriptions. By tracking MRR and the reasons behind churn, startups can implement strategies to reduce churn, improve customer retention, and enhance revenue stability.

Startups can further analyze MRR by segmenting it based on different customer cohorts, subscription tiers, or product lines to gain deeper insights into revenue drivers and optimize their offerings accordingly. MRR is a valuable metric for startups operating on a subscription model, providing a clear view of their recurring revenue, and enabling data-driven decision-making for growth and profitability.

Q. **Gross MRR Churn**: Also known as revenue churn, is a metric used by subscription-based businesses, particularly in the software-as-a-service (SaaS) industry, to measure the loss of revenue from existing customers over a specific period. It represents the total revenue lost from cancellations, downgrades, or reductions in subscription plans. The calculation of Gross MRR churn involves determining the lost revenue as a percentage of total MRR at the beginning of a given period. The formula, is as follows:

Gross MRR Churn = (Lost MRR / Starting MRR) x 100

Where:
- **Lost MRR:** The total MRR lost during the period due to customer churn, downgrades, or reductions in subscription plans.
- **Starting MRR**: The total MRR at the beginning of the period.

Gross MRR churn provides insights into the rate at which customers are discontinuing or reducing their subscriptions, which directly affects a business's revenue and growth. It helps businesses evaluate the impact of customer churn on their financial performance and assess the effectiveness of customer retention efforts.

It's important to note that Gross MRR churn does not take into account any expansion or upsells from existing customers during the period. It focuses solely on the lost revenue from churned or downgraded customers. To gain a more comprehensive understanding of revenue changes, businesses often analyze Net MRR churn, which considers both lost revenue and expansion revenue from existing customers.

Net MRR churn factors in the revenue gained from upsells, cross-sells, or upgrades, which can offset some of the lost revenue. By comparing Gross MRR churn and Net MRR churn, businesses can better assess their overall revenue retention and growth potential.

Monitoring and analyzing churn metrics like Gross MRR churn helps businesses identify patterns, understand customer behaviour, and make informed decisions to improve customer retention, enhance product offerings, and drive sustainable revenue growth.

R. **ARR**: Stands for Annual Recurring Revenue, and it is a key metric used by subscription-based businesses, particularly in the software-as-a-service (SaaS) industry, to measure their annualized revenue from recurring subscriptions.

ARR represents the total revenue that a business expects to generate from its subscription-based customers over the course of a year, assuming that their subscription plans remain unchanged. It provides a snapshot of the annual revenue stream and helps businesses gauge their financial performance and growth potential.

To calculate ARR, you sum up the Monthly Recurring Revenue (MRR) from all active customers and multiply it by 12 (representing the 12 months in a year). The formula is as follows:

ARR = MRR x 12
Where:
- MRR: Monthly Recurring Revenue, which represents the total revenue generated from active monthly subscriptions.

ARR is a valuable metric for several reasons:

1. **Predictability**: ARR provides a more predictable and stable view of a business's revenue compared to one-time sales or non-recurring revenue streams. It highlights the consistent revenue that can be expected from existing customers and helps businesses forecast their financial performance.
2. **Growth Measurement**: By comparing ARR over different periods, businesses can assess their growth rate and track progress. Increasing ARR indicates positive growth, while decreasing ARR could indicate customer churn or a decline in revenue-generating opportunities.
3. **Valuation**: ARR is often used as a basis for valuation in the SaaS industry. It helps investors and potential acquirers evaluate the financial health and potential of a subscription-based business.
4. **Customer Lifetime Value**: ARR is a key component in determining the Customer Lifetime Value (CLTV) metric. ARR is multiplied by the estimated customer lifespan to calculate CLTV.

ARR assumes that customers will remain subscribed and maintain their current subscription plans throughout the year. In reality, customer churn, upgrades, downgrades, and other factors can impact the actual revenue generated. Therefore, it's crucial to monitor additional metrics such as customer churn rate, expansion revenue, and net new ARR to gain a comprehensive understanding of a business's revenue dynamics.

ARR provides businesses with a standardized and meaningful way to assess their recurring revenue streams, track growth, and make informed decisions regarding pricing, customer retention, and business strategy.

S. **Annualised TPV (Total Payment Volume)**: It refers to the total value of payments processed by a company or platform over a specified period. It is typically extrapolated to represent the volume that would be processed in a full year. It is a metric commonly used in the payment industry to understand the scale and performance of a payment platform or processor.

The calculation of Annualised TPV involves taking the actual TPV for a shorter period, such as a month or a quarter, and multiplying it by an appropriate factor to estimate the annual value. The factor used depends on the growth or seasonality patterns of the business. For example, if the TPV for a quarter is Rs.1

million, and the business expects similar growth rates for the remaining three quarters, the Annualised TPV would be Rs.4 million (Rs.1 million x 4).

Annualised TPV provides a more comprehensive view of a company's payment processing volume by normalizing it over a full year. It helps businesses evaluate their performance, track growth, and compare their payment volume with competitors or industry benchmarks.

This metric is particularly relevant for startups that are payment processors, payment gateways, online marketplaces, or a business that handles a significant volume of transactions. It enables them to assess their revenue potential, negotiate better terms with payment partners, and attract investors or strategic partnerships based on their processing capabilities. Though Annualised TPV provides a useful snapshot of payment volume, investors should consider it alongside other metrics such as revenue, transaction fees, customer acquisition costs, and profitability to gain a more complete understanding of a startup's financial health and performance.

T. **Organic Digital Marketing**: It refers to content and community-driven marketing strategies that focus on attracting and engaging an audience through non-paid or naturally occurring channels. It involves creating valuable content, fostering relationships, and building a community of loyal customers and followers. Here are the key elements of organic digital marketing:
   1. **Content Creation**: Organic digital marketing emphasizes the creation of high-quality, relevant, and valuable content. This content can take various forms, such as blog articles, videos, podcasts, social media posts, infographics, and more. The goal is to provide helpful information, address audience needs and pain points, and establish the business or brand as an authority in its industry.
   2. **Search Engine Optimization (SEO)**: Organic digital marketing often incorporates SEO strategies to optimize content for search engines. By implementing best practices like keyword research, on-page optimization, link building, and user experience enhancements, businesses aim to improve their organic search rankings and visibility. This helps attract organic traffic from search engine results.
   3. **Social Media Engagement**: Leveraging social media platforms is a fundamental aspect of organic digital marketing. By actively engaging with followers, sharing valuable content, responding to comments and messages, and participating in discussions, businesses can build a community around their brand. This fosters brand loyalty and encourages word-of-mouth promotion.
   4. **Email Marketing**: Email marketing is another effective organic strategy for nurturing customer relationships. By offering valuable content, exclusive promotions, personalized recommendations, and timely updates via email newsletters, businesses can engage with their audience directly and maintain ongoing communication.

5. **Online Communities and Influencer Marketing**: Building or participating in online communities relevant to the business's industry or target audience can be a powerful organic marketing approach. Engaging in discussions, providing valuable insights, and establishing relationships within the community can help increase brand visibility and credibility. Collaborating with influencers who align with the brand's values and target audience can also amplify reach and engagement.
6. **Return on Ad Spend (ROAS)**: ROAS gauges the revenue generated for every rupee spent on advertising. It showcases the efficiency of marketing campaigns.
7. **Click Through Rate (CTR)**: CTR calculates the ratio of users who click on an ad to the total number of users who viewed it, providing insight into ad effectiveness.
8. **Cost per Click (CPC):** CPC reveals the amount spent on advertising of each click generated, enabling budget optimization.
9. **Referral Marketing**: Encouraging satisfied customers to refer others to the business is an effective organic strategy. Implementing referral programs or offering incentives for referrals can generate word-of-mouth recommendations and organic growth.

It is explained by the startup founders in terms of outcomes of the Digital marketing efforts:

a. Increase in new users.
b. Increase in search clicks.
c. Increase in monthly trials.
d. Organic Brand impressions.
e. In-Organic Brand impressions.
f. Highest volume in a day.

Organic digital marketing focuses on creating a genuine connection with the target audience by delivering valuable content, fostering engagement, and building a loyal community of customers and brand advocates. While it may take time and effort to see results, organic strategies can lead to sustainable growth, increased brand awareness, and long-term customer relationships. These figures are treated more authentically and with respect by the investors.

U. **Revenue Drivers:** The startup founders should ideally present the following information in some of their pitch deck slides:
1) Number of customers
2) Number/Size of transactions per customer
3) Average transaction size
4) Average value service contract
5) Average value from consumables per base sale in case it is required for the product that is initially sold. For example, monthly coffee powder sale that is happening per coffee machine sold/installed.
6) Frequency of add-on sales per installed base sale
7) Milestone payments

8) Royalty percentage on net sales in case the solutions are offered as a franchisee.
9) Ratio of paid to unpaid customers in case of a freemium model.
10) Paid subscribers along with subscription fee
11) Frequency of customer upgrades

V. **Pre-money Valuation:** Pre-money valuation is the estimated value of a company immediately before it receives an investment or additional funding. It is crucial because it determines how much equity investors will receive in exchange for their investment. It sets the baseline valuation at which the investment is made, and the ownership stake investors acquire is based on this valuation.

W. **Post-Money Valuation:** It represents the company's total value after the new capital has been injected. Post-money valuation is essential for determining the company's overall value after the investment round. It is used to calculate the percentage of ownership that investors receive in the company. The ownership percentage is calculated by dividing the investment amount by the post-money valuation.

Here's a simplified example to illustrate the concepts. Suppose a startup is seeking investment, and the founders and investors agree on a pre-money valuation of Rs.2 million. An investor then injects Rs.1 million into the company. Here's how pre-money and post-money valuations apply:
- Pre-money valuation = Rs.2 million (the valuation before the investment)
- Investment amount = Rs.1 million (the amount invested)
- Post-money valuation = Pre-money valuation + Investment amount = Rs.2 million + Rs.1 million = Rs.3 million (the valuation after the investment.

In this scenario, the investor's ownership stake in the company is determined based on the post-money valuation of Rs.3 million. If the investor injected Rs.1 million, they would own one-third (33.33%) of the company because Rs.1 million is one-third of the post-money valuation.

Both pre-money and post-money valuations are essential for investors and entrepreneurs to negotiate the terms of an investment accurately. They provide clarity on the company's value before and after the infusion of capital and help determine the ownership stake that investors will receive in exchange for their investment.

Valuation of a Startup

"If calculus or algebra were required to be a great investor, I'd have to go back to delivering newspapers." - **Warren Buffett**

A business valuation is a general process of determining the economic value of a whole business or a company unit. Startup founders should develop a basic understanding regarding valuation, what could be the value of their startup, and how angel investors usually value the businesses before going out and making a pitch.

It's important because in case the founders' pitch is impressive, the very next questions usually are: how much funding are you looking for? According to you, what is the valuation of your enterprise? How much equity you are willing to dilute to raise that amount?

Reasons for Valuing a Startup

Business valuation is undertaken not only for raising funding but also for many other reasons, like the following:
- Securing Grants
- Employee Stock Options (ESOP)
- Company investments
- Shareholder conflicts/Disputes
- Buy/Sell Agreements
- Bankruptcy and Litigation
    - Liquidation or Reorganization
    - Patent Infringement
    - Marital Dissolutions
    - Economic Damages
- Spin-offs
- Divestitures
- Mergers
- Initial Public Offer
- Strategic Planning/Transaction
    - Value Enhancement
    - Business Plan/Capital Raising
    - Acquisitions, Due Diligence

Why Venture Valuation is Difficult?

Venture valuation is both an art and a science. It is difficult because of the following reasons:
- Sometimes there is a lack of a proper track record to undertake the valuation, especially the pre-revenue and research-based startups.

- Valuation is more dependent on qualitative factors.
- Valuation, how so ever may be undertaken through rigorous quantitative methods, usually requires some assumptions to be made. The final outcome is as good as the assumptions.
- Uncertainty is higher (team, market, and technology)
- Potential rewards higher
- Exit and liquidity are more important.
- Growth
- Not just a go/no-go decision; the actual valuations matter

Benefits of Valuation

Valuation of a startup is essential because of the following reasons:
- Valuation determines potential ownership.
- Valuation is essential to raise funding and investment.
- Higher valuation is an important feature helping the trade sale.
- Higher valuation provides a lot branding and visibility in social and professional media.

Valuation Process

A business valuation is a general process of determining the economic value of a whole business or company unit. It is the process by which an investor, such as an angel or VC, assigns a monetary value to a new venture.

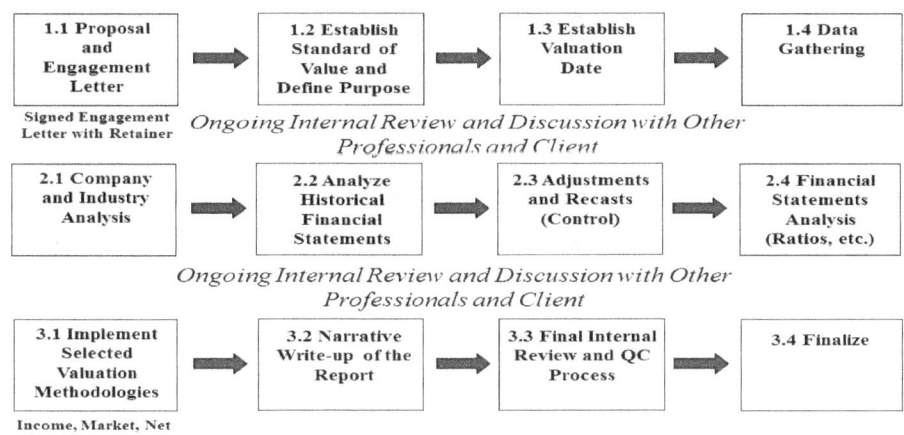

Valuation Methods

Valuation is more of an art than science. There are multiple methods for valuing startups at different stages of their evolution. Investors choose different methods based on their investment philosophy. Choosing the right one and then the appropriate inputs can be somewhat subjective.

Valuation methods can be classified on the basis of the following approaches:
- ❖ **Asset approach:** Determining the assets of the business by determining Book Value, Adjusted Book Value, and Liquidation Value.
- ❖ **Market approach:** By comparing to recently valued companies by using Price to Earnings, Price to Revenue, Price to Book Value, and Industry Comparable.
- ❖ **Income approach:** Present value of expected cash flows: NPV, VC method, and Discounted Future Earnings.

Broadly, the following methods are adopted for valuing a startup:

A. Valuation for Pre-Revenue Startup
B. Cost-based Methods
C. Asset-based Method
D. Market-based Methods
E. Future Projection-based Methods
F. Risk-based Methods
G. Investor/ROI Methods
H. Comprehensive Methods

Different Valuation Methods at Different Stages

Stage	Valuation Method	Principle associated with the Valuation Method
Pre Seed/ Seed Round	- **Berkus Method**	Assessment of 5 key success factors
Angel Round	- **Liquidation Value**	Scrap value of tangible assets
	- **Risk Factor Summation**	Base value adjusted for 12 standard risk factor
	- **Scorecard Valuation**	Weighted average value adjusted for a similar company
Series – A Round	- **Venture Capital Method**	RoI expected by the investor
Series – B/C and beyond	- **Private Company Comparables** - **Latest Financing Round**	Rule of 3 with a KPI from a similar company
Merger & Acquisition or Buyout	- **Discounted Cash Flow**	Sum of all future cash flows generated
	- **First Chicago Method**	Weighted average of 3 valuation scenario
IPO	- **Public Company Comparables**	Comparing with the discovered valuations

These methods are explained in the detail as follows:

A. **Valuation for Pre-Revenue Startup**

At the preliminary stage, Angels go by subjective assessment based on qualitative factors rather than quantitative tools.

Basis for Valuing Pre-Revenue Startup

- Traction: It is considered as a Proof of Concept
- The Value of the Founding Team
- Prototype /Minimum Viable Product
- Supply and Demand scenario for the solution
- Alignment with Emerging Industries & Hot Trends
- Current or Potential Margins

B. **Cost-based Methods**

1. **Book Value Method:**
   The book value is a straightforward approach that looks at the company's net worth based on its Balance sheet i.e., the tangible assets, the "hard parts." Book value helps in determining the valuation for investment-heavy business at a very early stage of establishment.

   Example

Liabilities	Amount	Assets	Amount
Debt	10,00,000	Land and building	20,00,000
Accounts payable	5,00,000	Plant and machinery	20,00,000
Long term debt	20,00,000	Accounts receivables	5,00,000
Capital	35,00,000	Patents	10,00,000
		Cash and cash equivalent	15,00,000
Total	70,00,000	Total	70,00,000
Net Book Value =70,00,000 - 10,00,000 - 35,00,000 = 25,00,000			

   Limitation:

   - This method is not that relevant for startups as it is focused on the "tangible" value of the company, while most startups derive value from intangible assets such as intellectual property, brand value, or customer base, which can be significant factors in valuing startups.
   - Based on historical cost and not the business model. Therefore, may not reflect the true economic value of assets or business.
   - **Ignores intangibles** like customer loyalty.
   - **Ignores risk**

2. **Cost to Duplicate Method:**
   This method works by estimating the amount it would cost to duplicate the startup at the time of valuation. It involves taking into account all costs and expenses associated with the startup and the development of its product and physical assets.

   This method requires extensive research, but it offers one of the most realistic valuations because it takes everything into consideration. For example, a software business might be figured as the total cost of programming time that is gone into designing its software. For a deep technology startup, it could be the cost of R&D, patent, prototype development, etc.

   Limitations
   The approach fails to take into account the future sales potential of a company along with its profit levels as well as it does not take into account intangible assets, like brand recognition.

C. **Net Asset Value Method**
   It is valuation of the company by determining net worth of the company at a particular time based on tangible and intangible assets of the company using the formula:
   A-L * (PV/PE)
   A = Value of all the assets
   L = Value of liabilities in the balance sheet
   But not including the following:
   - The amount set apart for payment of dividends on preference shares and equity shares where such dividends have not been declared before the date of transfer.
   - Reserves and surplus, even if the resulting figure is negative, other than those set apart towards depreciation.
   - Amount representing provision for taxation, other than amount of income-tax paid, if any, less the amount of income-tax claimed as refund, if any, to the extent of the excess over the tax payable with reference to the book profits
   - Amount representing provisions made for meeting liabilities, other than ascertained liabilities.

   PV = the paid-up value of such equity shares.
   PE = total amount of paid-up equity share capital as in the balance-sheet.

D. **Market-based Methods**

   1. **Market Multiple Method**:
      This is one of the most popular valuation methods.
      The method assumes that similar companies should be valued similarly, so it uses financial data from other companies to help determine a company's value. A financial ratio (or 'multiple') observed from these peer companies is applied to the company that is being valued. Recent

acquisitions of a similar startup are taken into consideration, and a base multiple is determined based on the value of recent acquisitions. The startup is then valued using the base market multiple.

Common Valuation Multiples	
Enterprise Value Multiples	**Equity Value Multiples**
Relevant for merger or acquisition kind of setting to consider overall effect of all sources of finance on company valuation	This is relevant for investor decision where the investment is just about acquiring a small stake in the company and goal is to maximize wealth through equity valuation
EV/EBITDA	P/E Ratio
EV/EBIT	Price to asset ratio
EV/Revenue	Price to sales ratio
EV/Invested Capital	

Enterprise Value Multiples
- **EV/EBITDA** – This valuation metric that is used as a **proxy for cash flow** [rm1] available to the company. Usually, it is in the range of **6x to 18x**.
- **EV/EBIT** – EBIT recognizes the **amortization** and **depreciation** in cases where non-cash charges reflect the expenses related to the use of assets. Generally, it stays between **10x and 25x**.
- **EV/Revenue** – EV/Revenue is affected by the **differences in accounting**. It is computed as a ratio of sales or revenue to enterprise value.
- **EV/Invested Capital** – This metric is helpful in cases where **capital assets** are the main drivers of earnings. That is why this multiple is commonly used in capital-intensive industries. It measures the rupee value in EV of each rupee of invested capital.

Equity multiples
- **P/E Ratio** – The Price-Earnings ratio is a multiple that is used to **determine the earnings per share**. This is one of the most used metrics. The P/E ratio is equal to EV/Net income which further is divided by the total diluted shares. It is usually in the range of **15x to 30x**.
- **Price/asset Ratio** – This ratio is used when the earnings are primarily driven by the **assets**,
- **Price/Sales** – This metric can be used in cases when a company is making losses to derive quick estimates.

For example, a mobile application software firm is selling for five times sales. We could use five times multiple as the basis for valuing a mobile apps venture. If the company is at an earlier stage of development than other businesses, it would probably fetch a lower multiple than 5, given that investors are taking on more risk.

Obtain Comp (V/EBIT) by using the value-to-earnings ratio of a "comparable" company or the average from a group of comparable companies.
Use EBIT from the firm or asset you are valuing.

$$V/EBIT = \frac{Market\ Value\ of\ Company}{Earnings\ Before\ Interest\ and\ Taxes}$$

Relevant Metrics/Indicators for different Industries

Indicator	Industry
Monthly Recurring Revenue (MRR)	SaaS
Number of outlets	Retail
Patent filed	Medtech/Biotech
Weekly Active Users (WAU)	Messengers

Limitations
- It simplifies complex information into just a single value or a series of values; this effectively disregards other factors that affect a company's intrinsic value, such as growth or decline.
- Simple but with many potential pitfalls

E. Future Projection-based Methods

1. **Discounted Cash Flow (DCF) Method**:
   The Discounted Cash Flow (DCF) method is used to determine the intrinsic value of a business. It is based on the principle that the value of any investment is the present value of its expected future cash flows. It focuses on projecting the startup's future cash flows and then discounting them based on the weighted average cost of capital to arrive at the present value to determine the valuation.
   Net Present Value (NPV) is what is the value of today when we discount the future cash flows with a 'risk & return' factor.
   It comprises of the following steps:
   1. **Step 1: Forecast Future Cash Flows:** Project the expected cash flows the investment is likely to generate over a specific period (often several years). These cash flows should be estimated based on realistic and comprehensive financial projections.
   2. **Step 2: Determine the Discount Rate:** Calculate the appropriate discount rate, often the company's cost of capital or weighted average cost of capital (WACC). This rate reflects the required return investors expect for bearing the risk of the investment. Since startups are just starting out and there is a high risk associated with investing in them, a high discount rate is generally applied.

3. **Step 3**: **Discount Future Cash Flows:** Apply the discount rate to each projected cash flow to convert them to their present value. The farther in the future the cash flow is expected, the more it is discounted.
4. **Step 4**: **Calculate Terminal Value:** Estimate the value of the investment at the end of the projection period. This is typically done using a terminal value formula, such as the perpetuity growth method or exit multiple method.
5. **Step 5**: **Sum the Present Values:** Add up all the present values of cash flows (including the terminal value) to arrive at the DCF value of the investment.
6. **Step 6**: **Determine company value**
7. **Step 7: Determine investor's stake in the company**

For example:
- Required return/risk-adjusted hurdle rate = 50%

Year	0	1	2	3	Exit 4
Cash flow	-3.000	50	350	500	25.000

NPV	€ 2.275
Discount rate	50%

Limitations
- It requires a lot of assumptions, so prone to errors if assumptions go wrong.
- It doesn't consider the relative valuation of the competitors.

F. Risk-based Methods

1. **Risk Factor Summation Method:**
   This method is based on the premise that the higher the number of risk factors present, higher the overall risk in achieving a strong exit. Therefore, this method values a startup by quantifying all risks associated with the business that can affect the RoI.
   The process starts by identifying the average valuation of similar startups in the similar region.
   To this initial value, the effect of different types of business risks are considered, and an estimate is deducted or added to the initial value based on the effect of the risk.
   It is generally done in multiple of 2,50,000 where:
   - +5,00,000 is very positive for growing the startup and exiting successfully
   - +2,50,000 is positive
   - 0 is neutral
   - -2,50,000 is negative for growing the startup and exiting successfully

- -5,00,000 is very negative.

After taking into consideration all kinds of risk and implementing the "risk factor summation," the final value of the startup is determined.

After the addition and subtraction, the valuation of a startup is determined,

Limitation
- Requires in-depth knowledge of concepts and their proper implementation.

2. **Liquidation Value Method**

The valuation we apply to a company when it is going out of business. Things that count for a liquidation value estimation are tangible assets: real estate, equipment, inventory, etc. In this method all the assets are discounted at appropriate rates.

The liquidation value is the sum of the scrap value of the tangible assets of a firm. For an investor, it is useful as a parameter to evaluate the risk of the investment. A higher potential liquidation value means a lower risk.

This method takes a more pessimistic view and determines the value of a company, based on premise what shall be realised if the company's assets were to be sold and its liabilities settled. In this scenario, assets are usually sold at a discounted rate since a quick sale may not yield the highest market value.

Liquidation Value = (Estimated Selling Price of Assets) - (Liabilities)
liquidation value < book value.

Limitation
- This may not be the right tool to measure a profitable company as it ignores the future growth potential.

G. Investor/ROI Methods

1. **Future Valuation Multiple Method/Decision Tree Analysis:** This Approach solely focuses on estimating the RoI that the investors can expect in 5 to 10 years. It begins with the startup's EBITDA (Earnings Before Interest, Taxes, Depreciation, and Amortisation).

Several projections are carried out, for example, sales projections over 5 years, growth projections, cost, and expenditure projections, etc., and the startup is valued based on these future projections.

Limitation
- It is unsuitable for continuous variables.
- It is difficult to handle numerous data points.

2. VC Method

As its name indicate, the Venture Capital Method stands from the viewpoint of the investor. It reflects the perspective of investors and works backward. Investors are looking for an exit within 3 to 7 years. An investor is always looking for a specific return on investment, let's say 10x and it also estimates the exit or harvest value. Based on those two elements, the investor can easily determine the maximum price he or she is willing to pay for invest.

Therefore, first, an expected exit price for the investment is estimated. From there, one calculates back to the current post-money valuation, taking into account the time and risk the investors take.

Return on Investment (ROI) = Terminal (or Harvest) Value ÷ Post-money Valuation

Then: Post-money Valuation = Terminal Value ÷ Anticipated ROI

But in this formula, we are missing out on an important concept of finance i.e., TVM (Time value of money, A rupee worth today is more than a rupee worth tomorrow). Meaning the terminal value is an absolute amount and considers TVM.

$$\text{Post money valuation} = \frac{\text{Terminal Value}}{(1+ROI)^{\text{time period}}}$$

Pre-money Valuation = Post-money Valuation – Investment

Terminal Value = Terminal Value is the anticipated selling price (or investor harvest value) for the company

Investment	Rs.5,00,000
Terminal Value	Rs.1,00,00,000
Expected ROI	50%
Years until exit	5
Post money valuation	Rs.13,16,872
Pre- money valuation	Rs.8,16,872

Typically, VC seeks a **multiple** on their investment based on a required rate of return and perceived risk.

Limitations

Doesn't look at aspects of the business (i.e., team, product, traction, risks, etc.) while determining the valuation, as it only depends on the required rate of return. It still requires a selection of representative startups to estimate future potential terminal values.

Though the mathematics is simple, but for ventures, there is a severe danger of over or under pricing, as:
- It assumes the risk of the venture does not change over time.
- It assumes a pre-determined course of development.
- Changes in discount rates lead to huge changes in valuation outcomes.
- Underestimation of the impact of taxes on the value.

3. **Pragmatic approach:**

It is based on the standard practice of the organisation. The decision is largely to select or not consider a startup for investment. The money they invest and the %age of equity they take if they like the business proposition, and the impractical ideas are rejected.

Limitation

For averaging, it requires investors to make a large number of deals.

H. Comprehensive Methods

1. **Scorecard Valuation Method (Bill Payne Valuation Method):**

   This method employed at seed or early stage uses weighted percentages and market data to determine an acceptable average valuation of the company. In this method, the target startup seeking investment is compared with other similar funded startups. The pre-revenue company's pre-money valuation is taken in the same business sector and region of the target company to derive the median. The scorecard valuation model compares these companies based on following six criteria:

   1. Founder, the management team (30%),
   2. Size of opportunity (25%),
   3. Technology/Product or service (10%),
   4. Marketing/Sales channels (10%),
   5. Stage of business (10%), and
   6. Other factors (15%

   These percentages can be adjusted according to the investor's preferences Example – If XYZ Pvt Ltd a pre-revenue stage startup is looking for funds and investor chooses to value the company using Scorecard Valuation method.

   - **Step 1** – Define weights of each given factor as per investor preference
   - **Step 2**. – Identify industry or market specific median valuation of similar startups in same region
   - **Step 3.** – Identify if the XYZ Pvt Ltd is doing better than the industry in each factor and accordingly assign factors
   - **Step 4** - Calculate factor rate.
   - **Step 5** - Calculate valuation of XYZ Pvt Ltd by multiplying factor rate and medium market valuation.
   -

	Weight	comparison	Factor Rate
Entrepreneur, the management team	30%	125% (better than average)	0.375
Size of opportunity	25%	150%	0.375
Technology/product/service	10%	100% (as per average)	0.1
Competitive environment	10%	75% (below average)	0.075
Marketing/sales channel	10%	80%	0.08
Stage of business	10%	120%	0.12
Others	5%	100%	0.05
Sum			1.175
If average medium company valuation in industry			Rs.2 crore
Valuation of XYZ pvt ltd is (2*1.175)			Rs.2.35 crore

Limitation
It requires a lot of time, data, and competence to put it into practice.

2. **Berkus Method**
   It values a start-up at seed or early stage based on a detailed assessment of the following five key success factors (Value Drivers), which reduce five different types of risks:
   1. **Basic value (Sound idea):** adds up to Rs.50,00,000 of value.
   2. **Technology (Prototype):** adds up to Rs.50,00,000 by reducing technology risk.
   3. **Execution (Quality management team):** adds up to Rs.50,00,000 by reducing execution risk.
   4. **Strategic relationships in core market:** add up to Rs.50,00,000 by reducing market risk
   5. **Production and consequent sales:** adds up to Rs.50,00,000 by reducing production risk

   The Berkus Method prioritizes the reduction of risk, adding value for each element a startup has that can reduce risk and increase the chance that an investor can get a good return on their investment. It is based on the simple premise that the value of a startup is equal to the sum of its parts. A detailed assessment is carried out evaluating how much monetary value is assigned to the five key success factors. The startup valuation is the summation of those monetary values. This approach allocates up to Rs.500,000 per success factor for a theoretical maximum pre money valuation of Rs.2.5 million.

   Advantages
   - Ease of use (No need to analyse projected financial statements)
   - Good for pre revenue stage where financial information is not prominent

   Disadvantages
   - Too simplistic
   - Don't consider unique risks and opportunities
   - Easily manipulable

3. **First Chicago Method**
   This technique a continuation of DCF Analysis is of wide scope. The first element is to construct valuation estimation for three scenarios and assign a probability to each scenario and do sensitivity analysis. Probability of each case is defined and then multiple the expected valuation (as per DCF model),
   1. Best Case
   2. Average
   3. Worst Case

   Step 1: It gives the freedom and the opportunity to consider events with low probability but a huge impact on investment payoff. This freedom brings more complexity to the valuation.
   Step 2: Use data from professional data providers. The choice of the multiples depends on the peer group and the structure of the enterprise.
   Step 3: Investigate the market through a short-term analysis focusing on the potential of the business case and a long-term analysis to identify fundamental market trends.

   The average of all three scenarios is considered to be the value of company.

DCF Cases	Probability %age	Valuation
Base Case	65%	Rs.100 cr
Worst Case	25%	Rs.45 cr
Best Case	10%	Rs.160 cr
Weighted Company Valuation		Rs.92.3 cr

   Limitation
   - Very complex and time-consuming; requires a lot of knowledge of the business and future estimates to produce accurate results.
   - Not useful for pre-revenue startups.

Conclusion: Important Insights
- There is no magic formula that will give exact valuations. Valuations are nothing but formalised guesstimates. They never show the exact value of your company.
- The more one practices valuing companies, the better one becomes in determining the valuation.
- It's better to keep it simple, especially when starting out.
- As one becomes comfortable, one can try advanced methods.
- It's a matter of investor preference, but also impacted by how much is invested.
- Investors/founders can use multiple methods and then employ the football-field approach to visualize ranges and check how the outcomes of different methods compare with one another.
- Valuations often require information from similar companies to best understand how the company fits into this landscape.
- Comparables and a rough estimate of how much dilution is acceptable by the founders are used by a large number of investors.
- Investors look at financials, funding rounds, how much the company raised, and at what valuation.

Angel Investor Ecosystem in India

"Chase the vision, not the money; the money will end up following you." –
Tony Hsieh, Zappos CEO

Angel investors are individuals or groups of individuals who provide funding to early-stage startups in exchange for equity or ownership. They are individuals who invest their own personal funds into startups that may have limited or no revenue and uncertain prospects.

Angel investors typically invest in the company's development when the business is often too young or risky to attract traditional sources of financing. They often provide the initial seed funding that entrepreneurs need to turn their idea into a viable business. In addition to financial support, angel investors often bring valuable industry experience, expertise, and networks to the companies they invest in. Many angel investors have a background in entrepreneurship themselves and can provide mentorship, guidance, and strategic advice to help startups navigate challenges and make informed decisions.

Angel investors differ from VCs in several ways. Firstly, they invest their own money, whereas VCs manage funds from various investors. Secondly, angel investors are more likely to invest in smaller amounts compared to VCs. They may invest individually or as part of a group of angel investors known as angel networks or syndicates.

Angel investors generally take on higher risks compared to other types of investors, as they invest in early-stage companies with unproven business models and uncertain prospects. They understand that not all startups will succeed, but they are willing to take calculated risks in the hopes of achieving substantial returns on their investments. They can do this because they are usually from the same industry or because they are investing in their own money.

Guidelines for Angel Investors

Do's	Don'ts
Focus on Founder and Team	Focusing only on Returns
Proper Due Diligence	Not checking the financial health
Evaluate Problem and Solution	Not evaluating Team Potential
Future Potential of the Idea	No Hurry
Own Expertise or Expert Advice	No Expert Advice

Like VCs, angel investors typically seek an exit strategy to realize their returns. This could be through the sale of their equity stake when the company is acquired or selling their stakes in subsequent funding rounds, taking a complete or partial exit, or through an initial public offering (IPO) when the company goes public.

Angel Networks in India and Select Investment

Angel Network	Select Startups invested
ah! Ventures	Barbrew, Klassroom, and Playo
AngelList India	TrulyMadly, Pitstop and Bluepad
Indian Angel Network (IAN)	Dhruva Space, Unotag and Fyllo
JITO Angel Network	HomeCapital, Siply, Blusmart, vidyakul, S3V Vascular Technologies, Galaxy Card, Finance Peer, Taquanal Energy, Epigeneres, and Fello
JPIN Venture Catalysts	Chingari, CreditEnable, and TSLC
LetsVenture	MentorKart, Dukaan and Meddo
Mumbai Angels Network	Pixuate, goSTOPS, and Unlu
The Chennai Angels	as TrulyMadly, POPxo, Purplle, The Postbox, and Ketto
Venture Catalysts	TagZ Foods, TrulyMadly, and leap. club
9Unicorns	Fleek, Rage Coffee and LegalPay
We Founder Circle	YPay, Vidyakul, and Knocksense
Inflection Point Ventures	Vested Finance, Stylework, and LoanKuber

Angel Networks in North India

Name	Location	Focus	Contact Authority	Email	Mobile
Punjab Angel Network (PAN)	Mohali		Mr. Sahil Makkar		
Startup Accelerator Chamber of Commerce (SACC)	Chandigarh Tricity	Multi-sectoral	Mr. Vineet Khurana	info@saccindia.org	0172-4000712
Chandigarh Angel Network (CAN) Incubator	SCO 1088-89, Sector 22-B, Chandigarh	Multi-sectoral (Early-stage startups)	Mr. Deepak Bansal	info@canetwork.in	92168-88055

Active Angels in India

Name	Designation	Organisation	Prefers to invest in	Past Investments
Rajan Anandan	Managing Director	Sequoia Capital	B2B startups, Big data, Analytics, Online health care, Mobile commerce, Consumer internet, Digital media	Instamojo, Travelkhana, Explara, Social Cops, Letsventure, LBB, PopXo
Anupam Mittal	Founder & CEO	People Group	Technology, Consumer Internet, Mobile, Healthcare and SaaS	Shaadi.com, Ola Cabs, Drivezy, Kae Capital, Truebil, myHQ HackerEarth, Letsventure,
T.V. Mohandas Pai			Women entrepreneurs, Technology startups, Consumer Internet, Media	Zoomcar, Zimmber, YourStory, FairCent, Kaaryah
Girish Mathrubootam	CEO	FreshWorks	SAAS, customer support, Enterprise Softwares, Consumer Internet, Education, Content & Listing Platforms	Whatfix, The Ken, Innov8, GoBumpr and iService, Unacademy, Factor Daily, Inkmonk, The Ken, Zarget
Rohit Bansal	Co-founder	Snapdeal, AceVector and Titan Capital	Consumer Products, IT, Manufacturing, Payment Platforms, Real Estate, Community & Lifestyle, AI-Enabled Healthtech, Payment Platforms, API, AI-driven Chatbot, Lifestyle, Community,	Sanfe, Ola, Bira, Razorpay, Beardo, ANS Commerce
Harshil Mathur	CEO & Co-Founder	Razorpay	Fintech, Edtech, B2B cross-border trading platform, Assisted eCommerce, Payment Platform, Coworking Space	Newtown School, Contlo, BHIVE Workspace, BharatX, Birky App, GlobalFair, Volopay
Sandeep Tandon	Co-founder	FreeCharge	Internet Services, FinTech, Healthcare, Education	Razorpay, Inc42, Tablehero, Unacademy, Fabelio, Remitware Payments, Pocket Aces, Ziploan
Anand Ladsariya	Founder	Everest Flavours	Location-based services, customer support tools, content discovery, social media, games, web design sectors	Asiatic, Oyo, Myntra, Appsdaily, Tonbo Imaging, Uniphore, Assured Risk, Mobiquest
Sanjay Mehta	Founder	MAIA Intelligence	Social, mobility, analytics & cloud. Clean technology, Enterprise	Loginext, Lawrato, OYO, Box8, Orange Scape, Fab Alley

Name	Role	Company	Sectors	Investments
			Software, Consumer Internet, and Healthcare	
Gokul Rajaram	Founder	Chai Labs and Flight.vc	Saas, Internet Services, Analytics & AI, Media & Entertainment	LivSpace, Edu Fire, Daily.co, Buffer, Loop, Flipora, Whatfix
Ratan Tata	Ex-Chairman	Tata Industries	Technology Sector, E-commerce, Affiliate Sectors, etc.	Urban Clap, Xiaomi, Moglix, Snapdeal, Urban Ladderm NestAway, One97 Communication, YourStory, Tracxn, Abra, niki.ai, Moglix, Teabox, ClimaCell Inc., GOQii, Lybrate, Crayon Data, MadRat Games, Cashkaro, Qikpod, Bombay Hemp Company, DogSpot, Invictus Oncology, Bollant, MUrgency, Idea Chakki, Printline Media (ThePrint).
Amit Somani	Managing Partner	Prime Venture Partners	Travel Industry, Consumer Internet	Qikwell Technologies India, Advises Phone Warrior Inc, Ixigo.com, HotelTravel.com, and MindTickle
Vijay Shekhar Sharma	Founder & CEO	Paytm	Consumer Internet, FinTech, Ed-Tech	Unacademy, GOQii, Flyrobe, sourceeasy, InnerChef, The Ken, Milaap
Sachin Bansal	Co-founder	Flipkart	Saas, Internet Services, Analytics & AI, Media & Entertainment,e-Commerce	Tracxn, Unacademy, Inshorts, Ather Energy, Sigtuple, SpoonJoy, Plabro Networks
Kunal Bahl	Co-founder & CEO	Jasper	Fintech, Consumer Internet, B2C Marketplace	Ola, Bira 91, Snapdeal, UrbanClap, Razorpay, Rapido, Belong, Supr Daily
Binny Bansal	Co-founder	Flipkart	Online commerce, Health Tech, Consumer internet	Flipkart, CureFit, Avail Finance, Roposo, Nymble Labs, Sigtuple
Kunal Shah	Founder & CEO	CRED	Coworking Spaces, Consumer Internet, Education Tech, E-commerce	Inc42, Razorpay, Unacademy, Innov8 Coworking, ShaadiSaga, Pianta, Cookifi, Bharat Bazaar.

Name	Role	Company	Sectors	Investments
Naveen Tewari	Founder	InMobi	Coworking Spaces, Online Games, Technology	Wooplr, Springboard, Razorpay, LetsVenture, Indus OS, Mettl, Zimmber, ZAPR, Mango Games
Zishaan Hayath	Co-founder	Toppr.com	Ed Tech, SaaS Products	Shadowfax, SquadRun, Wealthy, Qyk, AdPushup, Orobind Fitness Technologies
Sakshi Chopra	MD	Sequoia Capital		Purplle, Ladies Who Lead
Varun Alagh	Co-Founder	Manaearth, The Derma Co.	Advertising, AI, Business Support Services, Consumer Products, Community and Lifestyle, Health-Tech	Nestasia, Almabetter, Early Steps Academy, Shiprocket, Skye Air Mobility
Sujeet Kumar	Co-Founder	Udaan	Software, Business-in-a-box Platform, Cafe chains, Real Estate, Professional services, Sales & Marketing	Kofluence, Parentlane, Unacademy, Third Wave Coffee Roasters, Ximkart
Gaurav Munjal	Co-Founder	Unacademy and Flatchat	IT, Celebrity managementEnterprise Software, Games & Gaming Enablers, Health-Tech, Sales & Marketing	Trinkerr, NFTically, Bhanzu, Hoggy, Up
Ritesh Agarwal	Founder	OYO Rooms	Content and Publishing, ManufacturingTransportation, Agritech and Farming	Agrowave, Josh Talk, Unacademy, Vetic, Pepper Content
Ajeet Khurana	Founder	Reflexical	Blockchain Network, Bitcoin, Advertising, Community & Lifestyle, Consumer Electronics	Zorro, Leaf Studios, Sportzchain, Faaya
Anand Chandrasekaran	Director	Facebook	Consumer internet, B2C and P2P Marketplaces, Fintech & SaaS	LetsVenture, Fynd, InnerChef, Instalively, NoBroker, Wooplr
Dheeraj Jain	Director	Redcliff Capital	AI, IoT, VR, Big data analytics, Healthcare, Biotechnology	Mappr, Burger Singh, Shaadisaga, Qdesq, JustRide, Deyor Camps, Yumlane

Family Offices, and Accelerators

Name	Investment Stage	Sectoral Focus	Startups Invested	Cheque Size
Axilor Ventures	seed and Pre-Seed		DropShop, CanPe and Wiz Freight	$300k - $500k
Capier Investments / Cloudnine Hospitals	early-stage	Tech-focused ventures, healthtech, insurtech, fintech, agritech, social media, B2B SaaS, and D2C brands	Ambee, Cloudnine Hospitals, Doxper and Parentlane	
Entrepreneur First (EF)		Early-stage startups	UngearVR, Neuropixel, and Immunito AI	
Huddle Accelerator		D2C, EV, agritech, healthtech	Bold Care, Cell Propulsion, Wellversed, RACEnergy, F5, Celcius, The New Shop, Hapramp, StepSetGo, NeuroPixel, Yobee Research	$150K – $300K
Titan Capital			Ola, Snapdeal, Mamaearth, Supertails, kindlife.in, and Anar and UrbanCompany	
Y Combinator			Karbon Card, Snazzy and Gobillion	

Pitching

"In business, you don't get what you deserve, you get what you negotiate."
– **John Mariotti, President/CEO & Founder of The Enterprise Group**

India has the third-largest startup ecosystem in the world with about 60,000 startups. And it successfully raised $42 billion last year. Pitching is the art of describing growth to the investor by the startup founder. But the startup founders should know that the success rate of accessing venture funding through pitching is less than 1 percent.

Why one should not Raise Equity Investment

While raising equity from angel investors and venture capitalists (VCs) can be an attractive option for many startups and growing companies, these are some common reasons why a company might choose not to pursue raising equity from angel investors and VCs:

1. **Ownership Dilution**: When a company raises equity from investors, it typically involves issuing new shares, which dilutes the ownership stake of existing shareholders, including founders and early employees. Some companies may choose to avoid dilution by seeking alternative funding sources or using debt financing instead.
2. **Loss of Control**: Angel investors and VCs often require a certain level of involvement and decision-making power in the company in exchange for their investment. Founders who want to maintain full control over their company's operations and strategic direction may opt for alternative funding methods. With investors come obligations that fact must be kept in mind by the founders.
3. **Stringent Investor Requirements**: Angel investors and VCs typically have specific requirements and expectations from the companies they invest in, such as growth targets, exit strategies, or operational milestones. Meeting these requirements can be challenging or conflicting with the company's long-term vision and strategy.
4. **Long-Term Commitment**: Equity investments from angel investors and VCs often come with an expectation of a significant return on investment within a specific timeframe. This pressure to deliver rapid growth and profitability may not align with the company's preferred pace of growth or its ability to focus on long-term sustainability.
5. **Complex Due Diligence Process**: Angel investors and VCs conduct thorough due diligence on a company before investing. This process can be time-consuming and resource-intensive for the company, diverting valuable time and effort away from other business priorities.
6. **Loss of Confidentiality**: Sharing sensitive business information during the due diligence process with potential investors can carry the risk of confidentiality breaches. Companies may choose to limit their exposure to external

stakeholders and protect their intellectual property by exploring alternative financing options.
7. **Alternative Funding Sources**: There are various alternative funding sources available that may better suit a company's specific needs. These include debt financing, government grants or loans, crowdfunding, bootstrapping, strategic partnerships, or revenue-based financing. Depending on the company's circumstances, these sources may be more appropriate or advantageous than equity funding.
8. **Stage of Development**: Early-stage companies may find it challenging to attract angel investors or VCs due to a lack of proven track record or market traction. In such cases, the company may opt to focus on initial development and revenue generation before seeking equity funding.
9. **Time that goes into raising investment**: One of the founders has to dedicate him/herself for networking/pitching for raising investments.

The decision not to raise equity from angel investors and VCs can be influenced by a combination of factors specific to each company's situation. The following sections in this chapter can guide the founders step by step with regard to raising investment.

Elevator Pitch

An elevator pitch is a concise and compelling summary of a product, service, business idea, or personal brand that can be delivered within the span of an elevator ride, typically lasting 30 seconds to 2 minutes. An elevator pitch is usually a short, impactful presentation that tells your audience: what your business is and who your customers are and summarizes your key USPs in a very interesting and interest arousing manner to know more about it.

The goal of an elevator pitch is to communicate the value proposition, unique selling points, and key benefits to capture the attention and interest of the listener quickly and effectively. Its name originates from the idea that the pitch should be succinct enough to deliver during a brief encounter, such as riding an elevator with a potential investor or customer.

Key Constituents of Elevator Pitch

The key constituents of an elevator pitch typically include the following:
1. **Introduction/Hook**: Start your pitch with an attention-grabbing introduction or hook that immediately captures the listener's interest. It could be a thought-provoking question, a compelling statement, or a surprising statistic that relates to the problem you're addressing.
2. **Problem Articulation**: Clearly and concisely define the problem or need that your product, service, or idea addresses. Why does the world need what you're doing right now? Explain the pain points or challenges that your target audience faces, highlighting the importance and relevance of the problem. For Dropbox, it could have been: 'In this digital world, no matter where you're

in the world, your share-ready, compress-friendly data will be with you'. For Airbnb, it would be, 'Soaking customised local culture in affordable pricing and independence that big hotels around the world can't deliver'.
3. **Solution**: Present your unique solution or offering that solves the identified problem. Clearly articulate the benefits and value that your product, service, or idea brings to the table. Focus on how it addresses the specific pain points mentioned earlier. Too early, you're shunned; too late, you're oblivious.
4. **USP (Unique Selling Proposition)**: Highlight the key differentiators or unique selling points of your offering. Explain what sets it apart from competitors and why it is superior or more compelling. Emphasize the aspects that make your product, service, or idea stand out in the market.
5. **Target Market**: Clearly identify and describe your target market or customer segment. Explain who stands to benefit the most from your offering and why. Paint a picture of the ideal customer and how your solution fulfills their needs.
6. **Call to Action**: End your elevator pitch with a call to action, which is a clear and specific next step you want the listener to take. It could be scheduling a meeting, requesting a demo, or visiting your website. The call to action should be actionable and encourage further engagement.
7. **Elevator Ride Test**: Finally, ensure that your pitch is concise enough to fit within the duration of an elevator ride. Practice and refine your pitch to ensure it can be delivered smoothly and confidently within the given timeframe.

By incorporating these key constituents into your elevator pitch, you can effectively convey the essence of your offering, capture attention, and generate interest from potential investors, customers, or partners. Remember to tailor your pitch to the specific audience and context to make it more relevant and impactful.

How to Develop Elevator Pitch

Developing an effective elevator pitch is crucial for capturing the attention of potential investors, customers, or partners in a concise and compelling manner. Here are some steps to help you develop an elevator pitch:
1. **Define Your Goal**: Clarify the purpose of your elevator pitch. Are you trying to attract investors, secure partnerships, or engage customers? Having a clear goal in mind will help you tailor your pitch accordingly.
2. **Identify Your Unique Selling Proposition**: Determine what sets your product, service, or idea apart from others in the market. Identify the key benefits, features, or value proposition that makes it unique and compelling.
3. **Keep It Concise**: An elevator pitch is typically delivered in a short amount of time, typically 30 seconds to 2 minutes. Focus on delivering your message succinctly and avoid getting too detailed or overwhelming the listener with information.
4. **Structure your Pitch**: Structure your pitch in a logical and engaging manner. Start with a hook or attention-grabbing statement to pique interest, then provide a brief overview of the problem or need you address. Clearly articulate

how your product, service, or idea offers a solution or benefit. Finally, end with a call to action or next steps.
   5. **Use Clear and Compelling Language**: Choose words and phrases that are easy to understand and resonate with your target audience. Avoid jargon or technical terms that may confuse or alienate listeners. Use vivid language and storytelling techniques to make your pitch more memorable and engaging.
   6. **Practice and Refine**: Practice delivering your elevator pitch to ensure it flows smoothly and confidently. Time yourself to ensure it fits within the desired timeframe. Seek feedback from trusted colleagues, mentors, or advisors and refine your pitch based on their input.
   7. **Customize for Different Audiences**: Tailor your elevator pitch to the specific audience you're addressing. Adjust the language, emphasis, and examples to resonate with their interests, needs, or priorities. Show that you understand their challenges and demonstrate how your offering can benefit them specifically.
   8. **Be Authentic and Passionate:** Show genuine enthusiasm and belief in what you're pitching. Passion and authenticity can be contagious and help create a memorable impression. Let your personality shine through and connect with your audience on an emotional level.
   9. **Adapt and Iterate**: Be open to adapting and iterating your elevator pitch based on feedback, market conditions, or new insights. As you gain experience and learn more about your audience, you may discover ways to refine and enhance your pitch for better results.

An elevator pitch is a starting point for capturing interest and opening doors for further conversation. It should be concise, compelling, and tailored to your specific audience. By effectively communicating the essence of your idea, product, or business, you increase your chances of making a lasting impression and generating further interest in what you have to offer.

Startup Deck

A short and crisp overview of a business idea often used when presenting to investors and raising funds. It is a presentation comprising 10 to 15 slides that founders use to showcase their startups to investors when looking to raise money.

Important Constituents of Startup Pitch Deck

A startup pitch deck is a presentation that provides an overview of a startup's business plan, value proposition, market opportunity, and potential for growth. While the specific content may vary depending on the startup and its target audience, are some important constituents commonly found in startup pitch deck:
1. **Company Description:** Briefly describe the general nature of your company and provide a short summary of the company background. The investor must be convinced of the uniqueness of the business and gain a clear idea of the market in which the company operate. For example: We transform MSME's into agile organisations by helping them develop a scalable and viable business model and a strong and dedicated team. We help them in terms of not just funding,

but also in terms of high-quality mentorship and networking and competence building on strategy and execution.
2. **Problem Statement:** Clearly define the problem or pain point that your startup aims to solve. Explain why this problem is significant and how it affects the target market. Validate the problem with real life examples.
   For example, India is one of the fastest growing economies in the world, drawing the attention of many international investors. Now, private investors who've had success in markets like America and the UK are looking to India to find their next great investment. The founders of Google and Yahoo! actively seek out investment opportunities in India. Even lesser-known angel investors - wealthy individuals who invest smaller amounts of money at the start-up level - have taken an interest in India's growing number of entrepreneurs, providing them not only with start-up capital, but also with their business knowledge and networks from previous investments. In turn, these new businesses promote more business, which attracts more investors from abroad, creating more jobs and stimulating the economy throughout India - from Delhi and Mumbai to smaller rural communities. Our investors are finding opportunities to invest in fields as broad as gaming, travel and manufacturing, and our Indian entrepreneurs are given the initial footing to jumpstart their businesses and revitalize their economy.
3. **Solution**: Convey to the investor that the company and product truly fill an unmet need in the marketplace. Present your startup's unique solution or product offering that addresses the identified problem. The characteristics that set the product and company apart from the competition need to be identified (competitive advantage). What characteristics make your solution a "never-before" solution? Explain how your solution is innovative, effective, and differentiates from existing alternatives. Explain how your product/ service adds value. Try and explain in layman terms.
4. **Market Opportunity:** Showcase the size and growth potential of your target market. Provide relevant market data, including market size, trends, and potential customer segments. Highlight any market gaps or untapped opportunities that your startup can capitalize on. Include potential market size and growth rate.
5. **Business/Revenue Model**: Describe how your startup plans to generate revenue and sustain its operations. Explain your pricing strategy, revenue streams, and any unique or disruptive aspects of your business model. How do you make money off your solution? For Example: Subscription Model, Direct Sales, Ad-based 3 to 5 year projections. Top cash burn reasons.
6. **Competitive Analysis and Barrier to Entry:** Analyze the competitive landscape and identify key competitors or potential direct and indirect competition. Highlight your startup's competitive advantages, such as intellectual property, technology, expertise, or unique value proposition. Clearly articulate how your startup stands out and how it can gain a competitive edge. How do the current solutions compare with your solution? How easy is it to replicate your solution? What category of competitors do you belong to? Enumerate some of the company's strengths and some weaknesses.

7. **Target Market**: Define your target customer segments and their characteristics. Provide insights into their needs, behaviours, and preferences. Explain how your product or solution addresses their pain points and offers value to your target market. The size of the market vs the percentage you are targeting. A granular profiling of your customer. For ex: age, geography, purchase habits, traits.
8. **Go-to-Market Strategy**: Outline your plan for reaching and acquiring customers. Discuss your marketing and sales strategies, what channels will you use to get to this market? Indicate which channels will be used to deliver your products/service to your target markets (i.e., website, retail, amazon, direct sales force, VARs, channel partners, etc...). customer acquisition costs, and customer retention plans. Present traction or early adopter success stories, if applicable.
9. **Clients:** Briefly describe the people who need or want your product / service by giving some characteristics like their age, gender, income, geographic localisation, why they buy, when they buy, where they buy, tastes, aspirations.
10. **Team**: Introduce your core team members and their relevant expertise, experiences, credentials, and accomplishments. Highlight their roles and responsibilities in driving the startup's success. Showcase any advisors, mentors, or industry experts associated with your startup. Along with you can mention why they're involved. Exhibit unity in thinking, in strategy.
11. **Financials and Projections**: Present key financial information, including revenue projections, expenses, and funding requirements. Outline the expected timeline for achieving profitability. If available, include metrics like unit economics, customer lifetime value (CLV), and customer acquisition cost (CAC).

Sales, the unit/quantity, the anticipated profit for the next 1, 3 and 5 years

	YEAR 1	YEAR 3	YEAR 5
SALES			
UNIT/QUANTITY			
EBIT			
NET PROFIT/ LOSS			

12. **Milestones and Roadmap**: Highlight significant milestones achieved to date and outline your future development plans. Show a clear roadmap that demonstrates your startup's growth trajectory and key milestones, such as product launches, partnerships, or expansion plans. For ex: prototypes, patents, pilots etc. Milestones for the next 1, 3, and 5 years. Milestones for what you would do if you got funded. What founders want to achieve: Briefly explain the goals and objectives. Explain the measure that will be used to measure the goals.
13. **Funding so far:** Funds raised through other investors & soft commitments It helps build credibility and validation.
14. **Investment Ask**: Clearly articulate the amount of funding you are seeking and how it will be utilized. Specify the equity or ownership stake offered in return. Explain how the investment will help accelerate your startup's growth and generate returns for investors. Mention realistic numbers for expected funding.

15. **Appendix**: Include additional information, such as testimonials, press coverage, product demos, user feedback, or any other relevant supporting materials that strengthen your pitch.

Remember to keep your pitch deck concise, visually appealing, and compelling. It should effectively communicate your startup's value proposition, market potential, and growth prospects to capture the interest of potential investors or stakeholders.

How do Angel Investors work?

Before making a pitch to angel investors, startup founders should understand how angels work. With this understanding they can make their pitch more effective. In terms of how angel investors work, they typically engage in the following process:

1. **Sourcing Opportunities**: Angel investors actively seek investment opportunities through various channels, including personal networks, startup events, pitch competitions, and referrals from other investors or industry experts.
2. **Due Diligence**: Once an investor identifies a potential opportunity, they conduct thorough due diligence. This involves examining the business, reviewing financials, assessing the market, evaluating the team, and validating the claims made by the startup.
3. **Term Negotiation**: If the due diligence process is favourable, angel investors negotiate the terms of the investment, including the amount of funding, valuation, ownership stake, and rights or preferences associated with their investment.
4. **Investment and Support:** If the terms are agreed upon, the angel investor provides the agreed-upon funding to the startup. Beyond funding, many angel investors also offer mentorship, guidance, and access to their networks to support the growth and success of the startup.

What are Angel Investors looking for? How do they evaluate?

When evaluating investment opportunities, angel investors typically consider several key factors:
1. **Business Potential**: Angel investors look for startups with high growth potential. They assess the market size, target audience, competitive landscape, and unique value proposition of the business. They evaluate whether the product or service addresses a significant problem or fulfils a market need.
2. **Strong Entrepreneurial Team**: Angel investors place great importance on the entrepreneur or founding team. They look for experienced, passionate, and dedicated individuals who have the skills and vision to drive the business forward. A capable team with complementary skill sets increases the chances of success.
3. **Scalability and Market Traction:** Angel investors seek startups with scalable business models that have the potential to generate substantial returns on investment. Traction simply means "quantitative evidence of market demand."

It is proof that somebody wants the product, and it communicates momentum in market adoption. They assess the startup's ability to scale operations, acquire customers, and achieve market traction. Demonstrating early customer interest or revenue growth can be favourable.

It's like dancing on the edge of being fairy tale and believable, too much on either side hurts credibility. In order to address the same, Uber proposed—best, realistic and worst-case scenario in the same slide of their 2008 pitch.

4. **Competitive Advantage**: Investors evaluate the startup's competitive advantage or unique selling proposition. They assess factors such as intellectual property, proprietary technology, barriers to entry, or a differentiated product or service that gives the business an edge over competitors.
5. **Financials and Projections**: Angel investors review the financials of the startup, including revenue projections, cost structure, and profitability potential. They evaluate the assumptions and underlying data supporting the financial projections to assess the feasibility and growth prospects of the business.
6. **Exit Strategy**: Angel investors consider the potential exit options for their investment. They assess whether the startup has a clear strategy for generating liquidity for investors, such as through an acquisition, initial public offering (IPO), or secondary market sale.

Angel investors have their own individual preferences, investment criteria, and evaluation methods. The evaluation process can vary from investor to investor, and each may have its unique focus areas and decision-making criteria.

Summary: Guidelines for Startups' Pitch Presentation

When making a startup pitch presentation to investors for raising funding, it's important to keep in mind some key guidelines to make a compelling and effective presentation. Here are some important guidelines to consider:

1. **Pitch less like a presentation, more like a story!**
2. **Know Your Audience**: Research and understand your target investors. Tailor your pitch to their interests, preferences, and investment criteria. Customize your presentation to resonate with their investment thesis and goals.
3. **Make a connection**:
4. **Start Strong:** Capture investors' attention from the beginning with a strong and engaging opening. Clearly communicate your startup's value proposition and why it matters. Hook investors with a compelling story or problem statement.
5. **Keep It Concise for a crisp delivery**: Investors receive numerous pitches, so keep your presentation concise and focused. Use a limited number of slides (usually 10-15) and aim for a presentation duration of around 15-20 minutes. Avoid overwhelming the audience with excessive information.
6. **Clear and Simple Messaging**: Use clear, concise, and jargon-free language. Avoid technical terms or complex explanations that may confuse or alienate investors. Keep your messaging simple, easy to understand, and compelling. A good pitch makes its concept clear for a high school student or even a grandma.

7. **Vibrant Pitch Deck for sual Appeal**: Design your pitch deck with clean and visually appealing slides. Use high-quality graphics, charts, and images to support your key points. Ensure that the text is legible, and the overall design is professional and consistent.
8. **Focus on the Problem and Solution:** Clearly articulate the problem or pain point your startup addresses and how your solution provides a unique and effective remedy. Highlight the market need and demonstrate why your solution is compelling and differentiated.
9. **Master your Business Model**: The logic why anyone should pay for your product/service.
10. **Showcase Traction and Validation:** If your startup has achieved any traction, such as revenue, user growth, partnerships, or significant milestones, highlight them. Showcase customer testimonials, case studies, or any validation that demonstrates market demand or product-market fit.
11. **Emphasize the Market Opportunity:** Present a clear and compelling market opportunity. Demonstrate the size, growth potential, and attractiveness of your target market. Back your claims with market research, data, and insights to build confidence in the opportunity.
12. **Highlight the Team: Showcase the strength and expertise of your team**. Highlight relevant experience, track records, and achievements of key team members. Investors want to see a capable and committed team that can execute the business plan.
13. **Financial Projections and Use of Funds**: Provide realistic and well-supported financial projections that outline revenue growth, profitability, and return on investment. Clearly articulate how the funding will be utilized to achieve specific milestones and accelerate growth.
14. **Validate every possible slide with data:** Numbers don't lie. It is usually not a great idea because you think so, rather it is because your target market said so. A great pitch makes audience believe in it through undeniable numbers. Presenters should have every data point handy before starting the pitch and not just the top line, bottom line and burn rate.

Industry	Important metric
Content industry	DAU (daily active users) to MAU (monthly active users) ratio, retention curve, and average time spent per user
FMCG	Basket size (AOV), sale frequency, and CPA (cost per acquisition)

15. **Address Risks and Mitigation Strategies:** Acknowledge and address potential risks and challenges your startup may face. Demonstrate your understanding of these risks and present strategies to mitigate them. This shows that you have thought through the potential pitfalls and have plans in place to overcome them.

16. **Practice and Rehearse**: Practice your pitch thoroughly to ensure a smooth and confident delivery. Rehearse your presentation with a focus on timing, clarity, and engagement. Anticipate and prepare for potential questions or objections from investors.
17. **Be Authentic and Passionate**: Show genuine passion and belief in your startup. Investors are not only investing in your business, but also in you as an entrepreneur. Be authentic, confident, and enthusiastic about your vision, and let your passion shine through.
18. **Be Open to Feedback**: Be open-minded and receptive to feedback from investors. Be prepared to answer questions and engage in a constructive dialogue. Investors may provide valuable insights or perspectives that can help refine your business strategy.
19. **Timing**: Timing is very crucial while raising funding. Founders must be aware regarding the global and domestic macro level headwinds and tailwinds as well as the changing preferences of investors for various sectors. Its good to stay ahead of the curve.
    This can be understood from the negotiation process and changing valuations during the funding discussions going on for GoMechanic for Series D round in the year 2022. The founders of GoMechanic were pushing for a valuation of around $1.2 billion, while Tiger Global was offering a valuation of $1 billion. The founders were adamant about achieving the higher valuation. Simultaneously, GoMechanic also started engaging with SoftBank's Vision Fund to raise funds. SoftBank was initially willing to invest at a valuation of around $800-900 million. Then during the negotiation period there came "Funding Winter" impact, wherein the Indian startup ecosystem experienced a slowdown in funding activities, which resulted in caution among investors, including SoftBank and Tiger Global. As a consequence of the funding winter and investor caution, SoftBank's willingness to invest decreased, and they were only willing to come in at a valuation of approximately $600-700 million. The founders of GoMechanic ultimately signed a term sheet with SoftBank at a valuation of $650 million (Remember initially they were getting a valuation of $1 billion) due to financial constraints and the need for cash. This highlights the impact of changing market conditions and investor sentiments on funding process.
20. **Follow-up and Follow-through**: After the pitch, follow up with investors promptly. Send a thank-you note and additional information if requested, or schedule further meetings or due diligence. Maintain clear communication and transparency throughout the fundraising process.

Every investor pitch is an opportunity to tell a compelling story, showcase your startup's potential, and build trust and confidence in your venture. By following these guidelines, you can increase your chances of making a positive impression and attracting the funding you need.

Exit Strategy of Investors

"Exits are great, but it's better to do it as a choice, not a consequence of bad modus operandi." — **Richie Norton**

An exit strategy is a planned approach to terminating/exiting from a venture. This helps minimise risk and maximise returns.

Guidelines for Founders for Planning Exit Strategy for Angel Investors and VCs

When it comes to raising funding, startup founders should pitch, keeping in mind that investors are looking for an exit after some time. There should be some indication in the pitch regarding the Investors' exit. If startup founders know what investors expect regarding exit, they can plan their pitch accordingly. Angel investors or VCs consider these guidelines while planning their exit strategy, which outline how and when they plan to cash out investment to maximize their returns:

1. **Investment horizon**: They like to determine the timeframe in which they expect to achieve their investment objectives. This timeframe may vary depending on the industry, growth potential, and specific investment. It's important to have a clear understanding of how long they are willing to wait for a return on their investment.
2. **Understand the entrepreneur's vision:** Investors want to have open and transparent discussions with the entrepreneur or management team to understand their long-term vision for the company. Then they align their exit strategy with their objectives and ensure both parties are on the same page regarding the potential exit opportunities.
3. **Evaluate potential exit routes**: Investors identify and evaluate various exit options available for their investment. Common exit routes include:
    - Initial public offerings (IPOs)
    - Mergers and Acquisitions (M&A)
    - Strategic partnerships

   Investors research market trends and consider the specific dynamics of the industry to determine the most viable exit routes.
4. **Establish milestones and triggers**: Investors work closely with the entrepreneur to establish key milestones and triggers that will influence your decision to exit. These milestones can include achieving certain revenue targets, market share, or profitability. Having specific triggers in place will help you make informed decisions about when to exit.
5. **Consider secondary markets**: VCs explore possibility of selling their shares in secondary markets such as private equity exchanges or dedicated platforms for private companies. This can provide liquidity before a traditional exit event and might be suitable for smaller investments or early-stage companies.
6. **Prepare the company for exit**: By actively participating in the growth and development of the company, investors try to increase the likelihood of a

favourable exit. This includes optimizing operations, financials, governance, and intellectual property.

As each investment and entrepreneur is unique, so investors tailor their exit strategy to the specific circumstances. Therefore, startup founders need to both understand as well as embed the potential exit strategy of their investor into their strategic plan.

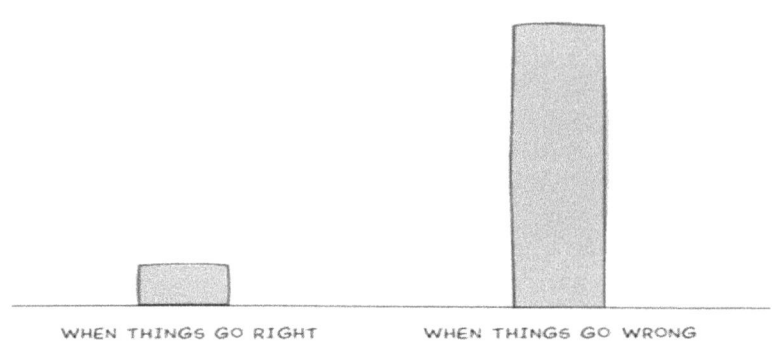

Term Sheet

"It is impossible to unsign a contract, so do all your thinking before you sign." **- Warren Buffett**

A term sheet is a non-binding agreement most often associated with start-ups that outline the basic terms and conditions concerning a proposed potential investment. Though Term sheets are non-binding, the signing of Term sheet by two parties is an indicator of evidence that both parties intend to carry out and execute a full agreement. The term sheet is usually developed after the initial in-principal agreement to fund while the due diligence is on.

It serves as a template and forms the basis for more detailed, legally binding documents and agreements. Terms included in this document, such as the company valuation, investment amount, percentage stake, voting rights, liquidation preference, anti-dilutive provisions, and investor commitment, are crucial to investors, such as angel investors or venture capitalists (VC) conducting due diligence after listening to the pitch and agreeing in principle but before funding an enterprise.

Once the parties involved reach an agreement on the details laid out in the term sheet, a binding agreement or contract is drawn up.

Uses of a Term Sheet

The term sheet should cover significant aspects of a deal without detailing every minor contingency which would be covered later by a binding contract. The term sheet essentially lays the groundwork for ensuring that the parties involved in a business transaction agree on most major aspects. The term sheet reduces the likelihood of a misunderstanding or unnecessary dispute. Additionally, the term sheet ensures that expensive legal charges involved in drawing up a binding agreement or contract are not incurred prematurely.

Term Sheet: What's Included in it?

The details to be included in a term sheet are highly dependent on the agreement at hand. Commonly included details in Equity Term sheets are as follows:

- Information on the assets included in the deal.
- Company valuations and initial purchase price, the percentage of stakes, and investment amounts.
- Contingencies that may affect the price.
- The preferred payment method.
- What is excluded from the deal.
- Anti-dilutive provisions.

- Liquidation preference.
- Voting rights.
- How long the investor is required to remain vested.
- How the proceeds of a sale will be distributed between the entrepreneur and the investors.
- Items considered requirements by one or both parties.
- Timeframe for a response.

The commonly included details in the debt Term sheet, are as follows:

❖ **Economic details:** This includes the term, loan size, interest rate, and other financial matters common to debt.
❖ **Risk mitigation preferences:** Specific conditions to be met and specific information to be provided in a recurring, timely manner.
❖ **Extension rights:** The term sheet identifies the conditions and cost of the extension if the extension of debt is required beyond the initially agreed-upon terms.
❖ **Due diligence at closing:** Includes a list of requirements that the lender requires from the borrower for the loan to be approved when the loan agreement is drafted.

Terms found in a Term Sheet

Term sheets often have the following standardized terms or phrases:

A. **Investment Term Sheets**
   - **Valuation (Pre-Money & Post-Money):** Investors may want to see the pre-money valuation (before the investment is made) and post-money valuation (value of the company after including the new investment) before an official investment agreement is drafted.
   - **Valuation Cap:** It is the value when convertible notes become eligible to convert into equity. This figure should be agreed upon early to arrive at a fair valuation for the startup and adequate protection for the investor.
   - **Tag Along Clause:** The tag-along right gives minority shareholders the ability to "tag along" and sell their shares alongside the majority shareholders. If a majority shareholder or a group of shareholders intends to sell their shares to a third party, the tag-along right allows minority shareholders to join the transaction on the same terms and conditions. The purpose of the tag-along right is to ensure that minority shareholders have the opportunity to sell their shares and participate in the liquidity event or exit in the same transaction, effectively "tagging along" with the majority shareholder. It protects their interests by preventing a situation where majority shareholders can sell their shares to a third party without providing a similar opportunity to minority shareholders. The tag-along right is typically subject to certain conditions and limitations, which may include:
     a. Minimum purchase price thresholds,
     b. The requirement that the third-party offer is a bona fide offer.
     c. Timeframe within which the tag-along right can be exercised.

- **Drag Along Clause:** Guarantee that minority stakeholders will follow the guidance of majority stakeholders; drag-along clause requires that smaller investors lead larger investors in business decisions. It grants majority shareholders the right to force minority shareholders to sell their shares in the event of a sale or exit of the company. It provides the majority shareholders with the ability to sell the company to a third party without the potential obstruction or dissent from minority shareholders.

    The drag-along provision is invoked when the majority shareholders receive an offer to sell their shares or the entire company. If the majority shareholders choose to accept the offer and sell their shares, they can require the minority shareholders to also sell their shares on the same terms and conditions. This enables the majority shareholders to present a unified ownership interest to the buyer and simplifies the transaction process. The drag-along provision is typically subject to certain conditions and limitations, which may include:
    1. **Majority Shareholder Threshold**: The provision may specify a minimum ownership percentage, or a number of majority shareholders required to trigger the drag-along right. This ensures that the minority shareholders are not forced to sell their shares if only a small group of majority shareholders want to sell.
    2. **Sale Terms:** The provision usually stipulates that the minority shareholders must receive the same sale terms and price per share as the majority shareholders. This ensures fairness in the transaction and prevents the majority shareholders from offering preferential treatment to themselves.
    3. **Notice and Consent**: The provision may require majority shareholders to provide advance notice to the minority shareholders regarding the proposed sale and give them an opportunity to review the terms. In some cases, the consent of a specified percentage of minority shareholders may be required for invoking the drag-along provision.

    It protects the interests of majority shareholders by enabling them to complete a sale or exit transaction without being impeded by minority shareholders who may have different objectives or preferences. It provides a mechanism to achieve a unified ownership position and ensures a more efficient transaction process. For minority shareholders, the drag-along provision can present a risk of being forced to sell their shares, potentially at a price or under circumstances they may not prefer. Therefore, it's crucial for minority shareholders to carefully review and negotiate the terms of the drag-along provision and seek legal advice to protect their interests.

- **Dividends:** What net income distributions they will be entitled to, and what the timing will be (i.e., monthly, quarterly, or annually).
- **Anti-dilutive Provisions**: These are clauses commonly included in investment agreements or stock option plans to protect existing shareholders, typically investors, from dilution of their ownership stake in a company. These provisions adjust the conversion or exercise price of certain

securities in the event of a subsequent issuance of new securities at a lower price than the original purchase price. The purpose of anti-dilutive provisions is to maintain the economic value of existing shareholders' investments and preserve their ownership percentage. The two common types of anti-dilutive provisions are as follows:

1. **Full Ratchet**: Under a full ratchet anti-dilution provision, if the company issues new shares at a price lower than the price originally paid by existing shareholders, the conversion or exercise price of the existing securities is adjusted downward to the new lower price. This ensures that existing shareholders' ownership and economic value are protected by effectively giving them additional shares at the lower price.

2. **Weighted Average**: The weighted average anti-dilution provision takes into account the number of new shares issued and the price at which they are issued to determine the adjustment to the conversion or exercise price. This provision mitigates the impact of significant downward price adjustments by calculating a weighted average price that reflects both the new and existing share prices.

Anti-dilutive provisions are designed to protect shareholders from the potential negative effects of future equity issuances at lower valuations. By adjusting the conversion or exercise price of existing securities, anti-dilution provisions provide shareholders with additional shares or a lower cost basis, allowing them to maintain their ownership percentage and economic interest in the company.

The specific terms of anti-dilutive provisions can vary depending on the negotiations between the parties involved and the terms of the investment agreement. Founders and investors should carefully consider the implications and potential effects of anti-dilutive provisions, as they can impact the ownership structure and economic value of the company. Legal and financial professionals should be consulted to ensure a clear understanding of the provisions and their impact on the shareholders' rights and obligations.

- **Liquidation Preference:** It refers to the rights and priorities regarding the distribution of proceeds in the event of a company's liquidation or exit. The order in which investors and founders are paid out their respective share of the proceeds from a sale, merger, or winding up of the company in the event the company gets sold. This is important to investors as it reduces investment risk. Some common types of liquidation preferences that can be included in a term sheet are as follows:
    1. **Non-Participating Preferred**: Under this preference, the investors have the option to either receive their initial investment amount (the liquidation preference) or participate with the common shareholders on an as-converted basis. If the liquidation preference is chosen, the

investors receive their investment amount before the remaining proceeds are distributed to the common shareholders.
2. **Participating Preferred**: With participating preferred, the investors receive their liquidation preference (typically their investment amount) first and then participate with the common shareholders in the distribution of the remaining proceeds on an as-converted basis. This means that the investors can receive multiple payouts—one as per their liquidation preference and another through their ownership stake.
3. **Capped Participation**: Capped participation is a variation of participating preferred that includes a cap or limit on the total return an investor can receive. Once the investor reaches the cap, they convert their preferred shares into common shares and participate in the distribution of the remaining proceeds along with the common shareholders.
4. **Multiple Liquidation Preferences**: In some cases, investors may negotiate for multiple liquidation preferences, where they receive their investment amount back multiple times before sharing any remaining proceeds with the common shareholders. For example, an investor may have a 2x liquidation preference, which means they receive twice their investment amount before any distribution to the common shareholders.
5. **Seniority**: Liquidation preferences can also be structured based on seniority, where different classes of preferred shares have priority over other classes in terms of receiving their liquidation preferences. Senior preferred shares are paid first, followed by junior preferred shares, and then the common shareholders.

The specific terms and conditions of liquidation preferences can vary depending on negotiations between the founders and investors, the company's stage of growth, and market conditions. Founders should carefully consider the potential impact of liquidation preferences on their ownership stakes and the ultimate value they can derive from an exit event. Consulting with legal and financial professionals is recommended to ensure a thorough understanding of the terms and implications before agreeing to any liquidation preference provisions.

- **Voting Rights:** Voting rights refer to the say that the investor(s) would have over the operations of the company or the number of votes the investor receives or any restrictions on matters in which they are not eligible to vote in. In a term sheet, various types of voting rights can be negotiated between founders and investors to determine the decision-making authority and influence of each party. Here are some common types of voting rights provisions:
    1. **Majority Voting**: Majority voting requires a simple majority (more than 50%) of the voting shares to approve a resolution or decision. This means that decisions can be made if the majority of shareholders, including both founders and investors, are in favour.

2. **Supermajority Voting**: Supermajority voting, also known as a special majority, requires a higher percentage of votes to approve certain important decisions. For example, a term sheet may stipulate specific actions such as amending the company's bylaws, issuing additional shares, or approving a merger or acquisition, require a two-thirds or three-fourths majority vote.
3. **Founder Veto Rights**: Founder veto rights grant the founders the ability to veto or block specific decisions or actions even if they don't hold a majority of the voting shares. This can be negotiated to protect the founders' vision, strategic direction, or key decision-making areas.
4. **Investor Protective Provisions:** Investor protective provisions are clauses that give specific rights and approval powers to investors for certain actions. These provisions may include the approval of significant financing rounds, changes to the company's capital structure, the appointment of key executives, or approval of the company's budget or business plan.
5. **Board Representation**: Board representation grants investors the right to appoint one or more representatives to the company's board of directors. Board members have a significant role in overseeing the company's operations, strategic decisions, and corporate governance.

The specific voting rights provisions can vary widely depending on the negotiations and the relative bargaining power of the parties involved. It's important for founders to carefully consider the implications of voting rights provisions and seek legal counsel to ensure a clear understanding of the decision-making dynamics and their potential impact on the company's future operations and strategic direction.

- **Vesting**: How long the investor is required to remain vested? The length of time an investor is required to remain vested depends on the specific terms negotiated between the investor and the company. Vesting is a mechanism used to incentivize long-term commitment and alignment between investors and the company by linking the investor's ownership rights to a specific vesting schedule.

The vesting schedule outlines the duration over which the investor's ownership rights gradually "vest" or become available. It is common for vesting to occur over a period of time, often referred to as the vesting period, which can range from several months to several years. The vesting period and schedule are typically determined through negotiations between the investor and the company. Some common vesting structures include:
1. **Cliff Vesting**: Under cliff vesting, the investor does not become vested in any ownership rights until a specific milestone or period of time has passed. Once the cliff period is reached, the investor becomes fully vested in their ownership rights.
2. **Graded or Monthly Vesting**: Graded vesting, also known as monthly vesting, involves the gradual vesting of ownership rights over a specified

period. For example, if the vesting period is four years, the investor may become vested in 25% of their ownership rights after the first year and then gain an additional percentage each month thereafter until they are fully vested at the end of the fourth year.
3. **Accelerated Vesting**: Accelerated vesting provisions can be included in certain circumstances, such as a change of control event or termination of employment. These provisions allow investors to become fully vested or have an accelerated vesting of their ownership rights in such situations.

It's important for both investors and companies to carefully consider the vesting terms and negotiate an arrangement that aligns with their objectives and long-term commitment. The specific vesting period and schedule can vary depending on factors such as the industry, the nature of the investment, the stage of the company, and market practices. Legal counsel should be sought to draft appropriate vesting provisions and ensure they are properly documented in the investment agreement or shareholders' agreement.

- **Pro-Rata Rights:** Pro-rata rights, also known as pre-emptive rights or anti-dilution rights, are provisions that can be included in a term sheet or investment agreement between founders and investors. Pro-rata rights give existing shareholders, typically investors, the right to maintain their proportional ownership in the company by participating in future financing rounds or the issuance of new shares. These rights enable shareholders to preserve their ownership percentage and avoid dilution when the company raises additional capital. Here's how pro-rata rights typically work:
    1. **Opportunity to Participate**: Pro-rata rights allow existing shareholders to participate in future equity offerings or financing rounds in proportion to their current ownership stake. If the company decides to issue new shares, the existing shareholders with pro-rata rights can purchase additional shares to maintain their ownership percentage.
    2. **Preserving Ownership Percentage**: By exercising their pro rata rights, shareholders can prevent their ownership stake from being diluted. For example, if an investor owns 10% of the company before a new financing round, their pro rata rights would allow them to purchase additional shares to maintain 10% ownership even after the round is completed.
    3. **Limitations and Timing**: Pro rata rights may be subject to certain limitations or conditions defined in the term sheet. For instance, there may be a cap on the maximum percentage of new shares that an investor can purchase or a time limit within which the investor must exercise their rights.
    4. **Waiver or Transferability**: In some cases, pro rata rights can be waived or transferred. For example, if an investor decides not to exercise their pro rata rights, they may choose to waive them and allow other shareholders to participate instead. Additionally, pro rata rights may be

transferable, meaning that investors can sell or assign their rights to another party if they do not wish to exercise them personally.

Pro rata rights are designed to protect existing shareholders' interests by allowing them to maintain their ownership positions and avoid dilution when new equity is issued. They provide investors with the opportunity to continue investing in the company's growth and future financing rounds on an equitable basis. Pro rata rights are commonly negotiated as part of the investment terms in early-stage startup financing, but the specific terms and conditions may vary depending on the negotiations and the preferences of the parties involved.

Differential Voting Rights: These rights for investors in startups refer to a structure where different classes of shares or stocks carry varying voting power or rights. This means that certain shareholders have more voting power or influence over the company's decisions compared to others. In a startup, this structure is often used to provide certain investors, such as founders or early-stage investors, with greater control or decision-making authority. It allows them to retain a larger influence on the company's strategic direction and protect their interests. Here are a few common scenarios where differential voting rights can be implemented:

a. **Founder's Control**: Founders may hold shares with higher voting power compared to other shareholders, such as common stockholders or later-stage investors. This structure enables founders to maintain control over key decisions, even if their ownership stake decreases over time due to dilution from subsequent funding rounds.
b. **Investor Protection**: Investors who provide substantial funding or strategic support to startups may negotiate for shares with enhanced voting rights. This can help safeguard their investment and ensure they have a say in critical decisions, such as major corporate transactions or changes to the company's structure.
c. **Class-Based Voting:** Startups can create different classes of shares with varying voting rights. For example, Class A shares might carry ten votes per share, while Class B shares have only one vote per share. This allows certain shareholders to have a disproportionately larger say in matters that require shareholder approval.

It's worth noting that while differential voting rights can provide benefits in terms of control and protection, they can also raise concerns regarding governance and fairness. Some investors or shareholders might view this structure as giving undue power to certain parties and limiting the rights of others. Therefore, it's important for startups to carefully consider the implications and potential impact on their relationships with investors and shareholders before implementing differential voting rights.

- **Right of First Offer (ROFO) for future investment**: Whether investors are entitled to a right of first offer (ROFO) for future investment offerings depends on the specific terms negotiated between the founders and investors in a term sheet or investment agreement. The right of first offer is a provision that grants existing shareholders the first opportunity to invest in future equity offerings before shares are offered to external parties. It gives existing investors the right to maintain their proportional ownership and participate in subsequent funding rounds.

    The inclusion of a right of first offer in a term sheet can be beneficial for both founders and existing investors. Founders may prefer to offer the opportunity to existing investors first, as they are already familiar with the company and its operations. Existing investors, on the other hand, may want to protect their ownership stakes and have the chance to continue investing in the company's growth. The specific details of a right of first offer can vary. Here are some key considerations:

    1. **Notification**: The right of first offer typically requires the company to notify existing investors of any future equity offerings or financing rounds. This allows investors to evaluate the opportunity and decide whether they want to participate.
    2. **Terms and Pricing**: The terms and pricing for the shares offered under the right of the first offer should be clearly defined. It may be based on the same terms and conditions as offered to external investors or negotiated separately.
    3. **Timing**: The term sheet should specify the timeframe within which existing investors must respond to the right of the first offer. This ensures that the company can proceed with the offering promptly if existing investors decline the opportunity.
    4. **Exclusivity and Withdrawal**: A right of first offer may include a period of exclusivity, during which existing investors have the sole opportunity to participate in the offering. If existing investors decline the offer, the company can then proceed to offer the shares to external investors.

    The inclusion of a right of first offer is subject to negotiation and agreement between the founders and investors. The specific terms and conditions can vary based on the company's circumstances, the bargaining power of the parties involved, and market practices. Founders should carefully consider the potential benefits and implications of granting a right of first offer to investors and consult with legal and financial professionals to ensure the terms align with their objectives and the company's future funding requirements.

- **Penalties for Investors for not Partaking in future Rounds**: The penalties for investors who decide not to participate in future rounds of investing are typically negotiated and outlined in the terms of the Term sheet or investment agreement, or shareholders' agreement. These penalties, if any, are intended to incentivize investors to continue supporting the company's growth by participating in subsequent funding rounds. The specific penalties can vary based on the negotiations between the parties involved; a few potential penalty provisions that may be included in the term sheet are as follows:

1. **Dilution**: One common penalty for investors who choose not to participate in future funding rounds is dilution of their ownership stake. The investment agreement may include provisions that automatically adjust the investor's ownership percentage downward in proportion to their decision not to invest. This means that their ownership stake will be reduced when new shares are issued to other investors.
2. **Loss of Rights or Privileges**: The investment agreement may specify that investors who opt out of future rounds forfeit certain rights or privileges they would have otherwise enjoyed. For example, they may lose their board representation rights, voting rights on certain matters, or specific information rights. This loss of rights can act as a disincentive for investors to opt out of subsequent financing rounds.
3. **Limited Exit Opportunities**: Investors who choose not to participate in future funding rounds may face limitations on their ability to exit the investment. This can be in the form of restrictions on selling their shares, limitations on the timing of sales, or a requirement to offer their shares to existing shareholders before selling to external parties.
4. **Reduced or No Follow-On Investment Rights**: By not participating in subsequent funding rounds, investors may lose their right to make additional investments in the company. This means they may not have the opportunity to invest further in the company's growth and benefit from future value appreciation.

While penalties can be included in investment agreements, they are typically used as a means to align the interests of investors with the company's long-term success. The inclusion and severity of penalties will depend on the specific circumstances, negotiations, and market practices. It's important for both founders and investors to seek legal counsel to ensure that the penalty provisions are fair, reasonable, and legally enforceable.

- **No-Shop Agreement:** Included for the protection of investors from other investors or other investment rounds, a no-shop agreement outlines the terms that restrict the company from taking investment money from other people for a specific period of time. No-Shop Agreement, also known as an exclusivity provision, is a common clause included in a term sheet or letter of intent (LOI) between a potential investor and a company. This agreement restricts the company from actively seeking or engaging in discussions with other potential investors or parties for a specified period of time while negotiations with the current investor are ongoing. The purpose of a No-Shop Agreement is to provide the potential investor with a period of exclusivity to conduct due diligence and negotiate the terms of the investment without competition from other parties. Key features and considerations related to a No-Shop Agreement include:

1. **Exclusivity Period**: The agreement specifies a defined period during which the company is prohibited from soliciting or engaging in discussions with other potential investors. This period typically ranges from a few weeks to a few months, depending on the complexity of the transaction and the negotiation process.
2. **Restricted Activities**: The No-Shop Agreement restricts the company from taking actions that could result in the solicitation or engagement of other investors. This includes refraining from actively seeking investment proposals, entertaining offers, or initiating discussions with other parties regarding financing or acquisition opportunities.
3. **Exceptions**: The agreement may include exceptions that allow the company to continue discussions with other parties under certain circumstances. For example, exceptions could include unsolicited offers that the company receives without actively seeking them or discussions related to alternative transactions that are deemed to be in the best interests of the company.
4. **Exclusivity Fees**: In some cases, the No-Shop Agreement may include provisions for the payment of exclusivity fees by the potential investor. These fees compensate the potential investor for the opportunity cost associated with the exclusivity period and the potential loss of other investment opportunities during that time.
5. **Termination and Withdrawal**: The agreement may outline conditions or triggers for termination or withdrawal from the exclusivity provisions. For instance, if the parties are unable to reach a definitive agreement within a specified timeframe, either party may have the right to terminate the exclusivity and pursue other options.

No-Shop Agreements provide potential investors with a level of confidence and assurance that they have an exclusive opportunity to negotiate and finalize the investment. However, founders should carefully consider the duration and terms of the No-Shop Agreement to ensure that it aligns with their objectives and doesn't unduly restrict their ability to explore alternative options or secure more favourable terms. Seeking legal counsel is recommended to understand the implications and negotiate appropriate provisions in the agreement.

- **SAFE (Simple Agreement for Future Equity) Notes**: These are the documents that startups often use to raise seed capital. Essentially, a SAFE note acts as a legally binding promise to allow an investor to purchase a specified number of shares for an agreed-upon price at some point in the future. It is a financial instrument commonly used in early-stage startup financing as an alternative to traditional equity financing. It was introduced by Y Combinator, a startup accelerator, as a simplified and standardized approach to investment. Some key features and characteristics of SAFE notes are as follows:

1. **Convertible Instrument**: SAFE notes are a type of convertible instrument, which means that they are designed to convert into equity at a future trigger event. The trigger event is typically a priced equity financing round, such as a Series A funding round.
2. **Future Equity Conversion**: When the trigger event occurs, SAFE note holders have the right to convert their investment into equity at the predetermined terms specified in the SAFE agreement. The conversion typically happens at a discount to the price per share in the priced financing round or may include a valuation cap that sets a maximum price for the conversion.
3. **No Fixed Maturity Date or Interest**: Unlike traditional debt instruments, SAFE notes do not have a fixed maturity date or accrue interest. They are designed to be a simple and streamlined investment mechanism, focusing on the future equity conversion rather than debt repayment.
4. **No Voting Rights or Control**: SAFE note holders generally do not have voting rights or control over the company. They are not considered shareholders until the conversion event occurs.
5. **No Dividends or Liquidation Preferences**: SAFE notes typically do not carry dividend rights or liquidation preferences. Note holders participate in the distribution of proceeds upon a liquidity event on a pari passu (equal footing) basis with other shareholders, except for any specific terms negotiated in the SAFE agreement.
6. **Standardized and Customizable**: Although SAFE notes were initially introduced with a standardized template, they can be customized to some extent based on negotiations between the parties involved. Certain terms, such as conversion provisions, discount rate, and valuation cap, can be adjusted to fit the specific circumstances of the investment.

SAFE notes have gained popularity in early-stage startup financing due to their simplicity, flexibility, and investor-friendly features. They allow startups to raise funds without the immediate need to determine a valuation and offer investors the potential for future equity upside. However, it's important for both founders and investors to carefully consider the terms and implications of SAFE notes and seek legal counsel to ensure they align with their respective objectives and the specific circumstances of the investment.

B. **Loan Term Sheet**

- **Loan Amount:** This term may be a fixed amount, subject to Loan to Value (LTV) metrics or subject to Debt Service Coverage Ratio (DSCR) and Net Operating Income (NOI) calculations.

- **Guarantee:** The legal entity with more established credit that may vouch for the debt and can be held liable in the event of default by the company.
- **Interest Rate:** Depending on the type of loan, these terms may vary widely. For long-term loans, the interest rate may include a fixed spread rate in addition to a variable rate.
- **Term:** By when the loan is expected to be fully payable or due. For open lines of credit or development loans, this is the period in which the loan is assessed interest, but principal payments may not be due.
- **Collateral:** The underlying asset that is often supported by the debt is presented by the borrower to substantiate value in the event that they default on a loan.
- **Financial Covenants:** externally certified financial statements, guarantee statements, or other financial records submitted by the borrower to a lender to substantiate financial health.
- **Loan Costs:** In addition to interest assessments, a lender may require an annual administration fee or a one-time loan closing fee, or upfront costs that must be paid before the loan is disbursed.

Tips for Writing a Term Sheet

Every term sheet will vary, as the parties, conditions, situation, and agreement will rarely be repeated. Still, the following tips that apply to nearly every situation can be of help in drafting a term sheet:

- ❖ **Summarize the Conditions.** At the beginning of the term sheet, draft a summary that identifies:
    - ❖ Overall purpose of the agreement and the intended outcome.
    - ❖ Identify each of the legal parties that are involved.
- ❖ **State Binding/Non-Binding Terms.** A term sheet should explicitly state expectations early in the Term sheet regarding that what terms are binding and what are non-binding.
- ❖ **List the Terms.** Provide enough information covering the primary, most important aspects of a deal to engage the other party without being too overwhelming with details. The minor aspects can be sorted out later.
- ❖ **State Timeframes.** Though the term sheet is non-binding, it should still come with a date that requires the parties to take action by a certain time. This not only encourages participation and action but also ensures the deal is held by either of the parties for too long.
- ❖ **Encourage Feedback.** Share the first draft of the term sheet in the Word format in "Tracks changes" and add "Comment" mode allowing each side to easily identify the areas not yet in agreement.

Documents required for Due Diligence after Signing of the Term sheet

After signing a term sheet, the due diligence process begins, which involves a comprehensive review of the company's legal, financial, operational, and other relevant aspects. The specific documents required for due diligence can vary depending on the nature of the investment and the preferences of the parties involved. However, here are some common documents that are often requested during the due diligence process:

- ❖ **Corporate Documents:**
    - o Certificate of Incorporation or Articles of Organization
    - o Bylaws or Operating Agreement
    - o Shareholder or Member Agreements
    - o Board and Shareholder Meeting Minutes
    - o Corporate Registers and Records
- ❖ **Financial Statements and Accounting Records:**
    - o Audited or Reviewed Financial Statements (if available)
    - o Unaudited Financial Statements (Balance Sheet, Income Statement, Cash Flow Statement)
    - o General Ledger and Trial Balance
    - o Tax Returns and Filings
    - o Accounts Payable and Accounts Receivable Aging Reports
    - o Revenue and Expense Breakdowns
    - o Capitalization Table (cap table) detailing ownership and securities issued
- ❖ **Contracts and Agreements:**
    - o Customer Contracts and Agreements
    - o Supplier and Vendor Contracts
    - o Lease Agreements
    - o Employment Agreements
    - o Partnership or Joint Venture Agreements
    - o Licensing Agreements
    - o Non-Disclosure Agreements (NDAs)
- ❖ **Intellectual Property (IP) Documentation:**
    - o Patents, Trademarks, Copyrights, and other IP registrations
    - o License Agreements for IP
    - o IP Assignment Agreements
    - o Documentation related to IP litigation or disputes
- ❖ **Regulatory and Compliance Documentation:**
    - o Permits, Licenses, and Certifications
    - o Regulatory Filings and Reports
    - o Compliance Policies and Procedures
    - o Environmental or Safety Compliance Documentation
- ❖ **Litigation and Legal Matters:**
    - o Litigation or Claims History
    - o Pending or Threatened Legal Actions
    - o Intellectual Property Disputes
    - o Regulatory Compliance Issues
- ❖ **Human Resources and Employee Matters:**
    - o Employee Contracts and Offer Letters
    - o Employee Handbook and Policies
    - o Organizational Structure and Job Descriptions
    - o Employee Benefits and Compensation Details

It's important to note that the due diligence process may involve additional documents and information specific to the industry, market, or concerns of the investor. The due diligence process is typically conducted by legal and financial professionals representing the investor, and they will request the necessary documents to assess the company's risks, financial performance, legal compliance, and overall viability.

The company should be prepared to provide the requested documentation in a timely manner to facilitate the due diligence process and build trust with the investor. Legal counsel should be consulted to ensure compliance with applicable laws and regulations and to assist with the preparation and organization of the due diligence documentation.

Business Plan

"If you just work on stuff that you like and you're passionate about, you don't have to have a master plan with how things will play out." **–Mark Zuckerberg, Facebook Founder & CEO**

A business plan developed by startup founders while raising funding is a comprehensive document that outlines the key aspects of the startup's business model, strategy, and financial projections. It serves as a roadmap and a tool to communicate the startup's vision, market opportunity, and growth plans to potential investors. Here are the key components typically included in a startup's business plan:

1. **Executive Summary**: Provides a concise overview of the business plan, highlighting the startup's value proposition, market opportunity, competitive advantage, and funding requirements.
2. **Company Description**: Provides detailed information about the startup, including its mission, vision, legal structure, location, founding team, and key milestones achieved.
3. **Problem Statement**: Clearly defines the problem or pain point that the startup aims to solve. Describes the market need and the significance of addressing this problem.
4. **Solution**: Presents the startup's unique solution or product offering that addresses the identified problem. Explains how the solution is innovative, valuable, and differentiated from existing alternatives.
5. **Market Analysis:** Conducts a thorough analysis of the target market, including the size, growth rate, trends, and dynamics. Identifies the target customer segments, their characteristics, and their needs.
6. **Competitive Analysis**: Evaluates the competitive landscape and identifies key competitors. Assesses their strengths, weaknesses, and market positioning. Highlights the startup's competitive advantages and how it differentiates itself from competitors.
7. **Business Model**: Describes the startup's business model, including how it plans to generate revenue, pricing strategies, and revenue streams. Discusses the cost structure, key partnerships, distribution channels, and customer acquisition strategies.
8. **Marketing and Sales Strategy**: Outlines the startup's marketing and sales approach to reach and acquire customers. Describes the target market segments, marketing channels, promotional activities, and customer acquisition tactics.
9. **Product or Service Description**: Provides a detailed description of the startup's product or service, including its features, functionalities, and benefits. Highlights any unique selling points or intellectual property associated with the product or service.

10. **Operations and Management**: Describes the startup's organizational structure, key team members, their roles, and relevant experience. Discusses the operational processes, production or service delivery, and quality control measures.
11. **Financial Projections**: Presents the financial forecasts, including revenue projections, expenses, profit margins, and cash flow statements. Demonstrates the financial viability and growth potential of the startup. It may include historical financial data if available.
12. **Funding Requirements**: Specifies the funding required to support the startup's growth plans, including the amount and the purpose of the funding. Explains how the funds will be utilized and the expected return on investment for potential investors.
13. **Exit Strategy**: Outlines the startup's exit strategy, providing a plan for how investors can realize their returns on investment. It may include options such as acquisition, IPO, or buyback.
14. **Risks and Mitigation Strategies**: Identifies the potential risks and challenges that the startup may face and provides strategies to mitigate those risks. Demonstrates an understanding of the risks and a proactive approach to managing them.
15. **Appendices**: Includes additional supporting materials, such as market research data, customer testimonials, product demos, legal documents, and any other relevant information that strengthens the business plan.

A well-developed business plan provides a comprehensive and compelling overview of the startup's business model, market opportunity, growth potential, and financial projections. It is a critical document that helps startup founders articulate their vision and strategy to attract investors and secure funding.

Guidelines for Developing Business Plan

While developing a business plan as a startup founder, it's important to follow certain guidelines to ensure that your plan is comprehensive, well-structured, and effectively communicates your startup's value proposition. Here are some guidelines to consider:

1. **Be Clear and Concise**: Keep your business plan clear, concise, and to the point. Avoid jargon and technical terms that may confuse readers. Use simple language to ensure that your plan is easily understandable.
2. **Know Your Audience**: Understand who will be reading your business plan and tailor it to their needs. Investors may have different priorities and areas of interest, so customize your plan to resonate with their expectations and investment criteria.
3. **Do Thorough Market Research**: Conduct comprehensive market research to understand your target market, including its size, growth potential, trends, and customer needs. Use credible sources and data to support your market analysis and projections.
4. **Clearly Define Your Value Proposition**: Clearly articulate your startup's unique value proposition. Explain how your product or service solves a

problem or fulfils a need in the market. Highlight the benefits and advantages that differentiate your offering from competitors.
5. **Address the Competitive Landscape**: Conduct a thorough analysis of your competition. Identify key competitors and their strengths and weaknesses. Clearly explain how your startup differentiates itself and its competitive advantages.
6. **Define Your Target Market**: Clearly define your target market and customer segments. Describe their characteristics, demographics, behaviours, and preferences. Demonstrate a deep understanding of your customers and their needs.
7. **Develop a Strong Marketing and Sales Strategy**: Outline your marketing and sales approach. Define your marketing channels, promotional activities, customer acquisition strategies, and pricing. Clearly explain how you plan to attract and retain customers.
8. **Provide Realistic Financial Projections**: Develop realistic financial projections that demonstrate the potential profitability and growth of your startup. Use sound assumptions based on market research and industry benchmarks. Include income statements, cash flow projections, and balance sheets.
9. **Showcase a Strong Management Team**: Highlight the skills, expertise, and experience of your management team. Clearly define the roles and responsibilities of key team members and their contributions to the startup's success.
10. **Be Realistic About Risks and Mitigation Strategies**: Identify and assess the risks and challenges your startup may face. Provide strategies and contingency plans to mitigate those risks. Demonstrating a proactive approach to risk management enhances your credibility.
11. **Use Visuals and Graphics Effectively**: Incorporate visuals, charts, and graphs to present data and key information effectively. Visuals can make complex information more understandable and help to engage readers.
12. **Be Transparent and Honest**: Be transparent and honest about your startup's strengths, weaknesses, opportunities, and threats. Address potential challenges openly and discuss how you plan to overcome them. Investors appreciate honesty and realism.
13. **Revise and Update Regularly**: Your business plan should be a living document that evolves with your startup. Regularly revise and update it as your business progresses, incorporating new information and insights. Keep it current and relevant.
14. **Seek Feedback**: Share your business plan with trusted advisors, mentors, or industry experts. Seek their feedback and incorporate their insights to improve your plan. Constructive feedback can help strengthen your business strategy.
15. **Proofread and Edit**: Pay attention to grammar, spelling, and formatting. Proofread your business plan carefully to eliminate errors and ensure a professional presentation.

A well-developed and thought-out business plan can communicate your startup's potential and increases your chances of success in raising investment.

Developing a Business Plan

Before developing a business plan the founder and the team should have clarity regarding the following three C's:

1) **Concept:** What the startup is all about
2) **Customers/clients:** Knowing who your customer or client are and will be
3) **Cash flow**: Knowing how the cash flow is/and likely to the startup

Business Plan: An Outline

Executive Summary

In no more than a short paragraph for each point, summarize the sections of your business plan:
Fast Facts:
Founded:
Founder:
Problem you are aiming to solve
Describe how your product or service solves the problem
Market Size:
Target Audience:
Synopsis of Sales and Marketing Plan
Our Mission:
Our Vision:
Company Synopsis:
Team Overview: Introduce key Management
- Name, Qualification, Relevant experience, Achievements/Accolades

Financial plan
Funding Allocation:
→.....% Manufacturing →...% Sales & Marketing →....% Key Hires →....% Operational

Close Executive summary with a brief but clear explanation of product-market fit, why it is needed, and how it will benefit future customers and investors.

Company Description

Describe what makes your company different. This section should convince readers that your business idea is important and that the product or service that you will offer is needed.

Present your company's name, location, type of business, ownership, and significant assets.

Describe your company's mission: What is your reason for existence? Describe the values on which you are founding the company.

List the company's goals and objectives and explain how you fit into the industry.

Company Timeline

Products and Services

Product:
Key Features and Benefits:
Inter-operability:
Cost-Saving Benefits:
Pricing and Revenue

Market Opportunity and Marketing Plan

Competitive Landscape
Primary competitors for …… include other companies that are currently operating in the ……..space, such as …….

Target Audience
We are directly targeting ….. specific target populations for our product:
a. :
b. :
c. :

Marketing Strategy
…… has carefully developed a diverse marketing plan intended to keep our brand in the hearts and minds of our existing and prospective customers, enabling us to continue expanding our reach and grow our business. Between our massive social network followings and email database contacts, we regularly communicate directly with over ……. consumers.

Strategic Partnerships:
We are in the process of building relationships with notable industry leaders, influencers, and development teams in the ……. sector. We are also in advanced-stage partnership discussions with a number of major name ……. providers.

Consumer Validation:

Company Milestones:

SEO & Social:
We will drive traffic and conversions to our website using social media marketing via Facebook, LinkedIn, Twitter, Instagram, Snapchat, YouTube, and others. We are also exploring SEO and SEM.

Content Marketing:
We consistently release marketing content through our blog that aims to educate our audience about the value that our product provides. Our content marketing

efforts aim to influence and persuade readers without having to rely solely on conventional direct selling tactics.

Influencer Marketing:
We will launch an initiative to guest blog articles and features in ……….. publications like ……….., and other outlets in our industry.

5-year Revenue Projection

Future Development
Our initial focus on the consumer space with our launch product is just the first step in our long-term roadmap to growth. In order to capture a larger market share and continue scaling the company exponentially, we are planning on rolling out a B2B model in the future. This will provide us with new revenue streams and will offer a valuable, tech-driven solution for businesses.

Operational Plan

Proprietary Technology:
We have applied for and have been granted a provisional patent for our ……. technology.

Manufacturing:
A ……. contract manufacturer has been secured and is ready to begin production with the capacity to produce around ….. units per month as we scale.

Management and Organization

Team
- Overview of your existing team
- Organization structure
- Predicted hires, with their salaries.

Startup Expenses and Capitalization

Capital Structure

Investor-Backed:
We have secured a total of …………. in funding from angel investors, founder capital, friends and family, and VCs.

Financial Plan

Income statement
- Revenue sources
- Expenses over a given period

- Bottom line, or the profit or loss business experienced during that time.
- If not operating business yet, put a forecast for the same information.

Balance sheet

- Business assets (what you own)
- Liabilities (what you owe).
- Business' shareholder equity which is calculated as: **Assets - Liabilities = Equity**

Cash-flow statement and/or Projections

- Showcases when revenues are collected.
- When expenses are paid.

Financial Statement Summary

Appendices

- Contracts
- Leases
- Purchase orders
- Intellectual property certificates
- Key managers' resumes
- Market research data and Background literature that supports the assumptions made in the plan
- Press mentions:

Tax on Investment in Startups in India

The best things in life are free, but sooner or later the government will find a way to tax them.

The taxation treatment pertaining to investment in startups in India depends on the type of investment, the stage of the startup, and the nature of the transaction. Here are some key considerations:

a. **Investment in equity shares:** When an investor acquires equity shares of a startup, the taxation treatment depends on whether it is a long-term capital gain (LTCG) or a short-term capital gain (STCG). If the shares are held for more than 12 months, the gains are considered LTCG and are subject to tax at a concessional rate of 10% without indexation benefits. If the shares are held for 12 months or less, the gains are considered STCG and taxed at the applicable individual income tax rates.
b. **Angel Tax:** Under the angel tax provisions, if the valuation of a startup exceeded its fair market value, the excess amount could be treated as income and taxed at the individual income tax rates. However, the Indian government has introduced various measures to address this issue and provide relief to startups. Discussed in detail in the subsequent section.
c. **Tax incentives for eligible startups**: The Indian government has introduced various tax incentives to promote investments in startups. For example, the "Startup India" initiative offers eligible startups certain tax benefits, including a three-year tax holiday on profits, exemption from the angel tax subject to certain conditions, and capital gains tax exemptions on the sale of specified assets.
d. **Taxation of exit events**: When a startup is acquired or undergoes an initial public offering (IPO), the taxation of capital gains on exit events depends on the holding period and the type of investment. If the shares are held for more than 12 months, the gains are considered LTCG and may be eligible for certain exemptions or benefits. If the shares are held for 12 months or less, the gains are considered STCG and taxed at the applicable individual income tax rates.

Angel Tax

The Income Tax Act of 1961's Section 56 (2) (viib) discusses the concept of angel tax. According to the Finance Act, 2012, in the IT Act, every startup (i.e., unlisted companies whose shares are not available for buying on the stock market) that receives funding from an angel investor must contribute a certain amount in the form of tax. Angel tax is levied at a rate of 30.9% on investments received by a startup greater than its fair market value. But it is subject to following conditions:

a. A startup earning an investment from venture capital and non-resident investors are not eligible for the deduction of angel tax.

b. This tax comes into play only if the total investment value exceeds the company's FMV or Fair Market Value. Investment greater than FMV is categorised as "income from other sources", and the tax imposed on it is called angel tax. For example, a firm receives an investment from an angel investor of Rs 15 crore in exchange for equity. But the fair market valuation (FMV) of the shares issued is Rs 10 crore. The remaining Rs 5 crore is considered excess money and, therefore, taxable at a rate of 30.9%.

Angel Tax Exemption

As Angel tax was applicable only to startups that are funded by a resident Indian, and startups tend to lose a significant part of the investment in the form of taxes as angel tax. The notification by the Central Board of Direct Taxes also excluded certain classes of investors from the ambit of the angel tax levy. These includes VC funds registered with Sebi as Category-I FPI, Endowment Funds, Pension Funds and broad-based pooled investment vehicles, which are residents of 21 specified nations, including the US, UK, Australia, Germany, Spain, and others.

Therefore, after numerous pleas made by the startups, the Indian government has made some provisions for the following relaxations/exemptions from Angel tax in the 2019 Union budget:

a. If the startup is registered under the DPIIT or Department for Promotion of Industry and Internal Trade, it would not be subject to such tax. To be eligible, the startup needs to send an application along with the necessary documents to the Central Board of Direct Taxes or CBDT. After CBDT approval, they will be exempted from paying angel tax.

   Criteria that a startup needs to fulfil for angel tax exemption are as follows:

   a. After issuing the shares, the startup's maximum paid-up capital and share premium should not exceed Rs 25 crore.
   b. As per Rule 11 UA (2)(b) of the Income Tax Act of 1961, it is imperative for the merchant banker to evaluate the fair market value of the startup.
   c. The amount raised from venture capital firms, NRIs, and other specific companies is not included in the calculation.
   d. The startup's yearly turnover should not be more than Rs 100 crore in any of the past fiscal years.
   e. Angel investors are eligible for a 100% tax exemption on investing in startups with higher fair market value. However, to avail of this exemption, the average income of angel investors should not be more than Rs 25 lakh and should have a net worth of Rs 2 crore in the previous 3 fiscal years.

Until the 2023 Budget, the tax was applicable only to domestic individual investors. However, in the 2023 Budget, both foreign investors and NRI investors were also brought under the ambit of the angel tax.

VC Funding

"The biggest secret in venture capital is that the best investment in a successful fund equals or outperforms the entire rest of the fund combined." **-Peter Thiel**

Venture Capitalists (VC)

VCs firms are professional investors who provide capital to high-potential startups and early-stage companies in exchange for an ownership stake or equity in the company. They typically invest larger amounts of capital compared to angel investors and often play an active role in guiding the growth and strategic direction of the invested companies.

They specialize in funding early-stage and high-growth companies by identifying promising investment opportunities and providing financial support to help these companies scale and succeed. They typically invest in businesses that have the potential for rapid expansion, disruptive technologies, innovative business models. In addition to capital, VCs often bring valuable expertise, experience, and industry connections to the companies they invest in. They may provide guidance and strategic advice to help the entrepreneurs navigate challenges and make critical business decisions. They may also assist with recruiting key talent, building partnerships, and accessing additional sources of funding.

VCs play a crucial role in supporting entrepreneurial ventures by providing the necessary capital, expertise, and resources to help them grow, succeed, and potentially become significant players in their respective industries. VCs generally take on higher risks compared to traditional lenders or investors as they invest in early-stage companies. In return, VCs expect a significantly higher return on their investments. This comes in the form of exit during an initial public offering (IPO) or an acquisition, where the VC can sell their equity stake and realize their gains.

How VCs work

VCs, typically follow a process that involves:
1. **Sourcing and Screening:** VCs actively source investment opportunities through various channels, including referrals, industry networks, pitch events, and their own research. They screen potential opportunities based on their investment criteria and initial evaluation.
2. **Due Diligence:** VCs conduct thorough due diligence on selected startups. This involves analyzing the business, financials, market, technology, team, legal aspects, and any other relevant factors. They assess the risks and potential upside of the investment.
3. **Term Negotiation:** If the due diligence process is positive, VCs negotiate the terms, the investment amount, valuation, ownership stake, and any specific terms or conditions associated with the investment.
4. **Investment and Support:** Once the terms are agreed upon, VCs provide the funding to the startup. In addition to the capital investment, venture

capitalists often provide strategic guidance, industry connections, and mentorship to help the startup succeed and maximize its growth potential.

What do VCs look for? How do they evaluate?

VCs have specific investment criteria and preferences, and not all companies are suitable for venture capital funding. Startups seeking venture capital often need to demonstrate a high growth potential, a scalable business model, and a market opportunity that justifies the investment. Here's an overview of how VCs work and what they typically look for when evaluating investment opportunities:

1. **Investment Focus:** VCs have specific investment focus areas or sectors they specialize in, such as technology, healthcare, fintech, or consumer goods. They often seek startups with disruptive or innovative business models that have the potential for high growth and substantial market impact.
2. **Strong Management Team:** Venture capitalists place great importance on the management team. They look for talented and experienced entrepreneurs who demonstrate leadership skills, domain expertise, and the ability to execute the business plan effectively. A capable team with a track record of success enhances the likelihood of investment.
3. **Market Potential:** VCs assess the market size and growth potential of the startup's target market. They evaluate the market dynamics, competition, and the startup's ability to capture a significant market share. The potential for scalability and a large total addressable market (TAM) are attractive to VCs.
4. **Unique Value Proposition:** VCs look for startups with a unique value proposition or competitive advantage. They seek businesses with innovative products or services, proprietary technology, intellectual property, or a differentiated approach that offers a compelling advantage over existing solutions in the market.
5. **Traction and Growth Potential:** VCs evaluate the startup's current stage of development and traction. They assess metrics such as customer acquisition, revenue growth, user engagement, and market adoption to gauge the potential for rapid growth. Demonstrating strong traction and a clear path to scaling the business is important for VC investment.
6. **Business Model and Monetization Strategy:** VCs scrutinize the startup's business model and monetization strategy. They assess the revenue streams, pricing, cost structure, and the potential for profitability. VCs seek startups with a clear plan for generating revenue and achieving sustainable profitability in the long term.
7. **Exit Strategy:** VCs consider the potential exit options for their investment. They look for startups with a credible and realistic exit strategy, such as a strategic acquisition by a larger company or an initial public offering (IPO). The potential for generating significant returns on investment is a crucial aspect for venture capitalists.

VCs have their own investment preferences, strategies, and evaluation methods. The evaluation process can vary among VCs, and each may have its unique focus areas, decision-making criteria, and involvement levels post-investment.

VC Funding in India: Recent Trends

Out of 61,400 start-ups launched till January 2022, only around 7 % were able to raise funds from PE or VC investors. A brief description regarding VC funding in India over a period of time is discussed below:

A. **Before 2021:**
The data recorded at the end of Q3 of 2019 indicated that the top 10 most active VC firms in India contribute 32% of the total deal count in the startup ecosystem. The Indian startups secured over $12.1 billion from the VC funds in the first 6 months of 2021, which is $1 billion more than the overall funding that they received last year.

B. **During 2021**
During 2021, Indian startups raised over $42 Bn in funding and most of them came from the VC funding for startups and private equity investments, which increased by 3X from the previous year. Over 2,487 investors participated in the Indian startup funding in 2021.
According to a report by KPMG, VC investment in India more than doubled from Q2 2021 quarterly high of $6.7 billion to $14.4 billion during Q3 2021. Different investors raised about $6.2 Bn by 62 funds comprising VCs, Debt, CVC, and Micro VCs to invest in Indian startup story.

C. **During 2022**
According to India Venture Capital Report 2023 by Bain & Co., the trends in the VC funding landscape in India during 2021 and 2022 are as follows:
  a. **Global VC Funding Share**: In 2021 and 2022, India accounted for approximately 5% of global VC funding. Within the Asia-Pacific region, India's share of VC investments reached 20% for the first time in 2022.
  b. **Unicorn Growth**: India achieved a significant milestone by surpassing 100 unicorns in May 2022. For two consecutive years, India added more unicorns (23) compared to China (11).
  c. **Funding Compression**: The total deal value in India experienced a decline from $38.5 billion in 2021 to $25.7 billion in 2022. This reduction was in line with the global slowdown and was influenced by macroeconomic headwinds.
  d. **Funding Momentum**: Despite the overall decline in deal value, investments in India grew by 1.4 times during the first half of 2021-2022. However, in the second half of 2022, there was a significant 70% decline compared to the second half of 2021 due to global macro headwinds.
  e. **Mega rounds Decline**: The number of "mega rounds" (deals with a value of $100 million or more) decreased from 92 in 2021 to 48 in 2022. Global investors exercised caution and showed a reduced appetite for large-ticket size deals.
  f. **Concentration of Investments:** The concentration of investments by large investors decreased to less than 20% in 2022 from 25% in 2021. Investment activity by global hedge funds and crossover funds slowed down during this period.
  g. **Early-Stage Rounds**: Despite the challenges faced in the VC funding landscape, early-stage rounds across sectors saw marginal growth, with

deal volume increasing by 1.1 times. The expansion was mainly driven by Seed to Series B deals. In 2022, more than 80% of deals for top funds like Sequoia, Accel, and Lightspeed were in the early-stage category.

These trends indicate that while there was a decline in overall funding and caution in large-ticket investments, the early-stage sector remained relatively resilient and attracted significant interest from VC investors.

Noticeable Differences in Funding Ecosystem in 2022

a. **Fundamental Shifts: Likely to Shape Funding Landscape:**
   In 2022, the Indian start-up ecosystem experienced the following fundamental shifts that are likely to shape the funding landscape in the near to medium term:

   - **Investors**: Investors shifted their focus from pursuing rapid growth at any cost to prioritizing sustainable unit economics. Additionally, venture debt emerged as a viable alternative funding option for start-ups.

   - **Regulators**:
     i. **Negative developments:**
        - The tightening of following regulatory guidelines for fintech companies
        - Ban on prepaid instrument-based credit.
        - New digital lending norms
        - Taxes on virtual digital assets impacting cryptocurrency, etc.
        - Corporate governance issues raising alarm bells (Discussed in detail in a separate chapter)
     ii. **Positive developments:**
        - Macro regulations playing a supportive role in the ecosystem.
        - Measures such as production-linked incentives (PLI)
        - Introduction of a framework on tech listings by the SEBI.

   - **Macro Highlights:**
     - **Macroeconomic headwinds**:
       - Russia-Ukraine war shadow on Europe
       - Rising inflation
       - Central banks across the globe raising rates.
       - Capital becoming expensive.
       - PE/VC firms negotiating hard for valuation.
       - Due diligence process getting longer and stringent.
       - Investors getting choosier over valuations.

     - **Secular Tailwinds**: Several positive factors that create favourable conditions for startups in India include:
       - Low data costs
       - Availability of digital infrastructure as public goods
       - Growing base of aspirational consumers

- More formalized economy,
- Presence of world-class software companies
- Significant amount of unused capital available for investment.
- Focus on building public digital infrastructure: the launch of initiatives like the Open Network for Digital Commerce (ONDC).

The combination of these favourable conditions and evolving ecosystem dynamics makes it an excellent time to start a business in India as these can provide opportunities for entrepreneurs to build successful ventures.

- **Startups:**
  - The ecosystem witnessed over 25,000 layoffs.
  - More than 10 deferred initial public offerings (IPOs)
  - Distress mergers and acquisitions (M&A).
  - Focus on diversity in leadership positions within start-ups.
  - Focus on Quality: The quality of businesses became imperative in 2022, the larger companies prioritized generating profits. This shift toward prioritizing sustainable business models demonstrates moving away from a growth-at-all-costs approach.
  - Creation of Robust Businesses: The emphasis on quality and profitability is expected to lead to the creation of robust businesses that can withstand challenges and stand the test of time. This suggests a long-term perspective in building sustainable ventures.

These shifts reflect a maturing and evolving start-up ecosystem in India. Investors' emphasis on sustainable growth, regulatory changes impacting certain sectors, and the overall ups and downs experienced by startups all contribute to the ongoing transformation of the landscape.

b. **VC Investment Themes**:
In 2022, different sectors experienced varying levels of deal momentum and investor interest in India. Some notable themes include:
- **Consumer Tech**: The deal momentum in consumer tech moderated due to higher cash-burn business models. Investors exercised caution in this sector.
- **SaaS:** The Software-as-a Service (SaaS) sector witnessed steady deal momentum, indicating sustained investor interest in this space.
- **Fintech:** Fintech, the intersection of technology and financial services, maintained its momentum with sustained investor interest.
- **Emergent Sectors:** There were green shoots of growth in emergent sectors such as electric vehicles (EV), Agritech, and Deep tech. These sectors, including space tech, generative AI, and climate/clean tech, attracted attention from investors.

c. **Capital Deployment Caution:**
    - **General Partners (GPs):** Despite the availability of unused capital, GPs remained cautious in deploying capital. GPs sought quality assets and, in some cases, awaited corrections in valuation expectations.
    - **Limited Partners (LPs):** LPs also exercised caution in making commitments due to potential slowdowns in realizations from prior investments.

d. **Exits:**
    - **Decline in Exits:** There was a dramatic decline in exits with VC participation in 2022 compared to 2021. The total exit value dropped from $14 billion (including the cancelled BillDesk exit) to less than $4 billion. Global tech stock rout and the deferral of potential IPO plans by some tech-first players affected this overall exit value.
    - **Exits by Secondary Transactions**: A significant portion (47%) of the exits involved secondary transactions. However, the overall exit value decreased due to a decline in large anchor exit deals. In 2022, there were only 11 secondary exits greater than $50 million, compared to 19 in 2021.
    - **Shift in Exit Mix**: Public market exits remained prominent, accounting for 40% of total exits. However, there was a shift from initial public offerings (IPOs) to trades, specifically exits by anchor VC funds as lock-ins on tech IPOs expired.
    - **IPO Exits**: Six IPOs included VC exits in 2022:
        → Sequoia, and Matrix from Five Star Business Finance
        → SoftBank from Delhivery
        → Sequoia, Accel, Elevation from Tracxn

e. **Funding Distribution spread**
    Here are some key points regarding noticeable changes in geographical spread of funding across India In 2022:
    - **Funding Distribution**: Emerging startup hubs beyond Bengaluru, Mumbai, and Delhi NCR and located in Tier 2+ cities started attracting a significant portion of funding and accounted for 18% of the total funding in India in 2022. These hubs not only received investments but also witnessed growth in their startup ecosystems.
    - **Unicorns from Emerging Startup Hubs:** Out of the 23 new unicorns added in 2022, 9 were from the emerging startup hubs. This highlights the growing potential and attractiveness of these cities for investors and startups.
    - **Tier 2+ Startup Success**: Citymall and Apnamart, startups from Tier 2+ cities, received large investments of $100 million each. This demonstrates the increasing recognition and support for startups beyond the traditional metropolitan areas.

f. **VC Fundraising:**
In 2022, despite cautious capital deployment, there was a record fundraising activity in India's VC landscape. Several Tier 1 investors and prominent domestic VC firms raised substantial India-focused funds in 2022. Here are some key points:
- Sequoia's $2 billion India Fund VIII
- Lightspeed India's $500 million India/Southeast Asia-dedicated fund
- Domestic VCs:
    → Fireside Ventures raised $225 million
    → Blume Ventures raised $250 million
    → Artha Select raised $55 million

These trends suggest a diversification and maturation of the Indian startup ecosystem, with emerging hubs gaining prominence and various sectors experiencing different levels of investment activity in 2022.

D. **Expectations for 2023**
The funding raised by the startup ecosystem in India increased 15% month-on-month (MoM) in May 2023 to $1 Bn. In comparison, Indian startups raised $900 Mn in the month of April 2023. VC, angels, and PE investors together announced 40 funds worth more than $3.6 Bn in 2023 till June 2023 to support Indian startups at various stages. The outlook for 2023 in the Indian start-up ecosystem is characterized by cautious optimism among stakeholders. Here are the key points mentioned:

a. **Impact of Global Macro Headwinds**: Global macro headwinds are expected to continue affecting India's start-up ecosystem.
b. **Emergence of a more resilient environment**
c. **Focus on Unit Economics**: Scale start-ups will maintain a laser focus on achieving sustainable unit economics. This suggests a shift towards prioritizing profitability and efficiency in the operations of larger start-ups.
d. **Significance of SaaS and Fintech**: SaaS (Software-as-a-Service) and fintech sectors will remain significant. While regulatory oversight may impact fintech to some extent, there will be a focus on the global expansion of India Stack, including cross-border Unified Payments Interface (UPI), identity solutions, and cross-border commerce, which can open up new opportunities.
e. **Investor Focus**: Investors are likely to increase early-stage dealmaking and innovation. According to Inc42, 65% (or 26 funds) of 40 funds announced in 2023 till June 2023 focus on early-stage, and early and growth stage startups. The following areas are expected to garner interest:
   - Gaming (hyper-casual games, e-sports)
   - Healthtech
   - Electric vehicles (EV)
   - AI-led startups
f. **Diverse Investor Base**: The participation of a wider investor base, including micro-VCs, family offices, and global funds entering the Indian market, is expected to sustain.

g. **M&A and Re-evaluation of Assets**: Some M&A-driven consolidation and potentially flat or down rounds may occur as investors reevaluate assets in their portfolios. This indicates a period of consolidation and strategic realignment in the start-up ecosystem.

While challenges remain, the ecosystem is expected to adapt and evolve, fostering a more resilient environment for Indian start-ups.

VC Funding Ecosystem in India

"VCs are slow until they think they're going to lose the deal."
— **Uri Levine**

India witnessed a 39% YoY growth in VC funding deal volume to 976 during H1 2022 (Fortune India, July 25, 2022). The disclosed funding value too rose by a 4.5% to $15.6 billion (GlobalData, a data and analytics company). "India witnessed a positive trend in both VC funding value and volume in H1 2022 compared to H1 2021 while several other key markets such as the U.S. and China experienced a decline," says Aurojyoti Bose, Lead Analyst at GlobalData.

Some of the prominent deals announced during H1 2022 include $805 million funding raised by Verse Innovation, $800 million series F funding raised by Think and Learn (Byju's), $700 million funding raised by Bundl Technologies (Swiggy), $450 million funding raised by Polygon, and $300 million funding raised by Xpressbees.

Select Top VCs operating in India

Name of VC Fund	Location	Focus Sector/ Sector Agnostic	Important Information	Contact Authority	Email	Mb
Accel Partners India	Bengaluru	Invests between $0.5 million and $50 million	Cloud-Enabled Services, Internet and Consumer Services, Infrastructure, Mobile and Software	Shekhar Kirani, Partner	shekharkirani@accel.com	8043539800
Sequoia Capital India	Bengaluru	invests $100,000 to $1 million in seed stage, $1 million to $10 million in early stage and $10 Mn to $100 million in growth stage	Healthcare, Outsourcing, Technology, Consumer, Energy, Financial	Sunder Ramdas – Senior Finance Manager	sunder.ramdas@sequoiacap.com	9845207940 8041245880
Blume Ventures	New Delhi, Mumbai, Bengaluru	Invest $0.05 million – $0.3 million in seed stage. Follow-on investments to companies from $.5 million to $1.5 mn	Internet and Software Sectors, Mobile App, Media, Telecommunications Equipment, Data Infrastructure, R&D Consumer Internet,	Karthik Reddy Co-Founder & MD	karthik@blume.vc info@blume.vc	02249746351

Kalaari Capital	Bengaluru	Invest in Early-stage technology companies	Portfolio: Cure-fit, SimpliLearn, Dream11, Myntra, Snapdeal, Urban Ladder		info@kalaari.com	8067159600
Nexus Venture Partners	Mumbai	Invests between $0.5 million and $10 million in early growth stage companies. Also, makes investments up to $0.5 million in their seed program	Infrastructure, Cloud, Storage, Internet, Rural Sector, Outsourced Services, Agribusiness, Energy, Media, Mobile, Data Security, Big Data analytics, Consumer and Business services, Technology	Suvir Sujan Co-Founder and MD	suvir@nexusvp.com plans@nexusvp.com	8066260000
Helion Venture Partners	Gurugram	Healthcare, Education and Financial Services, Retail, Outsourcing, Mobile, Internet, Retail Services	Invests between $2 million to $10 million in company with revenues of less than $10 million	Sanjeev Aggarwal – Founder and MD	sanjeev@helionvc.com	9810248407 01244615333
Chiratae Ventures	Bengaluru	The firm invests $1 million to $10 million in India-based companies as well as in companies outside India	Digital Consumer – Media and Tech-Enabled Consumer Services, Internet, Mobile, Enterprise, SaaS, Software Products and Enterprise services, Engg – Medical Devices, Clean-tech, IP-led Businesses		contact@chiratae.com	01149457700 08040434836
Matrix Partners India	Bengaluru, Delhi, Mumbai	Invests in Early-Stage Venture, Seed	Entertainment and Media, Consumer Internet, SaaS, E-commerce	Megha Kaul Executive Assistant		02267680000 8025196000
Elevation Capital	Delhi/Bengaluru	Have invested in PayTM, Swiggy, MakeMyTrip. Organisation has track record of returning investors funds	Multiple sectors whether new or old like consumer internet, healthcare, fintech, logistics, B2B	Mukul Arora	info@elevationcapital.com	9350956872

	Headquartered in New York	Worldwide internet, software, consumer and financial technology	Invests in businesses driven by excellent management teams. Have invested in Ninjacart, Mongolix.			+1 2127162363
Inventus Capital Partners	Bengaluru	leads the first venture round with $1 million to $2 million, and as the businesses grow, it invests from $0.25 million up to $10 million	Media, Internet and Catalog Retail, Healthcare, IT, Hardware and Equipment, Telecom, Consumer, Hotels, Restaurants and Leisure	Vivek Balakrishnan, Principal Associate	deals@inventuscap.com contact@atheravp.com	804126747 01414435541
Venture East	Hyderabad	Invests between $1 million to $10 million in multiple rounds.	Internet of Things (IoT), Education, E-commerce, Financial Services, Digital Healthcare, Life Sciences, IT		info@ventureast.net	8029986994 8025580045 4065510491

Investments made by Sequoia Capital in India

Sequoia is not only leading the pack of VC firms in India, it started backing Indian founders well before startup and entrepreneurship became buzzwords in the country. According to the market research firm Venture Intelligence, Sequoia participated in 50 deals in 2018, followed by 94 and 93 in 2019 and 2020 respectively and peaking at 110 in 2021, when India produced a record number of unicorns. Even in 2022, it participated in 74 deals.

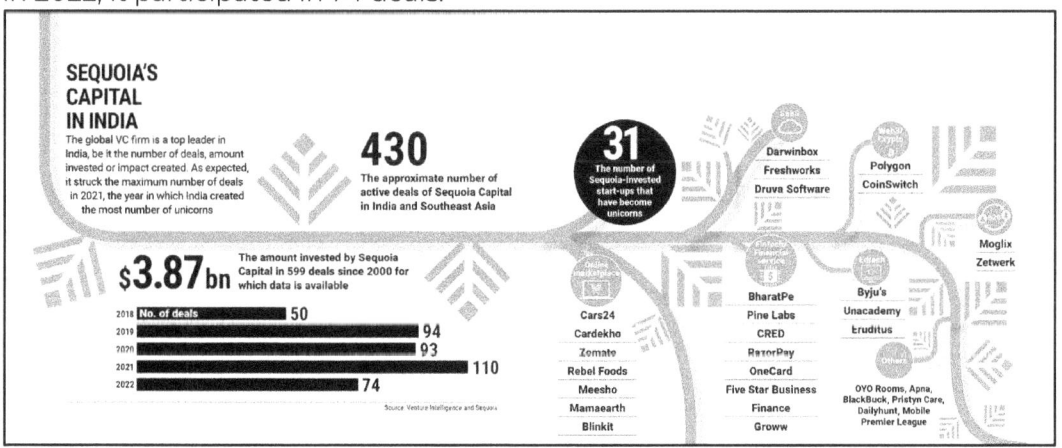

Source: https://www.outlookbusiness.com/the-big-story-1/lead-story-8/sequoia-stuck-between-start-up-frauds-and-controversies-6722

VCs Classification

VCs can be classified based on stage at which they make an investment. Given below is brief description of VCs based on investment stage, sectoral focus, and the cheque size. Very Early-Stage Micro VCs or Angel Funds of VCs in India

Micro-VCs invest at very early stage (Pre-seed or Seed fund rounds)

Name of Fund	Sectoral Focus	Startups Invested in	Cheque size
IvyCap Ventures	tech startups	Purplle, Clovia, Bewakoof Biryani By Kilo, and Get My Parking,	INR 60 Cr to be invested in 30-40
Anicut Capital		Neeman's, Deepsync Technologies, Burgerama, Blue Tokai, ShareChat, Astrogate Labs, Agnikul and Grip Invest	
First Cheque	data-driven organisations	Loopin, ClainBuddy, Questt	INR 25 Lakhs & INR 75 Lakhs
Matrix Partners		Dukaan, Captain Fresh and Rocketlane	
Redcliffe Capital	Telecom, Enterprise IT, Fintech, Digital Media	Shoopy and RevFin	
Antler India	ecommerce, edtech, mobility, fintech, web3.0	Flow Club, Humit, and PeakPerformer	$175K to $250K at 10%
Better Capital	Crypto and Web 3.0, cleantech and creator-economy	OneCard, Zingbus, and Virohan	$300k
iSeed	SaaS, remote work enabling tools and tech enterprise software	PagarBook, BimaPe, GoKwik, Velocity, FloBiz, RocketLane, DELOS, and Park+.	$150K
ITI Growth Opportunities Fund	edtech, fintech, media & entertainment	REVOS, ten3THealthcare, Evolve Snacks, and Redwing	$100K and $600K
Gemba Capital	SaaS, consumer tech, fintech, and deeptech startups	Plum, BimaPe, SleepyCat, Gripinvest, Strata, Unnati, Crejo, Zuper, ClickPost, Smartstaff and Cleardekho	$250k
Artha Venture Fund (AVF)	Edtech, fintech, media & entertainment, ecommerce, consumer services, & enterprisetech	Agnikul, HobSpace, PiggyRide, Daalchini, Kabbadi Adda InstaAstro, StarClinch and Immensitas	INR 1 to 2 Cr with INR 10 Cr and INR 15 Cr for follow-on
Unicorn India Ventures	SaaS, fintech, robotics, healthtech, gaming and digital content	ChitMonks, boxx.ai, Finsall, libryo, Open, and SmartCoin	Initial & follow on INR 50 Lakh to INR 10 Cr.
100X.VC		Healthy Barks, PensionBox, Super Scholar, Broomees, Utsav, Wizzy.ai, Red Basil Technologies,	
Eximius Ventures	Fintech, edtech, gaming, healthtech, B2B SaaS, and media & entertainment	EsportsX	$150K to $300K

Venture Capitalists for Early-Stage Startups in India

These VCs usually invest in Series A and early series rounds:

Fund Name	Sectoral Focus	Startups Invested in	Cheque size
3one4 Capital	AI/ML-driven actionable intelligence services, enterprise automation, ambient intelligence technologies, consumer products, fintech, media, multilingual content and digital health	Betterplace, Open, Zorro, Koo, WeRize, Everstage, Dozee and Breathe Well	$500k and $4 Mn
2am VC	Edtech, fintech, healthtech, ecommerce, enterprisetech, media & entertainment, and consumer services	Karbon Card, BurnCal. Invact Metaversity and Bimaplan	
Ankur Capital	Edtech, fintech, agritech, healthtech, SaaS, EVs, and D2C brands	mycaptain, WASABI, Captain Fresh, Krishify, Cropin, String Bio, Niramai, BigHaat, and Jiny, VeGrow, Health Sutra, Offgrid Energy Labs, numen	$1,500K
Beenext		AppsForBharat, Agrikul, and Jupiter	
Fireside Ventures	Consumer brands across sectors such as food and beverages, personal care, lifestyle and home products	Azani, Yoga Bar, Bombay Shaving Company, boAt, MamaEarth, The Ayurveda Experience, Samosa Singh, Kapiva, Wellbeing Nutrition, Pilgrim, and Fitterfly	
India Quotient		SUGAR, ShareChat, Saveo, WebEngage, Fleetx, Vyapar, Pagarbook, Powerplay, FRND	
Kae Capital	Fintech, gaming, healthtech, logistics, SaaS and ecommerce	HandyHome, Myntra, InMobi, Fynd Truebil, Nudgespot, Disprz, Nua, 1k Kirana Bazaar, Yojak, Zetwerkand The Porter	
Orios Venture Partners	B2C, B2B and software spaces	Battery Smart, Krishify, and ShopG	
Whiteboard Capital	fintech, consumer and healthtech startups	ApnaKlub, Supertails, Zeda.io	
RTP Global	tech startups	DeHaat, Khatabook and MPL	
Sauce.vc	food & beverages, personal care, apparel and lifestyle	Gobbl, AroLeap, and Perfora	
Endiya Partners	healthtech, enterprise SaaS, cybersecurity	Zluri, Upside AI, and SuperBeings	$1 Mn - $1.5 Mn between $4 Mn and $5 Mn in follow-on rounds
W Health Ventures	healthtech companies	Ryse Health, Jasper, BeatO, Wysa and Mars by GHC	$3.5 Mn

CDC Group		Bizongo, Indifi, and Betterplace.	$1.7 Bn in India & developing countries
Chiratae Ventures	consumer media and tech, cloud and software, healthtech and fintech	Questt, BeepKart, and ShopSe	$700 Mn under management
DSG Consumer Partners	consumer brands	OYO, Zipdial, Redmart, Veeba, Epigamia, Chai Point, Vista Rooms, EazyDiner Koparo, Ugaoo	
Eight Roads Ventures	technology and healthcare companies	Quizizz, Uni, and PharmEasy	
Elevation Capital	consumer brands, consumer tech, enterprise, SaaS, financial services and logistics startups	Chaayos, Country Delight, The Souled Store, Urban Ladder, AppsForBharat, ixigo, MakeMyTrip, CityMall, Yellow Class, Sugar Cosmetics	
Alpha Wave		CRED and Mensa Ola Electric, and Lenskart	
Goodwater Capital	social, education, healthcare, housing, transportation, fintech and commerce	ByteLearn, Snazzy, and Stack Finance.	
Info Edge Ventures		Zomato, Geniemode, Lumiq, and Attentive	
Kalaari Capital		Myntra, Dream11, Medplus and Snapdeal, Skit, Koo, and Elevar	
Moore Strategic Ventures	electronics, advanced materials, energy, cleantech, information technology, transportation, distribution	ShareChat, Shiprocket, and Khatabook	
Nexus Venture Partners	enterprise technology and consumer internet	Quizizz, Postman, and Zepto	
Omidyar Network India		Doosra, Kutuki, and CredFlow	
Omnivore	agritech and foodtech, farmer fintech, B2B agri marketplaces, farm to consumer brands, precision agriculture, post-harvest technologies, life sciences	Pixxel, ReshaMandi, and Onato	
Prosus Ventures	consumer internet investment group	Meesho, Urban Company and DeHaat	
Ribbit Capital	to change the world of finance'	Groww, Razorpay, and CoinSwitch Kuber	

Sequoia Capital India	BYJU's, Carousell, Druva, Gojek, OYO Rooms, Tokopedia, Truecaller, Zilingo, Zomato	Mamaearth, BharatPe, Purplle	
Sixth Sense Ventures	consumer-centric	Neeman's, Bombay Shaving Company, and Open Secret	
SoftBank	technology, energy, and fintech sectors	GlobalBees, Zeta and Swiggy	
Soma Capital		TagMango, Stack Finance, and PropReturns	
Steadview Capital	technology startups	Innovaccer, PharmEasy, and MoEngage	
Stellaris Venture Partners	personal care products, SaaS	Mamaearth, Whatfix, MFine, Splinter, LoadShare, Signzy, Propelld, LimeChat, Swiflearn, and BeepKart	

VCs for Multistage Funding

The following VCs invest at multiple stages from early funding round to growth stage

Name of Fund	Sectoral Focus	Startups Invested in	Cheque size
YourNest Venture Capital	Deeptech, AI, IoT (internet of things), AR/VR/MR, developer tools, digital products	Practically, UptimeAI, and Exponent Energy	
Lightspeed	Enterprise technology, consumer, and health sectors	GlobalBees, Hubilo, and ShareChat	
Accel Ventures	Internet and consumer services, infrastructure, cloud-enabled services, and mobile and software	Koo, Agrostar, Anar, Breathe Well, Captain Fresh, Powerplay	$500k and $50 Mn
B Capital Group		Byju's, Innovaccer, and CoinDCX	
SOSV	Technology sector	Kiko Live, The Money Club, and Supplynote	
WestBridge Capital		DealShare, Vedantu, Rapido.	
Temasek		upGrad, ShareChat, and Unacademy	
Aavishkaar Capital	fintech, agritech, transporttech	AgroStar, chqbook.com, fabelio, Grasshoppers, Paywell, and Vortex, GoBolt, Nalanda	

VCs for Late or Growth Stage Finding

These VC funds usually participate in the late or the growth stage:

Name of Fund	Sectoral Focus	Startups Invested in	Cheque size
Blume Ventures	consumer internet, SMB marketplace, SaaS and enterprise tech	Smartstaff, Exotel, Euler, Yulu, Koo, Purplle, Cashify, smallcase, Purplle, Stage3, ElectricPe, and Battery Smart	$1 Mn and $2.5 Mn
Lightbox Ventures	fintech, traveltech, transportech, agritech, healthtech, and consumer services	Truecaller, Cityflo, WayCool, Bombay Shirt Company, Flinto, Zeno Health, Furlenco, InnerHour, Nua, and Dunzo	
Insight Partners	technology, software and internet businesses	Twitter, Shopify, Tumblr, Wix, Slice, Postman and CRED	
Tiger Global	internet, software, consumer tech and fintech companies	Pristyn Care, Apna, and Captain Fresh	

Dedicated Funds by VCs for Startup Investment

The following table provides details concerning the dedicated funds raised by different VCs with a specific theme and for a specific period of time.

Name of Fund	Firm Type	Founded	Fund Size	Closed When	Sectoral Focus	Investment Stage	cheque sizes
3one4 Capital (Fund IV)	VC	2015	$200 Mn	May 2023	consumer internet, SaaS and fintech, health tech, climate tech	Pre-seed to Series A)	$0.5 Mn to $5 Mn
AdvantEdge (Fund III)	VC	2015	$80-$100 Mn		consumer sector focus on mobility solutions EV ecosystem	Early-stage tech fund	
Aeravti Ventures	VC		INR 100 Cr	May, 2023	New-age tech startups, deeptech, biosciences, agritech, climate, & enterprisetech	Early stage pre-seed to Pre-Series A	
Agri-Focused Accelerator Fund	Govt Fund	2023			credit, insurance, market intelligence		

Name	Type	Year	Size	Date	Sectors	Stage	Ticket Size
Airavat Global Technology Fund R			$40 Mn	June, 2023	consumer, financial services, technology and pharma		
B Capital (Growth Fund III) Healthcare Fund I	VC		$500 Mn		digital health and biotech segments.	early and late-stage startups	
Blume Continuity Fund	VC		INR 400 Cr	June, 2023			
BoldCap Fund			$25 Mn	April 2023	SaaS	early-stage startups	
Capria Ventures	VC		$100 Mn	April 2023			
Avaana Capital	VC		125 Mn	June, 2023	Energy transition & resource management, mobility & supply chains, sustainable agriculture		
B Capital third venture growth fund	VC	2015	$40 Mn		Enterprisetech, fintech, healthtech, B2B SaaS and cybersecurity	pre-seed and seed-stage	
CarTrade Ventures	VC		INR 750 Cr	Feb, 2023	auto-tech play, auto finance, leasing, insurance, servicing, EV & clean energy, ownership, AR, AI and visualisation.		
Chanakya (Opportunities Fund I)	Category-II AIF		INR 100 Cr	April 2023	Sector Agnostic		INR 2 Cr- INR 10 Cr
Chiratae Ventures (Growth Fund I)	VC	2006	INR 1,001 Cr	Nov 2022	Growth: SaaS, consumertech, healthtech, deeptech, agritech, fintech		

Name	Type	Launched	Size	Date	Focus	Stage	Ticket Size
Courtside Ventures (Fund III)	VC		$100 Mn		sports, fitness, collectables, gaming, lifestyle segments		
Dallas Venture Capital			INR 350 Cr	Jan 2023	enterprisetech		
Early Spring			INR 300 Cr	April, 2023		Seed and Pre-Series A	
Epiq Capital (Fund II)		April 2016	$225 Mn	June 2023	Tech		$20-25 Mn each
Grayscale Ventures	VC		$20 Mn	Feb 2023	AI, vertical SaaS and Dev-Infra	Pre-seed	$200K and $1 Mn
Iron Pillar (Fund II)	VC	2016	$129 Mn	April, 2023	SaaS startups	Series B and Series C	
Lighthouse Canton	Debt fund	2020	INR 550 Cr	Jan 2023	Debt capital to technology-enabled startups		INR 15 cr each
Lumikai	VC	2019	$50 Mn	June, 2023	Gaming-focused	Seed stage ventures	18-20 companies
Nexus Ventures (Nexus Ventures VII)	VC	2006	$700 Mn	March, 2023			
Omnivore (Fund III)	VC	2011	$150 Mn	June 2023	Agritech & Climate Sustainability Fund		$1 Mn and $5 Mn
Prath Ventures Fund	VC	2022	INR 225 Cr	Jan 2023	Consumer-focused startups		INR 5 Cr - INR 6 Cr
PeerCapital (Fund I)	VC		$75 Mn	Feb, 2023	fintech, healthtech, enterprisetech, climate tech, consumertech	: seed and Series A-stage	$2 Mn
Physis Capital	Category II AIF		$50 Mn	May 2023	sector-agnostic		$2.5 Mn
Pi Ventures	VC: SIDBI's Fund of Funds	2016	$83 Mn	April 2023		Early-stage	
Piper Serica Advisors	Angel Fund		INR 100 Cr	Jan 2023			

Fund	Type	Year	Size	Date	Sectors	Stage	Ticket/Companies
Rockstud Capital (Investment Fund II)	Asset management	2017	INR 300 Cr	March 2023	Digitalisation, sustainability, financial inclusion, consumption and health	Pre-Series A and Series A	INR 1 Cr and INR 10 Cr in 25 startups
Speciale Invest (Growth Fund I)	VC firm	2017	INR 300 Cr	April 2023	Spacetech, robotics, green mobility, quantum tech & AI-led platforms	early-stage	20-22 companies
Stride Ventures (Fund III)	Debt firm	2019	$200 Mn	May 2023	Sector agnostic		
Unitus Ventures (Opportunity Fund)	VC		$40 Mn	Feb 2023		80%: early-stage, 20%: Series A: AI and climatetech	
V3 Ventures	VC	2021	INR 900 Cr		digital and consumer businesses, new-age brands, tech, enablers, platforms	Early-stage: seed and Series A stages	
WinZO (Game Developer Fund IV)		2018	$50 Mn	March 2023	Game Developer Fund		
Women Entrepreneurs Early Growth Fund			$45 Mn		Gender equity climate tech, agritech, edtech healthtech, and fintech	Early stage fund Pre-Series A and Series A rounds	
Z3Partners	VC	2019	INR 550 Cr	Jan 2023	SaaS, fintech, ecommerce, agritech, big data, consumer tech	early and growth-stage	INR 50 Cr and INR 80 Cr
Zero To One	Investment firm	May 2022	INR 300 Cr	Jan 2023	Edtech, healthtech, agritech, medtech and cleantech	Pre-Seed and Series A	

Source: Adapted from https://inc42.com/features/sparks-funding-revival-startup-funds-worth-2-bn-announced-2023-full-list/

Venture Debt Funds for Startups in India

These VCs provide debt funding to the startups in India.

Name of VCs	Funded these Startups
Alteria Capital	Rebel Foods, BharatPe, Lendingkart, Zestmoney, Dunzo, Portea, Toppr, Spinny, Stanza, Vogo, Melora, Mfine, Generico, Loadshare, LBB, Beato, Maverix, Country Delight, Clover, Happay, Cropin, Cityflo, Onco, Nua, Damensch, Bombay Shirt Company
InnoVen Capital	PepperFry, Udaan, and Mensa Brands
Northern Arc	True Balance, BharatPe, slice
Stride Ventures	Pocket Aces, TenderCuts, and The Good Glamm Group
Trifecta Capital	Practo, The Good Glamm Group, and ixigo

Fund of Funds for Startup

"The greatest entrepreneurs are incredible salespeople. They know how to tell an amazing story that will convince talent and investors to join in on the journey." —
Alejandro Cremades

Fund of Funds for Startups (FFS) was announced with a corpus of Rs. 10,000 crores through budgetary support by the Department for Promotion of Industry and Internal Trade (DPIIT), Ministry of Commerce & Industry, Government of India. Under FFS, support is extended to SEBI registered Alternative Investment Funds (AIFs), which in turn invest in startups.

FFS, launched under the Startup India initiative in 2016, has committed Rs. 7,385 crores to 88 Alternative Investment Funds (AIFs) as of 24th September 2022. FFS has already helped anchor 67 AIFs out of these 88 AIFs. The amount committed under FFS by the government grew by a CAGR of over 21% since its launch in 2016. These AIFs, in turn, have invested Rs.11,206 crore in 720 startups. Investments into eligible startups are approximately 3.7 times of FFS disbursements which are well above the minimum stipulated 2 times under the Scheme. Performing startups supported through FFS show a valuation increase of more than 10 times, with some achieving unicorn status (valuation of over USD 1 billion). Dunzo, CureFit, FreshToHome, Jumbotail, Unacademy, Uniphore, Vogo, Zostel, Zetwerk, etc., are some of the notable startups funded through FFS. Thus, FFS has been playing a monumental role in mobilizing domestic capital in the Indian startup ecosystem.

FFS has not only made capital available for startups at an early stage, seed stage, and growth stage but also played a catalytic role in terms of facilitating the raising of domestic capital, reducing dependence on foreign capital, and encouraging homegrown and new venture capital funds. Collectively, the AIFs supported by FFS have a target corpus of over Rs.48,000 crore. Among the prominent AIFs of leading startup investment firms supported under FFS are Chiratae Ventures, India Quotient, Blume Ventures, IvyCap, Waterbridge, Omnivore, Aavishkaar, JM Financial, Fireside Ventures, and more.

Small Industries Development Bank of India (SIDBI), which is responsible for operationalising the scheme, has undertaken a series of reforms recently to expedite the drawdowns to enable AIFs assisted under FFS to avail accelerated drawdowns. This has created a positive impact and has resulted in year on year (Q1 FY 2021-22 vis-à-vis Q1 FY 2022-23) surge of 100% in the amount of drawdowns.

Accredited Investors

Given a 10% chance of a 100 times payoff, you should take that bet every time." —
Jeff Bezos

An accredited investor can be a business institution or an individual who is allowed to deal with securities that are not available to the general public. Also, these securities may or may not be registered with any financial regulatory authority. In order to become an accredited investor, an individual or a business entity has to fulfil the following eligibility requirement set by the market regulator, i.e., Security and Exchange Board of India (SEBI). Thus, accredited investors are high net-worth individual (HNI) investors who satisfy the regulatory body's requirements to invest in listed startups. SEBI has given stock exchanges and subsidiaries of depositories the power to issue accreditation certificates. The accreditation lasts for 3 years.

Who can be an Accredited Investor?

The entities that are automatically accredited:
- Central government
- State government
- Centra & state government funds
- Developmental agencies
- Qualified institutional buyers
- Category I FPIs
- Sovereign wealth funds
- Multilateral agencies

The entities that require manual accreditation:
- Individuals
- Hindu Undivided Families
- Family trusts
- Sole proprietorships
- Partnership firms
- Non-family Trusts
- Corporates

Requirements: Who Qualifies for SEBI Accreditation:

a. A business entity or institution who wishes to invest in listed startups need to have a net worth of Rs.25 crore to be considered an accredited investor.
b. An "accredited SEBI investor" is an individual or entity who has a net worth of at least ₹7.50 crores or an annual income of ₹2 crores. Furthermore, individuals or entities who have a combined liquid net worth of at least ₹5 crores and annual income of ₹1 crore can become Accredited SEBI investors.
c. An individual can be considered an accredited investor has to maintain a total annual gross of Rs.50 lakh.

d. Trusts and corporates (except a family trust) must have a net worth of at least ₹50 crores to become accredited investors. But there's a catch, as per SEBI guidelines. At least half of the net worth or annual income should be invested in financial assets.

These requirements are set to ensure that the accredited investors are financially stable enough to absorb any losses that can occur due to unregulated securities as the risk of losing capital on unfamiliar investments are generally high.

Process to become an Accredited Investor in India
In order to become an accredited investor in India, the investor or business entity:
a. Need to have a Demat account
b. Apply for accreditation to the depositories or the stock exchange.
c. The eligibility of the investor is determined
d. Investor granted accreditation for a period of three years by stock exchange.
e. Should keep the stock exchange and depositories informed of any change in the financial status.

Benefits of being a SEBI Accredited Investor

Accredited SEBI investors will have greater flexibility when it comes to investing in financial assets. The minimum requirement for AIFs has been slashed and more investments can flow into investee companies. Furthermore, accredited SEBI investors can gain more exposure to unlisted securities with a PMS. Accredited investors can access the following broad benefits across the AIF and PMS domains.

1. **Relaxed Alternative Investment Fund (AIF) Norms**: An accredited investor has the privilege of investing in assets at a lower minimum amount than the general Alternative Investment Fund (AIF) mandate. SEBI has introduced the term "large value funds" for accredited investors. It means an AIF in which the accredited investor has an investment of at least ₹70 crores. Large value funds for accredited investors can invest up to:
   ❖ 50% in a company directly or through AIF units (Category I & II)
   ❖ 25% in a company directly or through AIF units (Category III)
2. **Relaxed Portfolio Management Services (PMS) Norms**: Accredited investors can receive investment advice from the PMS to invest in unlisted securities. The PMS can offer discretionary or non-discretionary advisory services related to unlisted securities for 100% of the AUM. This is subject to agreements between the investor and the PMS.

How can Accredited Investors Invest in Startups?

Accredited investors have various alternatives when it comes to investing in startups. They typically do so through a VC company or by sourcing private placement deals. Accredited investors join investors with a venture capital fund, and the business subsequently invests capital from the fund in a variety of startups. A VC fund's liquidity is always limited, which means you won't be able to withdraw your money anytime you want. Accredited investors should constantly be aware of the risks associated with a VC fund's investment horizon.

When Funding Stops: Innovative Strategies to Overcome Financial Constraints

"Patience and diligence, like faith, remove mountains." — **William Penn**

Indian startups witnessed a significant fall in business funding in the first half of 2023 (January to June) by raising only $3.8 billion during the six-month period, a massive decline of 36% as compared to the fundraising in H1 of 2022. Last year, Indian startups raised $5.9 billion in the first half. To deal with such scenarios, startups have can adopt alternative financing options, which range from traditional methods like bridge or mezzanine financing to modern approaches such as crowdfunding and peer-to-peer lending. To overcome funding challenges, startups can implement the following:

a. **Lean business model:** That minimizes spending, optimizes resources, and maximizes a startup's runway can help companies to sustain themselves until market conditions stabilize in the funding ecosystem.
b. **Negotiating with vendors for better terms**
c. **Exploring alternative financing options (Based on the stage or requirement):**
    - Companies should look for funding-raising platforms like angel investors
    - Take advantage of government schemes under the Startup India Initiative
    - Exploring crowdfunding
    - Looking for grants
d. **Focusing on positive cash flows:** Build a business model that emphasizes positive cash flows which begins by focusing on positive unit economics and creating real value for customers, rather than pursuing only valuation.
e. **Factoring or Purchase order/Supply Chain:** Financing by processing customer orders and generating immediate cash inflow to support expansion efforts. Opting for leasing instead of purchasing can significantly reduce operational overhead and free up resources that can be directed towards fuelling growth.
f. **Forming Partnerships with other Companies:** This can help the company to cut costs or generate additional revenue by leveraging partnership with other entities.
g. **Using Resources wisely:** Finding ways to save money can free up funds that can be used more efficiently.
h. **Using Technology:** By embracing digital solutions, automation, and data analytics companies can adapt to market changes more efficiently and make informed decisions that either help them to cut costs or generate additional revenue with same resources.

Transition from Startup to Corporate

"As long as you're going to be thinking anyway, think big."
–Donald Trump, The Trump Organization President

Cultural Difference between Startup and Corporate

	Startup	Corporate
Operating Model	Trying to find out the best way to run the business.	Already knows what works best for them. Looking to grow it at a decent rate.
Focus	Young, innovative, collaborative, and focused on two crucial priorities: acquiring customers and expanding into new markets	focused on productivity
Roles & Responsibilities	One can grow one's skills by picking up new responsibilities **and taking more responsibility**. Work can differ from day-to-day, and roles and tasks can change entirely from one week to the next.	**Clear roles and well-defined tasks** Corporate positions usually have clear roles and well-defined tasks
Pace of decision-making	**Fast-paced environment** Everything can change at a moment's notice. Encourage involvement of junior and mid-level employees in decision making process, product development, and strategies for quick feedback	**Corporations move slower** Slow to adapt so many moving pieces that need to synchronize to implement change and it helps companies streamline efficiencies and allocate resources appropriately. But when change is implemented, impact is profound
Processes	**Processes are being done for first time.** Employees given responsibility for getting tasks done and the authority to decide on how they get done. Employees are encouraged to manage their own time and tasks. Flexibility of working in teams that are not hierarchical	**Well-defined processes** To create clarity and uniformity, adherence to strict processes, but this can also create quite a lot of bureaucracy, Process is as important as results. Rigorous systems to support a specific structure and provide accountability up the chain of command.
Communication	**Transparency in communication** Communication between the employees and the founders/management is open and transparent. Short and simple. Feedback is appreciated as a means to validate assumptions and understand customers and improve.	**Careful communication** Communication by the management with the employees and the outside world is well planned and respect the hierarchy. Usually undertaken by a specialized department supervising it.
Approach towards Risk	**Thrives on Risk** Encourage calculated risk to challenge the established practices and disrupt the status quo	**Risk-averse** Many people are involved in the decisions & decision process is often quite long and as logical as possible

Transition of a startup into a corporate involves a series of changes and developments as the company grows and evolves. Here are some key aspects of this transition:

1. **Scaling Operations:** Startups typically begin with a small team and limited resources. As the company grows, it needs to scale its operations to meet increasing demands. This includes hiring more employees, establishing processes and systems, expanding infrastructure, and optimizing workflow efficiencies.
2. **Formalizing Structure and Roles**: In the early stages, startups often operate in an informal manner with flexible roles and responsibilities. However, as the company transitions into a business organization, it becomes important to formalize the organizational structure. This includes defining roles, responsibilities, and reporting lines to ensure clarity and accountability.
3. **Implementing Policies and Procedures:** To ensure smooth operations and compliance with regulations, startups need to develop and implement various policies and procedures. These may include HR policies, financial controls, data protection measures, quality assurance protocols, and other relevant policies tailored to the specific needs of the business.
4. **Building a Strong Team:** As the company grows, attracting and retaining talented individuals becomes crucial. Startups need to focus on building a strong team with diverse skill sets and a shared vision. This involves developing recruitment strategies, establishing a robust onboarding process, fostering a positive work culture, and providing opportunities for professional growth.
5. **Enhancing Financial Management**: Startups often have limited financial resources and may rely on external funding. As they transition into a business organization, it becomes essential to strengthen financial management practices. This includes implementing robust accounting systems, budgeting and forecasting processes, financial reporting, and managing cash flow effectively.
6. **Expanding Market Reach:** Startups usually focus on validating their business model and gaining initial traction. During the transition into a business organization, there is a need to expand the market reach and increase customer acquisition. This may involve developing marketing and sales strategies, expanding distribution channels, and building brand awareness.
7. **Establishing Partnerships and Alliances**: To accelerate growth and leverage synergies, business organizations often seek strategic partnerships, alliances, or collaborations. This could include forming partnerships with suppliers, distributors, or complementary businesses to expand market reach, access new resources, or enhance product/service offerings.
8. **Embracing Long-Term Sustainability**: While startups are often focused on short-term survival and growth, business organizations need to prioritize long-term sustainability. This includes developing a strategic plan, setting long-term goals, conducting market research and analysis, and continuously adapting to changes in the business environment.

9. **Implementing Effective Governance**: Transitioning into a business organization necessitates establishing effective governance mechanisms. This may involve forming a board of directors or advisory board, developing corporate governance policies, and ensuring compliance with legal and regulatory requirements.
10. **Continuous Innovation**: Startups thrive on innovation, and the transition into a business organization should not dampen this spirit. It is crucial to foster a culture of continuous innovation, encourage creativity, and invest in research and development to stay competitive and adapt to evolving market dynamics.

Making a Transition from a Startup into a Large Corporation

	Startup	Large Corporation
Understand the business flows	In startup mode, business can be very reactive, and getting new customers is often about going out and making it happen.	Corporations have a better sense of its business flows, creating targets & customer segments, and developing a much more structured approach to its marketing and sales efforts.
Divide work into groupings	In startup phase, an overlap between teams is warranted	Grouping of activities and identifying the buckets of work that can be set up as specialized departments within functional business areas
Clearly define people's roles	Overlapping employee roles and responsibilities make sense in startup phase	Overlaps can sow confusion in large organisation. Need to define and differentiate between roles on different teams
Undertake detailed process mapping	In startup phase the focus is more on outcomes and getting things done.	Process mapping drives efficiency and consistency throughout organization. During this, new objectives & processes are identified
Develop internal support structures and systems	The systems are usually basic and department centric and sometimes not integrated across the company.	Need for more advanced and integrated employee systems, finance systems and data analytics systems to dig more deeply into its business performance requiring employees to transfer data into systems in more consistent manner.

Transitioning from a startup culture into a grown-up organization isn't easy. The challenge is to get the entire organization comfortable with adopting a more formal approach to doing business. It's important for managers to shape emerging processes and policies while maintaining the freedom to innovate and create. The transition from a startup to a business organization is an exciting and challenging journey. It requires careful planning, strategic decision-making, and a willingness to adapt to changing circumstances. By focusing on scalability, organizational structure, talent acquisition, financial management, market expansion, and sustainability, startups can successfully navigate this transition and position themselves for long-term success.

Modern CFO: A Function in Transition

"At the end of the day, finance leaders have to be proper storytellers. You have to be constantly on top of your data and tell the story behind the numbers." –
Gerardo Adame, VP Finance at XP Power

Over the last few decades, the role of the Chief Financial Officer (CFO) has undergone a profound shift. Historically CFO fundamentally had three main tasks:
- Books and records of the company
- Financial reporting
- Statutory compliance.

These tasks continue to be important but are now taken for granted; in addition, the role of the CFO is developing and expanding. The expectations from the CFO of today and tomorrow has undergone a profound transformation in recent years; he/she must be able to take financial data and use it to influence operational decision-making and strategy.

CFOs tended to be number crunchers who operated behind the scenes and were usually the ones who said "no" to things due to budgetary reasons. Strategy and decision-making were left to the rest of the C-Suite, while the CFO was confined to more of a "sign-off" role than anything else. Today's CFOs must break away from the number-cruncher stereotype and think of themselves as more of a strategic player in the company.

The CFO of yesterday was more of a support function; the CFO of today and of tomorrow is of strategic relevance to a company. Today's CFOs drive the direction and success of their organisation in the ever-changing business environment. "It's intriguing to discover that despite their significance, 30% of unicorns continue to rely on VPs of finance instead of embracing the full potential of CFOs," Harold D'Souza, Co-Founder and Director at WalkWater Talent Advisors.

Key Skills for the CFO of Today and Tomorrow

The CFO role is much more dynamic today. CFOs today need to be creative, understand best practices, and know how to create more value for the company. Today's CFOs are business partners who help guide and influence decision-making using the financial context as an integral driver of such decisions. Given the changing role of the CFO, these are the key skills and competencies that a CFO must possess in order to fulfil their responsibilities:
1. **Leadership**: To be an effective business partner, today's CFO must have the necessary leadership and communication skills. They must give advice and counsel as well as provide a voice of reason. They must be able to translate detailed financial information into clear, concise, and accessible messaging.

2. **Operations**: CFOs should possess a strong understanding of the company's business model and industry and be able to use this knowledge to provide an independent perspective and to constructively challenge the commercial and operations teams, ensuring that business decisions are grounded in solid financial criteria. They must navigate complex data and provide analytics and predictive scenarios that drive action and decision-making. The CFO should also identify opportunities for top-line growth and drive profit improvement, not just through the traditional methods of cost control but through product line/regional profitability analysis, benchmarking against industry peers, etc.
3. **Controls**: In an increasingly global and volatile environment, CFO is expected to ensure adequate assessment and mitigation of risk, and compliance with applicable regulatory or other legal requirements. They must understand risk through a commercial as well as a financial lens. Therefore, they need to manage risk as the business executes its strategies and initiatives and maintain a strong internal controls environment and financial reporting processes.
4. **Strategy**: Supporting strategy development and enabling its execution. The CFO also plays a role in prioritizing and ensuring the strategy can be funded. The finance skillset is very applicable to building predictive modelling, analyzing macroeconomic trends, and incorporating non-financial information. This also includes communicating the strategy and progress against it to external stakeholders and investors.

What Makes for a Successful Modern CFO

1. Behavioural competencies are key to the business partner role of the CFO. The CFO needs to be a visible leader in the business, an excellent communicator, and an influencer.
2. CFO should try to find out more about what is happening in the business and challenge where decisions are being taken without necessary financial input.
3. Finance must be embedded throughout the company. CFO should provide decision support to key functions such as commercial, operations, manufacturing, etc. CFO should have a dedicated finance analysis and support team attached to the most important functions in the business. This opens up the dialogue between finance and operations, and it fosters a better flow of data between areas of the business. This makes the functions more accountable for their financial metrics and also allows the finance team to provide more insightful commentary through a better understanding of the business.
4. It's not enough for finance just to produce static snapshots of the company's financial health. The CFO must paint the picture for the business and translate the financial data into meaningful commentary, trends, and actions.
5. Automation and technology are critical in an organisation; as access to timely, accurate data is a key enabler to finance productivity and decision support. Automated reporting and analytics allow more time to be dedicated to forecasting and predictive analysis. For businesses to succeed, CFOs will have to be champions and stewards of digital technology. CFOs must adapt to new technology and be at the forefront of ERP and cloud-based solutions.
6. As CEOs want "more for less" from their finance function, CFOs need to focus on results, not merely efficiency. The finance function is now increasingly being

assessed in terms of its effectiveness (to deliver what the business needs) rather than a narrower focus on its efficiency (its cost in serving the business).

The CFO of the future will add the most value as a business and strategic partner to the CEO by being commercially savvy as well as managing external relationships. According to the 2014 Accenture High Performance Finance Study, found that high-performance businesses are more likely to report high levels of satisfaction with their finance function across most dimensions.; tend to have CFOs whose strategic influence grew in recent years; Have finance leaders that are more engaged in assessing technology investments.

Focus Areas for CFO of the Future
- Gain a breadth of finance experience by having exposure to the commercial and operations functions in the business.
- Develop a global perspective through international exposure, especially in emerging markets. This experience can help them manage the volatility and complexity associated with modern-day businesses in these regions.
- Leadership opportunities and team-building skills through transformation initiatives and major change programs for developing the communication and influencing skills that are necessary for dealing with both internal and external stakeholders.
- Investment in digital technology for managing complexity and driving productivity.
- Expertise in managing, analyzing, and presenting data in a way that yields the greatest value for the business.
- Having the best talent and making an effort to retain them through coaching, mentoring, and leadership development is a big priority at all levels of the finance organization.

Importance of CFO in a Startup getting ready for IPO

The CFO plays a crucial role in a startup preparing for an Initial Public Offering (IPO). Here are some key reasons why the CFO's role is important in this process:

1. **Financial Strategy and Planning**: The CFO is responsible for developing and executing the financial strategy of the startup, especially during the IPO preparation phase. They assess the company's financial health, analyze market conditions, and develop a comprehensive financial plan to optimize the IPO process. This includes determining the offering price, timing, and capital structure to maximize investor interest and valuation.
2. **Financial Reporting and Compliance**: As part of the IPO process, the startup must adhere to rigorous financial reporting and compliance requirements set by regulatory bodies. The CFO ensures accurate and transparent financial reporting, manages the auditing process, and ensures compliance with regulatory guidelines, enhancing transparency and credibility for potential investors. Therefore, startups are preferring to hire CFOs who have worked at

large corporations. This is evident from the fact that almost 67 % of CFOs working at Indian unicorns do not have prior startup experience.
3. **Risk Management and Internal Controls:** The CFO establishes robust internal controls and risk management frameworks to mitigate financial risks, safeguard assets, and ensure compliance with relevant laws and regulations. This is crucial for building investor confidence and meeting the stringent requirements of the IPO process.
4. **Investor Relations and Communication**: The CFO plays a key role in communicating the financial performance, growth prospects, and investment value of the startup to potential investors. They collaborate with the executive team to craft investor presentations, financial statements, and other materials to effectively communicate the business's financial story and value proposition.
5. **Financial Due Diligence:** During the IPO process, potential investors conduct thorough due diligence to evaluate the startup's financial position, operations, and prospects. The CFO coordinates and facilitates this due diligence process, ensuring that accurate and relevant financial information is provided to potential investors. They work closely with legal counsel, investment bankers, and other stakeholders to address any financial concerns and optimize valuation.
6. **Capital Structure and Funding**: The CFO evaluates the startup's capital structure and funding requirements, optimizing the mix of debt and equity financing to support growth and expansion plans. They collaborate with investment bankers and financial advisors to determine the appropriate capital structure for the IPO, ensuring the startup's capital needs are met while attracting potential investors.
7. **Financial Performance Analysis:** The CFO provides valuable financial insights and analysis to the executive team and the board of directors. They assess the financial performance, identify key financial metrics, and provide recommendations to enhance financial efficiency and profitability, which are crucial for building investor confidence and long-term success post-IPO.

The CFO's strategic financial leadership, expertise in financial reporting and compliance, investor relations, and risk management are instrumental in positioning a startup for a successful IPO. They bring financial discipline, transparency, and credibility to the IPO process, ensuring the company's financial health and prospects are effectively communicated to potential investors. Therefore, in India, only 33% of unicorn CFOs were hired from other startups; remaining 67% of the CFOs were hired from non-startup talent pool from traditional industries such as BFSI, Industrial, and FMCG.

Mergers & Buyouts

The historical evidence shows that shareholders usually greatly benefit from mergers. - **Stephen Moore**

Mergers of startups, also known as startup-to-startup mergers, occur when two or more startups combine their operations and resources to form a new entity. These mergers are a strategic move to enhance growth, leverage synergies, pool resources, and increase market competitiveness. While startups often face challenges and risks individually, merging with another startup can offer several advantages. Here are some key aspects and benefits of startup mergers:

1. **Complementary strengths**: Startups with complementary strengths, such as complementary products, technologies, or customer bases, can merge to create a more comprehensive and robust offering. By combining their resources and expertise, the merged entity can provide a compelling value proposition to customers and gain a competitive advantage in the market.
2. **Increased market share and reach**: Merging startups can expand their market share and reach by leveraging each other's customer bases, distribution channels, or geographic presence. This broader market access allows the merged entity to penetrate new markets, attract more customers.
3. **Consolidation of resources**: By merging, startups can pool their financial resources, talent, intellectual property, and operational capabilities. This consolidation can result in cost efficiencies, improved R&D capabilities, and faster time-to-market for new products or services.
4. **Enhanced innovation and expertise**: Merging startups often bring together diverse teams with complementary skill sets, knowledge, and perspectives. This synergy can foster innovation, encourage cross-pollination of ideas, and create a more dynamic and creative work environment.
5. **Risk diversification**: Startups face various risks, including market volatility, funding challenges, and operational uncertainties. Through a merger, startups can mitigate some of these risks by combining resources, sharing responsibilities, and gaining access to new funding sources or investors.
6. **Competitive advantage**: By merging, startups can strengthen their competitive position in the market. They can combine their strengths to create a differentiated offering, compete against larger incumbents, and achieve economies of scale that were not possible individually.
7. **Talent retention and attraction**: A startup merger can provide more growth opportunities and career paths for employees. It can also attract top talent who may be attracted to the combined entity's enhanced resources, market presence, and potential for success.

Startup mergers, like any other business transaction, require careful planning, due diligence, and legal considerations. Merging startups should align their goals, culture, and strategic visions to ensure successful integration to maximize the potential benefits of the merger. Startups considering a merger should seek professional advice from legal, financial, and industry experts experienced in startup M&A to guide them through and address complexities that may arise.

Financial Consideration: Startup Mergers

Startup founders should be kept in mind the following financial considerations to ensure a smooth and successful transaction during startup mergers:

1. **Valuation**: Determining the value of each startup involved in the merger is crucial. It involves assessing their assets, liabilities, intellectual property, revenue streams, customer base, growth potential, and other relevant factors. Valuation methods such as discounted cash flow (DCF), comparable company analysis, or market multiples may be used to arrive at a fair valuation for each startup.
2. **Purchase Price and Payment Structure**: Consideration should be given to whether the purchase price will be paid in cash, stock, or a combination of both. The payment structure may involve upfront payments, earn-outs based on future performance milestones, or contingent payments tied to the achievement of specific targets.
3. **Due Diligence:** Conducting comprehensive due diligence is essential to assess the financial health, legal compliance, and potential risks of merging startups. It involves reviewing financial statements, tax records, contracts, intellectual property, legal and regulatory compliance, and any potential liabilities. Thorough due diligence helps identify any hidden financial risks or contingencies that could impact the merger.
4. **Financial Projections**: Developing detailed financial projections for the merged entity is crucial for assessing the potential synergies, growth prospects, and financial performance post-merger. These projections should consider factors such as revenue growth, cost savings, integration costs, and the impact of market dynamics. Financial models and sensitivity analysis can help evaluate different scenarios and assess the financial viability of the merged entity.
5. **Financing**: Consider the financing options available to support the merger. This may involve securing external funding from venture capitalists, private equity firms, or strategic investors. Alternatively, internal financing through cash reserves, stock swaps, or a combination of both can be considered. Evaluate the terms and conditions of the financing options to ensure they align with the long-term goals of the merged entity.
6. **Tax Implications:** Understand the tax implications of the merger, including any potential tax liabilities or benefits. Seek professional advice from tax experts to navigate the complex tax regulations related to mergers and acquisitions. Consider the impact of taxes on the purchase price, restructuring costs, capital gains, and any applicable tax incentives or exemptions.
7. **Integration Costs**: Consider the costs associated with integrating the operations, systems, and teams of the merging startups. This includes expenses related to restructuring, rebranding, IT integration, redundancies, and any legal or consulting fees. Carefully evaluate these costs and develop a comprehensive integration plan to minimize disruptions and maximize cost synergies.
8. **Post-Merger Financial Structure**: Determine the financial structure of the merged entity, including capitalization, ownership distribution, and the

allocation of financial resources. Consider the equity ownership percentages of each startup's shareholders, debt obligations, and the composition of the new management team.

It is essential to engage experienced financial advisors, investment bankers, and legal professionals specializing in startup mergers and acquisitions to guide you through the financial considerations and ensure compliance with relevant regulations. Their expertise can help you navigate the complexities, maximize value, and facilitate a successful merger.

Buyouts

Buyouts, also known as acquisitions or takeovers, refer to the process by which one company purchases a controlling stake or the entirety of another company. In a buyout, the acquiring company gains control over the target company's assets, operations, and decision-making processes. Buyouts can occur for various reasons, including strategic expansion, market consolidation, gaining access to new technologies or intellectual property, eliminating competition, or achieving synergistic benefits. They can be friendly, with the target company willingly agreeing to the acquisition, or hostile, where the acquiring company attempts to gain control against the target company's wishes. Innovation has its limits and some startups are adept at supplementing their growth with acquisitions.

There are different types of buyouts, each with its own characteristics:

1. **Leveraged Buyout (LBO)**: In an LBO, the acquiring company (often a private equity firm) uses a significant amount of debt to finance the purchase. The target company's assets are often used as collateral for the debt. The acquiring company aims to improve the target company's performance, increase its value, and eventually sell it for a higher price.
2. **Management Buyout (MBO)**: In an MBO, the existing management team of a company, often with the help of external financing sources like private equity firms or banks, purchases the company they are currently running. The management team becomes the new owners and takes the company private. Management buyout occurs when a large firm decides to sell a business that is no more part of its core business or when the owner decides to retire from his position. If the management team feels they have the expertise and resources to take over, they will opt for a buyout. Some of the largest Private Equity deals globally have been MBOs, and India is also moving in that direction. For instance, Oak Hill Capital Partners buying out exlService.com (I).

Considerations while Planning a Management Buyout
a. Investigate the transaction's viability.
b. Communicate openly and transparently with executives and shareholders.
c. Key employees cut out of the deal (share the equity)
d. Create a solid employee and customer retention strategy.
e. Develop a thorough understanding of company's worth (financial modelling and valuation)
f. Get financing in order.
g. Maintain a friendly behaviour.

h. Create a proper shareholders' agreement.
i. Don't neglect the business's operations while working on the deal.
j. Determine appropriate legal structure for the transaction.

3. **Merger and Acquisition (M&A)**: A merger occurs when two companies agree to combine their operations and form a new entity. An acquisition refers to one company purchasing another. Mergers and acquisitions can be friendly or hostile, depending on the agreement between the involved parties. Fintech saw the consolidation of 30 startups in 2021. Some prominent examples of acquisitions in the startup space are illustrated below:

Acquiring Startup	Acquired Startup	Acquisition value	Timing	Additional Information
Byju's		$2.5 billion	2021	Acquire the 10 companies in 2021. Aakash Educational Services for $1 billion, $600 million for Great Learning, $500 million for US-based Epic, and Tynker
PayU	BillDesk	$4.7 billion deal	2021	The largest in terms of deal size
Tata Digital	BigBasket	$1.2 billion	2021	Acquisition of a majority stake
CRED	Happay	$180 million	2021	
BharatPe	Payback	$27 million	2021	
Open	Finin	$10 million	2021	
Stripe	Recko	undisclosed amount	2021	
PayU	Citrus Pay	$130 million	Sept 2016	PayU expanded its user base to more than 30 million
Myntra	Jabong	$70 million)	July 2016	Despite raising $250 million, Jabong was facing a severe cash crunch when it was acquired by Myntra in all-cash deal
Snapdeal	Freecharge	$400 million	April 2015	Snapdeal sold Freecharge to Axis Bank for $60 million
Zomato	Urbanspoon	$50 million	January 2015	Marked Zomato's foray into US, Canadian and Australian market, taking its worldwide presence to 22 countries. Zomato also made investments in Indian delivery players Grab and Pickingo in 2015 to strengthen home delivery service.
Practo	Insta Health	$12 million	2015	Hospital information management solution provider, gave Practo access to over 500 hospitals in 15 countries. Practo, acquired four companies in 6 months: fitness solutions firm FitHo, product outsourcing firm Genii, and appointment booking platform Qikwell
Ola	TaxiForSure	$200 million	March 2015	adding TaxiForSure's 15,000-plus fleet across 47 cities. Ola shut-down TFS in Aug 2016 and laid off 1,000 of its employees
Flipkart	Myntra	$300 to 330 million	May 2014	Myntra founder & CEO Mukesh Bansal was appointed to Flipkart's Board and made head of fashion division of Flipkart

Acquisitions in 2021

According to data-tracking platform *Fintrackr*, more than 250 startups got acquired or acquihired by larger companies during 2021, Startups like Byju's, Unacademy, upGrad, Mensa Brands, GlobalBees, 10club, Upscalio, Cultfit (Curefit) made headlines for their acquisitions. Byju's was in the top position with 10 acquisitions in in 2021. Startups such as Mensa Brands, Upscalio, GlobalBees and 10club acquired 30 smaller brands during 2021. Goat Brand Labs announced that it took over 11 brands in 2021.

Buyouts can have significant implications for both the acquiring company and the target company. They can lead to changes in management, organizational structure, product offerings, and employee dynamics. Additionally, buyouts can affect shareholders, stakeholders, and the overall competitive landscape of the industry in which the companies operate.

Difference between Leveraged Buyouts and Management Buyouts

Leveraged buyouts	Management buyouts
Interested buyers opt for external financing to buy stocks to control company's equity. Banks and debt capitals offer funds to them. Thus, it comes with a lot of debts	The management team internally funds MBO financing
Management is likely to change	As company's manager acquires the company's ownership. Management team remains same

Guidelines for Startup Founders during Buyouts

While each situation is unique, here are some general guidelines that startup founders should consider when they are navigating the process of a buyout:

1. **Understand the terms and implications**: It's crucial for founders to thoroughly understand the terms and conditions of the buyout offer. This includes the purchase price, payment structure, potential earn-outs, and any post-acquisition roles or responsibilities. Startup founders should seek legal and financial advice to ensure they grasp the implications and consequences of the buyout.
2. **Evaluate the strategic fit**: Assess whether the acquiring company aligns with the startup's vision, values, and long-term goals. Consider how the acquisition can support the startup's growth, product development, market reach, and customer base. Ensure the acquiring company has the necessary resources and expertise to help the startup thrive.
3. **Advocate for the startup's interests:** Founders should actively advocate for the best interests of the startup and its stakeholders throughout the buyout negotiations. This includes negotiating favourable terms, protecting

intellectual property rights, preserving the startup's culture, and safeguarding the welfare of employees.
4. **Communicate with stakeholders:** Maintain transparent and open communication with key stakeholders, including employees, investors, customers, and partners. Keep them informed about the buyout process, address their concerns, and manage expectations to minimize disruption and build trust.
5. **Protect employee interests**: Consider the impact of the buyout on employees. Ensure their welfare is taken into account, and if possible, negotiate for retention packages or incentives to mitigate the risk of key talent leaving post-acquisition. Transparent communication about potential changes and opportunities can help alleviate uncertainties.
6. **Seek expert advice:** Founders should engage legal, financial, and tax professionals who specialize in mergers and acquisitions to guide them through the buyout process. Their expertise will help founders navigate complex agreements, assess tax implications, and protect their rights during negotiations.
7. **Plan for the future**: Founders should evaluate their role and vision for the startup after the acquisition. Discuss potential roles within the acquiring company, such as executive positions or advisory roles. Founders should consider long-term objectives and how the buyout fits into their personal and professional aspirations.

These guidelines are general and should be adapted to the specific circumstances of each buyout. Seeking personalized advice and support from professionals experienced in mergers and acquisitions is crucial to ensure the best possible outcome for the startup and its founders.

Private Equity Investment

The stock market has gone up and if you are stock picking, that's fine, you may do a bit better than the market. But if you want to play in another game where you can get rapid increases of value and so on and so forth, this apparently has become the new parlour game, to invest in these companies and many their cases, the private equity that has been piling in onto of the venture capital is creating the unicorn, in other words the company with the $1 billion valuation-
Kevin Kinsella

Private equity (PE) investment plays a significant role in the Indian start-up ecosystem alongside VC funding as a significant source of capital for growth-stage companies. Here is an overview of the characteristics of PE investment for startups in India:

a. **Investment Stage**: PE firms typically focus on more mature companies or growth-stage companies that have already achieved a certain level of scale and revenue and usually after the VC round.
b. **Larger Investment Size**: Compared to VC funding, private equity investments tend to be larger in size. PE firms have the capital resources to make substantial investments in companies, which can help fuel their growth and expansion plans.
c. **Strategic Partnerships:** PE investors often bring not just capital but also strategic expertise and industry connections to the table. They can provide guidance, operational support, and access to their network, which can be valuable for start-ups looking to scale rapidly.
d. **Exit Opportunities**: PE investors typically have longer investment horizons compared to VCs. They seek to realize their returns through various exit options, including secondary sales, mergers and acquisitions (M&A), and IPOs.

Leading PE Firms Investing in Startups in India

There are several leading private equity firms that actively invest in startups in India. Here are some prominent ones which have not been discussed under VC funding ecosystem chapter:

1. **Warburg Pincus**: Warburg Pincus is a global private equity firm that has been actively investing in India for many years. They have a broad investment focus, including sectors such as technology, healthcare, financial services, and consumer goods.
2. **General Atlantic:** General Atlantic is a global growth equity firm that has made significant investments in Indian startups. They have a long-term approach and focus on partnering with high-growth companies across various sectors.
3. **KKR**: KKR (Kohlberg Kravis Roberts) is a global investment firm that has a strong presence in India. They invest in a wide range of sectors, including technology, healthcare, consumer goods, and infrastructure.

4. **Ascent Capital:** This private equity firm has been in India for over a decade, and they have already helped more than 40 entrepreneurs achieve their dreams. They currently manage $600 million divided into three funds.
5. **Canada Pension Plan Investment Board (CPPIB):** It is a Canadian investment management organization that manages the funds of the Canada Pension Plan. CPPIB invests in Indian startups in the form of PE.
6. **Goldman Sachs:** It is a leading global investment banking, securities, and investment management firm. It offers a wide range of financial services to corporations, governments, and individuals. Goldman Sachs is involved in various activities, including investment banking, asset management, securities trading, and private equity investments.
7. **Silver Lake:** A global PE firm specializing in technology investments. focusing on investing in companies in technology, tech-enabled, and related industries.
8. **Kora Management:** It is an investment firm that primarily focuses on emerging markets, including India. It invests in technology, consumer goods, financial services companies with strong growth potential in emerging markets.
9. **Falcon Edge Capital:** It is an investment firm that focuses on both public and private investments. It invests in companies across various sectors, including technology, healthcare, consumer goods, and financial services and has made investments in several prominent companies, both in India and globally.
10. **TPG Growth:** It is the growth equity and middle-market investment platform of TPG, a leading global alternative asset firm. It invests in companies that exhibit strong growth potential across sectors such as technology, healthcare, consumer, and financial services. It supports companies in their expansion efforts and helps them scale their operations.
11. **Multiples PE:** It is an Indian PE firm that invests in mid-market companies across sectors such as consumer and healthcare. The firm focuses on growth-oriented investments and aims to partner with companies to accelerate their growth and value creation.
12. **ValueQuest Investment Advisors:** It is an Indian investment firm that primarily focuses on long-term value investing. The firm invests in public equities and follows a bottom-up research-driven approach and invest in high-quality companies with strong fundamentals and sustainable growth prospects.

Select Funds by PE Investors for Indian Startups

Name of Fund	Fund Size	Investment Stage/Sectoral Focus	cheque sizes
Multiples PE (Fund IV)	$640 Mn	Growth to late stage startup	$15 Mn and $50 Mn
ValueQuest Investment Advisors (VQ Scale Fund)	INR 1000 Cr		
Matrix Partners	$550 million	Series-B	$1-15 million
Catamaran Ventures	$1 billion	Deep tech, precision engineering, manufacturing and renewables	

Source:
1. https://inc42.com/features/sparks-funding-revival-startup-funds-worth-2-bn-announced-2023-full-list/
2. https://www.bizzbuzz.news/markets/india-focussed-pe-funds-raise-new-rounds-for-investing-in-startups-1221136

Significant PE Startup Deals in India

Large PE deals in the Indian startup ecosystem have become increasingly common as the sector matures and attracts significant investment. Here are a few notable examples of large private equity deals in Indian startups:

1. **Policybazaar** raised $75 million in a private equity round led by Falcon Edge Capital in 2021. The funding valued the company at around $2.4 billion.
2. **Byju's** attracted substantial private equity investments. In 2020, it raised $500 million in a funding round led by Silver Lake, bringing the company's valuation to around $10.8 billion.
3. **Zomato** raised $660 million in a private equity funding round led by Kora Management in 2021. The funding came ahead of the company's highly anticipated IPO.
4. **Nykaa** raised $100 million in a private equity funding round led by TPG Growth in 2020. The investment valued Nykaa at over $1.2 billion.
5. **Dream11** raised $225 million in a private equity funding round led by Tiger Global Management in 2020. The funding came ahead of the Indian Premier League (IPL) season and helped strengthen the company's position in the market.

PE Firms' Startup Deals in 2022

PE firms that demonstrated interest in select growth equity deals in 2022:

1. **Dailyhunt by CPPIB**: VerSe Innovation Pvt Ltd, which operates technology platforms: news and content aggregator Dailyhunt and short video editor Josh, has raised $805 million in April 2022 at 1.5 times jump in valuation as part of its Series J funding round. This investment took VerSe Innovation's valuation to around $5 billion. VerSe Innovation was last valued at $3.1 billion in January 2022 after it raised $28 million as a part of its Series I funding round from the Canada Pension Plan Investment Board (CPP Investments). The Series J round was led by CPP Investments ($425 million) and New investors Ontario Teachers' Pension Plan Board, Luxor Capital, Sumeru Ventures and Sofina Group, Baillie Gifford were among others who participated in this round.
2. **ElasticRun by Goldman Sachs:** ElasticRun, a rural B2B online commerce company raised $330 million in funding round which was led by SoftBank Vision Fund 2 and Goldman Sachs with participation from Chimera and Innoven, as well as existing investor Prosus Ventures.
3. **Amagi by General Atlantic**: Amagi, a leading media technology provider raised over $100 million in investment, which included $80 million from growth equity firm General Atlantic. With this investment Amagi's valuation rose to $1.4 billion, an increase from the $1 billion valuation that the company achieved in March 2022 when it raised $95 million from Accel, Norwest Venture Partners, and Avataar Ventures.

Startup Platforms on BSE and NSE

"The stock market is filled with individuals who know the price of everything, but the value of nothing." – **Phillip Fisher**

BSE Ltd has launched the BSE Startups Platform in December 2018 as per the rules and regulations laid down by SEBI. It became operational in August 2019. Alphalogic Techsys was the first startup to be listed on BSE startup platform on September 5 at a share price of INR 84 per share. The platform offers entrepreneurs and investors a regulated and convenient environment to list Startups. Till the end of 2021, 12 technology startups were listed on the platform.

Similarly, NSE EMERGE is the National Stock Exchange of India's initiative for SMEs and startup companies from India. These companies can get listed on NSE without IPO on this platform to connect with investors for funding.

As all startups do not get Angel, VC or private equity funding; they can raise funds by listing themselves on these platforms. These platforms assist listed startups to not only raise equity capital for their growth and expansion but also enable them to migrate into the Main Board of the stock exchange after a period of time. Thus, alongside it provides opportunities to investors to identify and invest in good companies at an early stage as well as offer an exit route.

Criteria for Listing

a. The Company shall be incorporated under the Companies Act, 1956 / 2013.
b. The "Start-up companies" seeking Listing on BSE Startup Platform should be in the sector of IT, ITES, Biotechnology and Life Science, 3D Printing, Space technology, E-Commerce, Hi- Tech Defence, Drones, Nano Technologies, Artificial Intelligence, Big data, Enhance/Virtual Reality, E-gaming, Exoskeleton, Robotics, Holographic Technology, Genetic Engineering, Variable Computers Inside body computer technology and other Hi-tech based companies.
c. The company should have a combined track record of at least 2 years at the time of filing the prospectus with BSE.
d. The company should be registered as startup with DPIIT. In case the company is not registered as Startup with DPIIT then the company's paid-up capital should be minimum Rs. 1 crore.
e. The post issue paid up capital of the company (face value) shall not be more than Rs. 25 crores.
f. There should be preferably investment by QIB investors (as defined under SEBI ICDR Regulations, 2009) / Angel Investors/Accredited Investors for a minimum period of 2 years at the time of filing of draft prospectus with BSE.
g. It should have a positive net worth.

Requirements
a. Company must have a website.
b. Company must facilitate trading in Demat securities and enter into an agreement with both the depositories.
c. There should not be any change in the promoters of the company in preceding one year from date of filing the application to BSE for listing under Startup segment.

Disclosures
The listing startup must provide a certificate stating the following:
a. The Company has not been referred to National Company Law Tribunal (NCLT) under Insolvency and Bankruptcy Code, 2016
b. There is no winding up petition against the company that has been accepted by the National Company Law Tribunal (NCLT).
c. None of the Promoter / Directors of the company has been debarred by any regulatory agency(ies).

List of Startups Listed on BSE Startups Platform

Name of Startup	Industry
Ascensive Educare Ltd	Consumer Services
CWD Ltd	Consumer Durables
Trekkingtoes.com Ltd	Services
Kuberan Global Edu Solutions Ltd	Consumer Services
Naapbooks Ltd	Information Technology
Net Pix Shorts Digital Media Ltd	Media, Entertainment & Publication
Niks Technology Ltd	Information Technology
Nirmitee Robotics India Ltd	Services
Transpact Enterprises Ltd	Healthcare
Tranway Technologies Ltd	Information Technology
Valencia Nutrition Ltd	Fast Moving Consumer Goods
Wherrelz IT Solutions Ltd	Information Technology

Investments in Startups through Exchanges

Retail investors, QIBs (Qualified institutional buyers), HNIs (High net worth individuals) have started investing in listed startups through the startup platform.

Migration from BSE Startups Platform to the Main Board

The companies seeking migration to Main Board of BSE should be listed and traded on the BSE StartUp Platform for a minimum period of two years and then they can migrate to the Main Board as per the guidelines specified by SEBI vide their circular dated 18th May 2010 and as per the procedures laid down in the ICDR guidelines Chapter IX. Listed startups can also migrate to the main board of the BSE if their paid capital crosses Rs.10 crore with market capitalisation of over Rs 25 crore and approval from two-third of non-promoters.

Profitability before IPO

"I'm convinced that about half of what separates the successful entrepreneurs from the non-successful ones is pure perseverance." **–Steve Jobs, Co-Founder, and CEO, Apple**

If 2021 was the year of startup IPOs, 2022 saw many startups like Droom, Oyo, boAt Lifestyle, Snapdeal, and Pharmeasy postponing their plans to go public because of multiple reasons. Concerns over valuations and rising global rates have taken the biggest toll on Paytm, Zomato, Nykaa, Delhivery and Policybazaar, the five of the most-hyped technology startup IPOs in 2021-22 in India. From August 2021 to November 2022, they floundered significantly since listing, shedding more than $18 billion in value turning the promoters and investors cautious.

"One or two years before a company goes for an IPO, founders should start practising the processes that best public markets follow by taking cue from their discourses in balance sheets, composition of board, investor communication. This will ensure that when a company is finally on the IPO stage, it doesn't have to reinvent the wheel. If you are planning an IPO, start behaving like a public company. That will make the transition really smooth.", said Sunil Sunil Singhania, Founder, Abakkus Asset Manager LLP.

Shekhar Kirani, a renowned startup investor and a Partner at Accel, a venture capital firm said, "Startups must show profitability for at least two quarters before they approach the public markets."

Importance to attain Profit or Profitability before Launching IPO

It is important for startups to attain profitability before launching an Initial Public Offering (IPO) for several reasons:

1. **Investor confidence:** Profitability demonstrates that a startup has a viable and sustainable business model. It shows that the company's products or services generate sufficient revenue to cover expenses and generate a profit. Profitability is a strong indicator of the company's ability to deliver returns to investors, which increases investor confidence and makes the IPO more attractive.
   While scaling, the process is an important aspect. So, it's important to lay down a process that established mechanism to ensure risk management, financial sustainability, and profitability. "At Infosys we followed the simple PSPD model – predictability, sustainability, profitability, and de-risking. It is not about not taking a risk, but more about how equipped we are to take a risk," said MD Ranganath, Chairman, Catamaran Ventures.
2. **Valuation**: Profitability positively impacts a startup's valuation. When a company is profitable, it has a track record of financial performance, making it easier for investors to assess its value. Profitability helps establish a solid

foundation for pricing the shares during the IPO, potentially leading to a higher valuation and allowing the startup to raise more capital.

3. **Market perception**: A profitable startup sends a positive signal to the market. It demonstrates that the company has a competitive advantage, market demand for its products or services, and effective cost management. This perception can attract more investors and potentially drive up demand for shares during the IPO.

4. **Access to capital:** Profitability can provide startups with access to alternative sources of capital before the IPO. When a company is profitable, it may be able to secure debt financing or attract private investors who are looking for a solid return on their investment. This additional capital can fuel growth, expand operations, and further strengthen the company's financial position before going public. Profitability opens up additional avenues for capital before the IPO. In India, profitable startups have greater access to debt financing and may be able to attract private investors who are seeking profitable ventures. This additional capital can be used to fuel growth, expand operations, strengthen the company's financial position, and make it more attractive to potential IPO investors.

5. **Risk reduction**: Achieving profitability reduces the risk associated with the IPO. Startups that are not yet profitable may face skepticism from potential investors who question the sustainability of their business model. Profitability demonstrates that the company has addressed key challenges, overcome initial hurdles, and has a higher likelihood of long-term success.

6. **Operating flexibility:** Profitability provides startups with greater operating flexibility. It allows the company to invest in research and development, marketing, hiring top talent, and other growth initiatives. Profitable startups are better positioned to weather economic downturns or market fluctuations as they have the financial resources to navigate challenging times.

7. **Regulatory requirements:** Stock exchanges and regulatory bodies have profitability requirements for companies looking to go public. These requirements ensure that companies listing on the stock exchange meet certain financial thresholds and are less likely to face financial distress shortly after the IPO. By attaining profitability beforehand, startups can meet these requirements and comply with the regulations.

    In India, there are certain regulatory requirements set by the Securities and Exchange Board of India (SEBI) that a company needs to meet before it can launch an IPO. One of these requirements is profitability. SEBI mandates that companies must have a track record of distributable profits in at least three of the preceding five years, including the year of the IPO. By attaining profitability, startups can meet this regulatory criterion and fulfil the eligibility criteria for launching an IPO in India.

8. **Compliance with listing requirements:** Stock exchanges in India, such as the Bombay Stock Exchange (BSE) and the National Stock Exchange (NSE), have specific listing requirements. These requirements often include profitability criteria for companies going public. By attaining profitability before the IPO, startups can meet these requirements and comply with the regulations set by the stock exchanges.

While profitability is not an absolute requirement for all IPOs, it significantly enhances a startup's prospects of a successful public offering. It instils confidence in investors, attracts higher valuations, provides access to capital, reduces risks, and grants the company greater operating flexibility. Attaining profitability before an IPO demonstrates the maturity and sustainability of the business, making it an important milestone for startups considering going public. Being profitable before going public is important for startups. Investors and stakeholders want to see evidence of sustainable and profitable growth. While startups can focus on scale and market share in the short term, they must show a path to profitability to attract investors to subscribe to its equity in primary and secondary market. The results show that the startup, which can generate a strong return on investment increases the confidence in its future prospects.

"An IPO need to be well thought through as there are a lot of regulator compliances. The journey needs to be well planned, and companies need to build a strong foundation, good sustainability practices, good governance framework. Investors will reward handsomely, if this is followed through," said Sonia Dasgupta, CEO of the Investment Banking Division at JM Financial.

IPO

What founders have to keep in mind is that an IPO is not the end but actually the beginning. - **Nithin Kamath, Zerodha**

An Initial Public Offering (IPO) is a process through which a privately held company offers its shares to the public for the first time, allowing individuals and institutional investors to purchase ownership stakes in the company. It is a significant milestone for a company as it transitions from being privately owned to becoming a publicly traded entity.

Indian unicorns are exploring the public listing avenues as a step to realise the growth potential. Some of the big unicorn names that have already launched an IPO before mid-2023 include: Zomato, Nykaa, PolicyBazaar, Paytm, MapmyIndia, Mobikwik, Tracxn, Cartrade, Delhivery, etc. Freshworks opted to list itself in the US. It all started when in 2010, Deep Kalra, the founder of MakeMyTrip, chose Nasdaq for its listing. Subsequently, in 2013, when JustDial went public, it adopted the 'safety net' scheme for retail investors that was proposed by SEBI. Safety net was a mark of promoters' confidence as it meant a buyback would get triggered after six months of the listing if the volume-weighted share price fell below the issue price in the two months prior to the completion of six months since listing. To encourage the reatail investors, Just Dial also offered 10 % discount on the issue price to them, twice the 5 % discount that was a historical trend.

The strength of domestic demand for startup equity can be understood from the fact that Indian investors at stock market have given $80 billion dollars back in 18 months from June 2021 to November 2022 to the foreign investors who invested in startups that got listed during this period, which is a big number.

Eligibility Conditions to Launch an IPO in India

To launch an IPO in India, companies need to fulfil certain eligibility conditions as per the regulations of the Securities and Exchange Board of India (SEBI), the regulatory authority for securities markets. Here are the general eligibility conditions for launching an IPO in India:

1. **Company Type**: The company must be registered as a public limited company under the Companies Act, 2013, or earlier applicable laws. It can be an existing unlisted company or a fresh issue of shares by a new company.
2. **Track Record**: The company must have a track record of at least three years in terms of its operations, profitability, and net worth. However, this requirement may be relaxed for certain sectors or companies under specific circumstances.
3. **Financials**: The company should have audited financial statements for at least three years, with a minimum net worth as prescribed by SEBI. The

financial statements should comply with Indian Accounting Standards (Ind AS) or Generally Accepted Accounting Principles (GAAP).
4. **Minimum Issue Size**: The company should meet the minimum issue size requirements as specified by SEBI. This is the minimum amount of shares to be offered to the public.
5. **Promoter Contribution**: The promoters of the company are required to contribute a minimum percentage of the post-issue capital. The exact percentage is determined by SEBI and may vary based on different factors.
6. **SEBI Approval**: The company must obtain the approval of SEBI for the IPO. This involves filing a draft offer document known as the Red Herring Prospectus (RHP) with SEBI, which is reviewed and approved by SEBI before the IPO can proceed.
7. **Compliance:** The company must comply with all applicable securities laws, regulations, and listing requirements of the stock exchanges where it intends to get listed. This includes complying with the SEBI (Issue of Capital and Disclosure Requirements) Regulations, 2018.
8. **Appointment of Intermediaries**: The company needs to appoint various intermediaries, including merchant bankers, registrars, and share transfer agents, to assist with the IPO process and ensure compliance with regulatory requirements.

These are general eligibility conditions, and specific requirements may vary depending on factors such as the nature of the company, its sector, and the prevailing regulatory framework at the time of the IPO. Companies should consult with legal and financial experts for detailed and up-to-date guidance on launching an IPO in India.

Red Herring Prospectus

In the Indian context, a Red Herring Prospectus (RHP) is a document filed with the SEBI by a company planning to launch an IPO. It is an important step in the IPO process and serves as a preliminary offer document to provide essential information about the company to potential investors. Here are some key points about the Red Herring Prospectus:
1. **Preliminary Document**: The RHP is called a "red herring" because it contains all the necessary information about the company and the IPO but excludes certain key details such as the price at which the securities will be offered to the public. These missing details are included in the final prospectus after the company receives approval from SEBI.
2. **Key Information**: The RHP provides comprehensive information about the company, its business, financials, promoters, management, risk factors, and the purpose of the IPO. It also includes details about the objects of the issue, the proposed utilization of funds, and the terms of the offer.
3. **Draft Filing**: The RHP is filed with SEBI for its review and approval before the company can proceed with the IPO. SEBI examines the RHP to ensure that it complies with all the relevant regulations, disclosure requirements, and investor protection norms.

4. **Marketing and Investor Education**: The RHP is used for marketing and investor education purposes during the "roadshow" phase of the IPO. Potential investors can study the document to gain insights into the company and make informed investment decisions. However, they cannot place any orders for shares until the final prospectus is filed.
5. **Book Building Process**: In the case of a book-built IPO, where the price of the shares is discovered through a bidding process, the RHP includes a price range within which investors can submit their bids. The final price is determined based on the demand generated during the bidding period.
6. **Final Prospectus**: After receiving approval from SEBI, the company publishes a final prospectus, which incorporates the offer price and other final details. This document is circulated to the public, and investors can then make applications for shares in the IPO.

The Red Herring Prospectus is an essential document that provides transparency and disclosure to potential investors while ensuring regulatory compliance. It helps investors evaluate the company's business prospects, financials, and risks before making investment decisions.

Book Building Process during IPO

The book building process is a mechanism used during IPO to determine the price at which the securities will be offered to the public. It involves creating a book of demand, known as the "book," by inviting bids from institutional and retail investors. Here's an overview of the book-building process during an IPO:
1. **Price Discovery**: The main objective of the book-building process is to determine the optimal price at which the company can issue its shares to the public. The issuer, along with the lead managers, decides a price range within which investors can submit their bids.
2. **Bidding Period**: The company announces the IPO and opens a bidding period during which investors can place their bids. The bidding period typically lasts for a few days.
3. **Investor Categories**: The book-building process caters to two categories of investors:
    a. **Qualified Institutional Buyers (QIBs)**: These include institutional investors such as mutual funds, insurance companies, banks, and foreign institutional investors. QIBs are generally allocated a separate portion of the shares in the IPO.
    b. **Retail Individual Investors (RIIs):** These are individual investors who are not classified as QIBs. They can participate in the book-building process with a smaller bid lot size compared to QIBs.
4. **Bidding Method**: Investors submit their bids specifying the quantity of shares they wish to purchase and the price they are willing to pay within the price range specified by the issuer. The bids can be revised during the bidding period.
5. **Demand Aggregation**: The lead managers collect and compile all the bids received from investors. They maintain a book that records the demand for

shares at different price levels. The book is categorized into different investor categories, such as QIBs and RIIs.
6. **Price Determination**: Based on the bids received and the demand aggregated in the book, the issuer, and lead managers analyze the demand at various price levels. They determine the final price at which the shares will be issued to the public, which is typically set at the price that generates the highest demand.
7. **Allotment and Refunds**: Once the price is determined, the shares are allocated to successful bidders. In the case of oversubscription, where demand exceeds the number of shares available, allotments may be scaled down proportionately. Refunds are issued to unsuccessful bidders.
8. **Listing**: After the shares are allotted, the company lists its shares on the stock exchanges, and trading commences. Investors who have been allotted shares can sell or hold shares based on their investment objectives.

The book-building process allows market forces to determine the price of an IPO and ensures efficient price discovery. It enables the company to gauge investor demand and optimize the issue price, benefiting both the issuer and investors.

Important guidelines regarding IPOs in India

During an IPO, the company typically hires investment banks or underwriters who help determine the offering price, prepare the necessary documentation, and facilitate the sale of shares to the public. The shares are listed on a stock exchange, such as the Bombay Stock Exchange (BSE) or the National Stock Exchange (NSE) in India, where they can be freely traded by investors.

1. **Regulatory Authority:** In India, IPOs are regulated by the Securities and Exchange Board of India (SEBI), which is the primary regulatory body overseeing securities markets in the country. SEBI lays down guidelines and regulations to ensure investor protection, fair disclosure, and transparency in the IPO process.
2. **Eligibility Criteria**: SEBI has established specific eligibility criteria for companies seeking to go public. These criteria include factors such as the company's financial performance, track record, minimum issue size, and compliance with disclosure requirements. The company must meet these criteria to be eligible for an IPO.
3. **Disclosure and Prospectus**: Companies planning an IPO must prepare a comprehensive disclosure document called the prospectus. The prospectus contains essential information about the company, its business operations, financials, risk factors, use of proceeds, and other relevant details. SEBI mandates that the prospectus provides accurate, complete, and material information to help investors make informed investment decisions.
4. **Book-Building Process**: In certain cases, IPOs in India may follow the book-building process. It involves the company and underwriters determining a price range for the shares, and investors indicate the quantity and price at which they are willing to subscribe to the shares. The final issue price is then determined based on the demand and investor response received during the book-building period.

5. **Lock-in Period**: SEBI imposes a lock-in period on the shares held by promoters, pre-IPO investors, and certain other categories of shareholders. This lock-in period restricts these shareholders from selling their shares for a specified duration after the IPO, which is typically three years.
6. **Listing and Post-IPO Compliance:** After a successful IPO, the company's shares are listed on the stock exchange for trading. The company must comply with ongoing disclosure requirements, periodic financial reporting, and other obligations stipulated by the stock exchanges and SEBI. Compliance with these regulations ensures transparency and investor confidence in the company's post-IPO activities.

IPO guidelines and regulations can evolve over time, and companies planning an IPO should refer to the latest guidelines issued by SEBI and consult with legal and financial professionals for accurate and up-to-date information.

How to Prepare Financial Statements Before Launching IPO

Preparing financial statements before launching an IPO requires careful attention to detail and adherence to regulatory guidelines. Here are some key steps and considerations for startups to prepare their financial statements:

1. **Engage professional assistance:** It is advisable for startups to engage professional accountants, auditors, and financial advisors with IPO experience to ensure accurate and compliant financial statements. These professionals can guide the company through the complex process and help meet regulatory requirements.
2. **Select applicable accounting standards**: Determine the accounting standards to be followed for preparing financial statements. In India, the Generally Accepted Accounting Principles (GAAP) or Indian Accounting Standards (Ind AS) may apply, depending on the size and nature of the company. Adhere to the prescribed accounting standards and ensure consistency and transparency in financial reporting.
3. **Historical financial statements:** Prepare historical financial statements for a specified period, usually three to five years, depending on regulatory requirements. These statements include the balance sheet, income statement (profit and loss statement), and cash flow statement. Ensure that financial statements provide a comprehensive and accurate view of the company's financial position, performance, and cash flows.
4. **Audited financial statements:** Get the financial statements audited by a qualified independent auditor. Auditing ensures the reliability and credibility of the financial information provided. The auditor will review the financial statements, assess the company's internal controls, and issue an audit report. The audit report should be included in the IPO prospectus.
5. **Compliance with regulatory requirements**: Adhere to the regulatory requirements of the market in which the IPO will be launched. In India, SEBI prescribes certain guidelines, including specific formats for financial statements, disclosures, and reporting requirements. Familiarize yourself with these guidelines and ensure compliance to avoid delays or rejections.

6. **Pro forma financial information:** In addition to historical financial statements, prepare pro forma financial information. Pro forma statements present the company's financial position and results of operations as if a particular event, such as an acquisition or merger, had occurred earlier. Pro forma information helps investors understand the impact of significant transactions on the company's financials.
7. **Key financial metrics and KPIs:** Identify and calculate key financial metrics and Key Performance Indicators (KPIs) that are relevant to your industry and business model. Examples include revenue growth rate, gross profit margin, customer acquisition cost, and customer lifetime value. These metrics provide insights into the company's financial performance and growth potential, which can be attractive to potential investors.
8. **Management discussion and analysis (MD&A)**: Prepare a comprehensive MD&A section that accompanies the financial statements. The MD&A provides insights into the company's financial condition, results of operations, liquidity, and future prospects. It should include a narrative explanation of financial performance, risks, opportunities, and other factors that may impact the company's financials.
9. **Disclosures and footnotes**: Include relevant disclosures and footnotes to the financial statements. These disclosures provide additional details about accounting policies, significant accounting estimates, contingencies, related party transactions, and any other material information that investors need to make informed decisions.
10. **Internal controls and governance**: Establish robust internal controls and governance mechanisms to ensure the accuracy and reliability of financial reporting. This includes implementing accounting systems, segregation of duties, periodic financial reviews, and compliance monitoring.

It's important for startups to work closely with professionals, such as accountants, auditors, and legal advisors, to ensure accurate and compliant financial statements. Regulatory requirements and market expectations may vary, so it's crucial to stay informed about the specific guidelines and regulations applicable to your jurisdiction and industry.

Professional Organizations to Launch IPO

In India, several professional organizations and regulatory bodies play a significant role in helping startups launch an Initial Public Offering (IPO). These organizations provide guidance, support, and regulatory oversight throughout the IPO process. Some of the key organizations involved in facilitating IPOs for startups in India are

1. **Securities and Exchange Board of India (SEBI)**: SEBI is the primary regulatory body overseeing the securities market in India. It regulates and supervises IPOs, ensuring compliance with relevant laws, rules, and regulations. SEBI plays a crucial role in setting guidelines and providing necessary approvals for IPOs, protecting the interests of investors, and maintaining market integrity.
2. **Bombay Stock Exchange (BSE):** BSE is one of the leading stock exchanges in India and operates the BSE SME Exchange, a dedicated platform for Small and Medium Enterprises (SMEs) to list their shares and raise capital. BSE aids

startups throughout the IPO process, including eligibility evaluation, listing requirements, and compliance with regulatory guidelines.
3. **National Stock Exchange (NSE):** NSE is another major stock exchange in India. It operates the NSE Emerge platform, which focuses on listing SMEs. NSE provides support and guidance to startups seeking to launch an IPO, facilitating the listing process and ensuring compliance with regulatory norms.
4. **Institute of Company Secretaries of India (ICSI)**: ICSI is a premier professional organization for company secretaries in India. Company secretaries play a critical role in the IPO process, ensuring compliance with regulatory requirements, drafting and filing necessary documents, and facilitating communication between the company and regulatory authorities. ICSI offers guidance and resources to startups and their company secretaries throughout the IPO journey.
5. **Institute of Chartered Accountants of India (ICAI)**: ICAI is the statutory body responsible for regulating the profession of Chartered Accountants in India. Chartered Accountants play a crucial role in the IPO process, conducting audits, preparing financial statements, and ensuring compliance with accounting and auditing standards. ICAI provides guidance, training, and technical support to Chartered Accountants involved in the IPO process.
6. **Merchant Bankers and Financial Advisors**: Merchant bankers and financial advisors, often affiliated with financial institutions and investment banks, play a significant role in assisting startups with IPOs. These professionals provide advice on valuation, structuring the offering, preparing the prospectus, coordinating with regulatory authorities, and managing the IPO process.

It's important for startups to engage with these professional organizations, seek guidance from experienced professionals, and stay informed about the regulatory requirements and processes involved in launching an IPO in India. Collaborating with these organizations and professionals can enhance the chances of a successful IPO and ensure compliance with relevant laws and regulations.

Steps to be followed for launching IPO in India

Launching an IPO in India involves several steps and requires compliance with regulatory requirements. Here is an overview of the typical process:

1. **Eligibility and Preparation**:
   ❖ Ensure that your company meets the eligibility criteria set by the Securities and Exchange Board of India (SEBI).
   ❖ Conduct a thorough internal assessment of your company's financials, operations, and governance structure.
   ❖ Prepare audited financial statements, prospectus, and other necessary documents.
2. **Appoint Intermediaries**:
   ❖ Engage intermediaries, including investment bankers, underwriters, legal advisors, and registrars, to the issue.

- ❖ These intermediaries will assist in the IPO process, due diligence, legal compliance, pricing, and marketing.

3. **Due Diligence:**
   - ❖ Conduct a comprehensive due diligence process, including legal, financial, and business due diligence.
   - ❖ Ensure compliance with SEBI regulations, disclosure requirements, and corporate governance norms.

4. **Draft Prospectus:**
   - ❖ Prepare a draft red herring prospectus (DRHP), which provides detailed information about the company, its business, financials, risk factors, and IPO offering.
   - ❖ File the DRHP with SEBI for review and approval.

5. **SEBI Approval:**
   - ❖ SEBI reviews the DRHP and provides its observations and clarifications.
   - ❖ Address SEBI's comments and make necessary amendments to the prospectus.
   - ❖ Once SEBI is satisfied, it issues the final observation letter, allowing the company to proceed with the IPO.

6. **Marketing and Roadshows:**
   - ❖ Engage in marketing activities to create awareness and generate investor interest.
   - ❖ Conduct roadshows to showcase the company's strengths, prospects, and investment potential to institutional and retail investors.

7. **Price Determination:**
   - ❖ Collaborate with investment bankers to determine the issue price based on market conditions, demand, and company valuation.
   - ❖ Decide the size of the offering, including the number of shares to be issued and the portion allocated to different investor categories.

8. **IPO Allotment:**
   - ❖ Open the IPO subscription period, allowing investors to apply for shares.
   - ❖ Allocate shares based on subscription received and SEBI regulations.
   - ❖ Refunds are issued to unsuccessful applicants.

9. **Listing:**
   - ❖ Obtain final approval from stock exchanges for the IPO listing.
   - ❖ Issue shares and credit them to investors' Demat accounts.
   - ❖ The company's shares are listed, and trading on the stock exchanges commences.

10. **Post-IPO Compliance:**
    - ❖ Fulfil post-listing requirements such as periodic financial reporting, corporate governance compliance, and regulatory disclosures.
    - ❖ Maintain transparency and adhere to SEBI regulations regarding shareholder communication and investor relations.

The IPO process in India is subject to regulatory changes, and it is advisable to consult with legal and financial professionals for accurate and up-to-date guidance.

Recent Startup IPOs: An Overview

Name	Year of Establishment	Year of IPO	Issue Size	Subscribed number of Times	Listing day Premium
Zomato	2008	2021	₹ 9,375 Cr	175.5	51.3%
Nykaa	2012	2021	₹ 5351.92 cr	81.78	80%
Policybazaar	2008	2021	₹ 5625 cr	16.59	17.35%
Paytm	2010	2021	₹ 16,600 cr	1.89	-9.3%
CarTrade	2009	2021	₹ 2,999 cr	20.3	-1.12%
Nazara Technologies	1999	2021	₹. 582.91 Cr	175.5	80.74%
MapmyIndia	1995	2021	₹ 1,039.61 Cr	154.71	54%

FOUNDER'S AGREEMENT: A TEMPLATE

This Founder Agreement (the "Agreement") is made among the founders of [**PROJECT NAME**] and effective [**DATE**],
The following individuals are hereby admitted as partners in the Project ("**Founders**")
[**FOUNDER 1**], (the "First Founder"), an individual with his main address located at [**SPECIFY**]
[**FOUNDER 2**] (the "Second Founder"), an individual with his main address located at [SPECIFY]
[**FOUNDER 3**] (the "Third Founder"), an individual with his main address located at [**SPECIFY**]
WHEREAS the undersigned individuals (each a "**Founder**", has and collectively, the "**Founders**") are collaborating as a team with a view to developing .... business and related product or service. Founders agree that all related technology to the business concept is also owned by the Founders pursuant to this Agreement.

AND WHEREAS it is the intention of the Founders that once the Product or Service is developed, or substantially developed to their satisfaction, the Founders shall form a corporation, upon the earliest of the following circumstances: [**SPECIFY**].

NOW THEREFORE in consideration of the covenants contained herein, and in connection with such collaboration of the business concept and technology, and in consideration for a mutually agreeable framework which shall serve as the foundation for the Founders to successfully develop the Business Concept and Technology, the undersigned hereby agree as follows:

1. **CAPITAL CONTRIBUTIONS AND EXPENSES**
    1.1 **Capital Contribution.** Each Founder hereby commits to contribute up to [**SPECIFY AMOUNT**] toward Company expenses when called by the Company, as non-refundable capital contributions. The Company must make capital calls of Founders on a *pro rata* basis. Each Founder has contributed such amounts as set-out at **Schedule 2** attached hereto towards the expenses of the Startup prior to incorporation.
    1.2 Additional **Capital Contribution**. The Founders may make additional capital contributions in the form of cash and prepaid expenses from time to time to fund the Company's ongoing capital and operating needs. The written consent of all Founders is required for any Founder to make a capital contribution. No Founder may be required to make a capital contribution except pursuant to such mutual written consent.
    1.3 **Expenses and budgeting:** The Founders will budget for Company expenses on a rolling basis. All budgets must be approved by all Founders in writing. Any Founder may pay budgeted expenses on the Company's behalf. Each Founder shall reimburse any Founder that incurs an expense

related to the Startup proportionately to such Founder's Equity Distribution pursuant to Section 4.1.

2. **ROLES AND RESPONSIBILITIES**

    2.1 **Founder's Contribution.** The Founders shall, using best efforts, contribute to the development of the Product or Service pursuant to each Founder's "Role and Responsibility" description as set-out at **Schedule 1** attached hereto.

3. **INCORPORATION AND FORMATION OF CORPORATION**

    3.1 **Actions Required.** Once it is determined by a Simple Majority that the Corporation will be incorporated and formed, each Founder shall grant and assign to the Corporation immediately upon its incorporation all of his or her right, title, and interest in and to the Product or Service (including all right, title and interest to intellectual property and all applications thereto), including waiving all moral rights, and assigning all patents, designs, industrial designs, trade-marks, copyrights, trade secrets, ideas (however formed or unformed) and labor and/or work product that results from any task or work performed by the Founder that relates to the Product or Service for the full term of such rights (the "**Transfer**").

    3.2 **Ownership of the Company:** Each Founder will have an equal ownership interest in the Company. The Founders' ownership interests need not be represented by a certificate or any other evidence beyond that contained in this agreement. If a Founder requests, the Company will issue a certificate evidencing the Founder's interest. The certificate must contain a legend noting that the ownership interest is subject to legal and contractual restrictions on transfer.

    3.3 **Transfer to Corporation.** The Founders acknowledge and agree that any discovery, invention, secret process or improvement in procedure made or discovered by any of the Founders in connection with or in any way affecting or relating to the Product or Service or capable of being used or adapted for use in the Product or Service shall immediately be disclosed to the Corporation and shall belong to and be the absolute property of the Corporation immediately as of and following the Incorporation Date.

4. **EQUITY DISTRIBUTION & VESTING**

    4.1 **Equity Distribution.** Subject to this Section 4, on the Incorporation Date, the Shares of the Corporation shall be issued to the Founders according to the distribution chart below (the "**Founder Equity**"):

Name	Equity Distribution (%)
[FOUNDER NAME]	[EQUITY PERCENTAGE]
[FOUNDER NAME]	[EQUITY PERCENTAGE]
[FOUNDER NAME]	[EQUITY PERCENTAGE]
[FOUNDER NAME]	[EQUITY PERCENTAGE]

Should the Founders wish to reserve any portion of the shares for future employees or for an option share pool, any such portion of shares reserved will dilute all Founders equally.

4.2 Ordinary Distribution. The Company may (but is not required to) make ordinary distributions to the Founders out of cash received by the Company (excluding new capital contributions or loans), less all accounts payable and reserves against anticipated expenses from time to time as determined by a majority of Founders. All distributions must be made in the following order:

4.2.1 First, in equal proportion to all Founders who have contributed cash that has not been repaid, until each Founder has been paid out to the extent of such contributions in full;

4.2.2 Second, to all Founders in equal proportion.

4.3 Vesting. The Founder Equity to be issued pursuant to point 4.1 shall vest to each Founder over **[SPECIFY NUMBER OF YEARS FOR VESTING]**, and each Founder shall enter into a customary stock restriction agreement on the Incorporation Date outlining such vesting:

4.4 Issuance of shares. The shares issued to each Founder shall come from the same series and class of shares, such that there are no differences in the rights (including but not limited to voting and distribution rights) accorded to the shares issued to each Founder.

5. **RESTRICTIONS**

    5.1 Restrictions. The Founders may not transfer, pledge or otherwise encumber any Shares or any ownership or entitlement to ownership of the Corporation or of the Product or Service described herein without the unanimous written consent of the Founders.

6. **MANAGEMENT AND APPROVAL RIGHTS**

    6.1 Management of the company. The Company will be managed by the Founders, and a majority of Founders may take any action on behalf of the Company except where explicitly stated otherwise in this agreement. The unanimous written approval of all Founders is required to:

    i. incur any debt on the Company's behalf or employ its credit, other than receivables to trade creditors in the ordinary course of business not to exceed Rs.2500 individually and Rs.5000 in aggregate;

    ii. initiate any voluntary bankruptcy proceeding;

    iii. liquidate or dissolve the Company, or distribute substantially all of its assets and business;

    iv. enter into any inbound or outbound license, transfer, or other assignment of protectable intellectual property used in the Project, including any patentable inventions, copyrights, trade secrets, or trademark rights (except for inbound end user licenses for software applications in the ordinary course of business);

    v. approve any contract with a Founder, or an immediate family member or domestic partner of a Founder, or an affiliate of any of the foregoing persons;

    vi. raise any equity capital in any amount from any person;

vii. admit any partner to the Company; and
viii. amend this agreement.

7. OPPORTUNITIES AND DUTIES TO THE COMPANY

7.1 Opportunities. The Founders must refer to the Company, in writing, all opportunities to participate in a business or activity that is directly competitive with the Project within **[GEOGRAPHIC REGION]**, whether as an employee, consultant, officer, director, advisor, investor, or partner. The Company will have **[SPECIFY]** days to decide whether to pursue any referred opportunity, and to notify the referring Founder of its decision in writing. If the Company elects not to pursue the opportunity, or if it does not notify the referring Founder of its intent in writing within the **[SPECIFY]** days period, then the referring Founder will be free to pursue the opportunity independently. If the Company elects to pursue the opportunity, but later abandons it, then the referring Founder will be free to pursue the opportunity independently at such time.

7.2 Duties. Other than as explicitly provided herein, no Founder will have any duty to the other Founders or to the Company, including any fiduciary duty, and including any duty to refer business opportunities to the Company, or to refrain from engaging in activity that is competitive with that conducted or planned by the Company.

8. CONFIDENTIALITY AND NON-COMPETE

8.1 Confidentiality. The Founders agree to keep all non-public information with respect to Project intellectual property (IP) confidential and not to disclose it to any other party, except (i) to attorneys and advisors who need to know in connection with performing their duties, (ii) to potential business development partners and/or investors approved by the Company in writing, and who are bound by a confidentiality agreement in writing, and (iii) in response to an inquiry from a legal or regulatory authority. The Founders agree to keep the Product or Service confidential; disclosure of the Product or Service will occur only on an as-needed basis and only upon consent of all Founders. Notwithstanding such unanimous consensual disclosures, the Founders shall take all necessary steps to keep the Product or Service confidential until the formation of the Corporation, at which time the Founders shall further detail and define any confidentiality obligations.

8.2 Non-Competition. Immediately after the incorporation of the Company, the Founders shall not at any time during their term as Founders and for a period of 12 months after they have ceased (i) to be a Founder; (ii) to provide services to the Company, whether as a partner, employee, contractor, officer, director or otherwise; or (iii) to hold Shares, whichever is later, alone or jointly or in any capacity whatsoever, directly or indirectly, of **[PROVINCE/STATE]** of **[COUNTRY]**, in connection with any of these transactions, either at a time when they became Shares or at any other time.

i. pursue, participate, assist, be engaged, concerned or interested in any business competing with the Product or Service;
  ii. interfere or seek to interfere or take such steps as may interfere with the continuance of supplies to the Startup (or the terms relating to such supplies) from any suppliers who have been supplying materials, components, products, goods or services to the Startup;
  iii. solicit or attract or offer employment or attempt to solicit or attract or offer employment to any person who was a founder, employee, officer or manager of the Corporation at any time without the express prior written consent of the founders; or
  iv. use or adopt or purport to use or adopt the name or any trade or business name of the Corporation for any purpose.

9. **EXTENSION OF AGREEMENT**
    9.1 **Shareholder Agreement.** Upon the formation of the Corporation, the Founders will enter into a Unanimous Shareholder Agreement to formalize all terms of this Agreement, unless otherwise agreed to by all the Shareholders.
    9.2 **New Founders.** Written consent of all Founders is required to approve any additional party to this Agreement. If a person not named as a Founder hereto joins the Founders in the Startup prior to formation of the Corporation on the basis that such person shall hold an equity interest in the Corporation when formed (a "**New Founder**"), the Founders shall require such New Founder to execute a counterpart signature page so that such person is a party to and bound by this Agreement and shall appropriately amend this Agreement.
    9.3 **Additional Investment**. The written consent of all Founders is required to approve any additional investment in the Company from any party, including a Founder, and to issue any equity securities or rights convertible into the Company's equity to any party. Any Founder who receives an offer from any party to invest in the Company will notify the other Founders of the same and provide each Founder an opportunity to participate meaningfully in the negotiations surrounding the potential investment in the Company.

10. **DISSOLUTION OF STARTUP**
    10.1 **Agreement Timetable.** Within **[SPECIFY NUMBER]** calendar months of the date of this Agreement, if the Founders have not yet incorporated the Corporation, the Founders agree to discuss the benefits of continued collaboration related to the Product or Service and will discuss a mutually agreeable timetable for the incorporation of the Corporation.
    10.2 **Dissolution.** If only one Founder remains a partner of the Company at any time, then the Company shall continue as a sole proprietorship of the remaining Founder until he resigns, without affecting any rights due to any Founder or former Founder under this agreement. In the event that no Founder remains as a partner of the Company at any point in time, then the Company will dissolve, and this agreement will terminate immediately upon completion of the winding up of the Company and distribution of its assets and liabilities in accordance with this agreement.

- **10.3 Resignation and Removal of Founders.** Any Founder may resign from partnership in the Company for any reason or no reason at all by giving written notice to the other Founders. A majority of Founders may remove a Founder from the partnership at any time, for any reason or no reason at all, by giving written notice to such Founder. Upon a Founder's resignation or removal, the Company will continue and will not dissolve, so long as at least one Founder remains as a member of the Company. The Company will pay out to the resigning or removed Founder his positive capital account balance (if any) within 180 days of resignation, either in cash or with an unsecured note payable within **[SPECIFY]** years and bearing interest at **[SPECIFY]** per year.
- **10.4 Dispute Resolution.** In the event that the Founders are unable to agree on a mutually acceptable separation pursuant to this Section 10, the Founders agree to submit to a binding confidential arbitration to be held in **[CITY]** and conducted by a mutually agreed arbitrator. The Founders agree and acknowledge that all provisions of this Agreement, including the confidentiality provisions, will be binding until the end of the arbitration process. The costs of the arbitration shall be borne equally by all the Founders.

11. **GENERAL PROVISIONS**
    - 11.1 **Good Faith.** All actions taken pursuant to this Agreement shall be made in good faith without intention to unduly deprive a Founder of any interests, rights or benefits.
    - 11.2 **Representations and Warranties.** Each Founder represents and warrants that he or she is not a party to any other agreement that would restrict such Founder's ability to perform its obligations as set forth in this Agreement. Each Founder represents and warrants that no third party can claim any rights to any intellectual property or other proprietary right possessed by that Founder as it relates to the Product or Service.
    - 11.3 **Unjust Enrichment.** Nothing in this Agreement prevents, blocks or eliminates in any way the ability of a Founder to bring an action against the other Founders or the Corporation for unjust enrichment or for any other similar cause of action.
    - 11.4 **Corporation to Enforce.** The Founders hereby agree that after incorporation, the Corporation shall enforce the rights and obligations of the Founders hereunder.
    - 11.5 **Assignment.** This Agreement shall not be assigned by any Founder without the written consent of all other Founders.
    - 11.6 **Successors / Assigns**. This agreement shall be binding upon and inure to the benefit of the Founders, the Company, their successors, and their permitted assigns.
    - 11.7 **Notices.** Any notice, consent or approval required or permitted with respect to this Agreement (referred to in this section as a "Notice") shall be in writing and shall be sufficiently given if delivered (in person, by courier or other personal delivery method) or transmitted by email to each founder.

11.8 Governing Law and Jurisdiction. This Agreement shall be governed by and interpreted in accordance with the laws of **[STATE/PROVINCE]** and the laws of **[COUNTRY]** applicable therein.

11.9 Severability. If any provision in this agreement is held to be invalid or unenforceable in any jurisdiction, the validity and enforceability of all remaining provisions contained herein shall not in any way be affected or impaired thereby, and the invalid or unenforceable provisions shall be interpreted and applied so as to produce as near as may be the economic result intended by the parties hereto.

11.10 Amendment / Waiver. This agreement may only be amended with the written consent of all Founders, and none of its provisions may be waived except with the written consent of the party waiving compliance.

11.11 Currency. Except as otherwise stated herein, all amounts are stated in **[COUNTRY]** currency.

11.12 Entire Agreement. This agreement contains the entire agreement between the parties hereto with respect to the subject matter hereof and supersedes all prior arrangements or understandings (whether written or oral) with respect thereto.

11.13 Agreement Confidential. The Parties shall keep the terms and conditions of this Agreement confidential except as may be required to enforce any provision of this Agreement or as may otherwise be required by any law, regulation or other regulatory requirement. Notwithstanding the generality of the foregoing, the Parties may disclose this Agreement to his legal and/or financial advisors.

11.14 Counterparts. This Agreement may be executed by the Founders in counterparts and may be executed and delivered by fax or other electronic means, and all such counterparts and facsimiles together constitute one agreement.

12. SIGNATURE

12.1 Acceptance. By signing below, each Founder indicates acceptance of the terms of this agreement in their entirety as of the date first written above, and represents and warrants to the Company and each other Founder that he has fully read and understood this agreement, and that to each Founder's knowledge, no law or third-party obligation would prevent each such Founder from entering into and performing this agreement in full. For the convenience of the parties, this agreement may be executed electronically and in counterparts. Each counterpart shall be binding, and all of them shall constitute one and the same instrument.

IN WITNESS WHEREOF, the parties hereto have duly executed this Agreement on the day and year set forth below.

FIRST FOUNDER	SECOND FOUNDER
Authorized Signature	Authorized Signature
_____	_____
Print Name and Title	Print Name and Title

SCHEDULE 1
Description of Founders Roles and Responsibilities

Name and Address	Role/Title	Responsibility
[FOUNDER NAME] Address:	[TITLE]	[RESPONSIBILITY]
[FOUNDER NAME] Address:	[TITLE]	[RESPONSIBILITY]
[FOUNDER NAME] Address:	[TITLE]	[RESPONSIBILITY]
[FOUNDER NAME] Address:	[TITLE]	[RESPONSIBILITY]
[FOUNDER NAME] Address:	[TITLE]	[RESPONSIBILITY]

SCHEDULE 2
Initial Capital Contribution of the Founders

Name	Contribution
[FOUNDER NAME]	[AMOUNT]
[FOUNDER NAME]	[AMOUNT]
[FOUNDER NAME]	[AMOUNT]
[FOUNDER NAME]	[AMOUNT]
[FOUNDER NAME]	[AMOUNT]

Term Sheet: A Template

Issue:	[Venture Capital FIRM] ("VC") and/or any member of its corporate group ("the VC Group") will purchase up to [AMOUNT] Series A Convertible Preferred Stock ("Series A") newly issued by [YOUR COMPANY NAME] (the "Company") at a price per share of [PRICE] (the "Purchase Price"). In addition, other investors shall purchase at least [AMOUNT] but not more than [AMOUNT] of newly issued Series A at the Purchase Price. The shares of Series A will be convertible at any time at the option of the holder into common shares of the Company ("Common Stock") on a one-for-one basis, adjusted for future share splits. The Purchase Price equates to a pre-money valuation of [VALUATION]. The calculation is based on [NUMBER] fully diluted shares of Common Stock. If the number of shares issued, or stock awards/options authorized increases before the closing the price per share for Series A Convertible Preferred Stock shall be reduced so that the pre-money valuation is unchanged. The Series A Convertible Preferred Stock shall be referred to herein as the "Preferred Stock."
Dividend:	The Preferred Stock is entitled to an annual [AMOUNT] per share dividend, payable when and if declared by the Board of Directors, but prior to any payment on Common Stock; dividends are not cumulative.
Liquidation Preference	The Series A will have a liquidation preference so that proceeds on a merger, sale or liquidation (including non-cumulative dividends) will first be paid to the Series A and will include a [%] per annum compounding guaranteed return calculated on the total amount invested. Upon completion of an additional round of funding of at least [AMOUNT] the compounding guaranteed return feature will expire. The liquidation preference will cease to operate if the proceeds due to Series A, on a merger, sale or liquidation on an as-converted basis, exceed the proceeds that would be due under the liquidation preference.
Use of Proceeds	The funds raised by Series A will be used principally for general working capital purposes.
Voting Rights	The holders of the Series A shall have the right to vote with the Common Stock on an as-if-converted basis
Redemption	If not previously converted, the Series A is to be redeemed in three equal successive annual instalments beginning [DATE]. Redemption will be at the purchase price plus a [%] per annum cumulative guaranteed return.
Pre-emptive Rights:	Holders of the Preferred Stock will be granted rights to participate in future equity financings of the Company based upon their pro-rata, as-if-converted, ownership of the Company.

Automatic Conversion	The Preferred Stock shall be automatically converted into Common Stock at the then applicable conversion rate (1:1 assuming no share splits) in the event of an underwritten public offering of shares of the Company at a total offering of not less than [AMOUNT] and at a per share public offering price of not less than three times the Series A purchase price per share, adjusted for splits.
Anti-Dilution	Series A shall have weighted average anti-dilution, based on a weighted average formula to be agreed, for all securities purchased as part of this transaction (excluding shares, options and warrants issued for management incentive and small issues for strategic purposes of under [NUMBER] shares).
Management Options	Simultaneously with this transaction, one million new shares shall expand the Company's management incentive stock option pool – bringing the total number of shares issued and stock incentives (awards and options) authorized to [NUMBER OF SHARES]. The Company and the Investors will have a right of first refusal with respect to any employee's shares proposed to be resold. Alternatively, the Investors will have the right to participate in the sale of any such shares to a third party (co-sale rights), which rights will terminate upon a public offering.
Information Rights	Monthly actual vs. plan and prior year. Annual budget [NUMBER] days before beginning of fiscal year. Annual audit by national firm. All recipients of financial statements to execute non-disclosure agreement acceptable to Company counsel. The aforementioned information rights shall be available to each holder of Preferred Stock for as long as such holder owns [NUMBER] shares of Preferred Stock or shares of Common Stock issued upon conversion of shares of Preferred Stock.
Negative Covenants	Approval by holders of Preferred Stock of organic changes outside normal course of business and sale, liquidation or merger, increase in board seats or change election procedures, new shares senior to or on par with and all distributions (dividends, repurchases).
Board of Directors	The Board will consist of [NUMBER] members. The holders of the Preferred Stock will have the right to designate [NUMBER] directors, the holders of the Common (exclusive of the Investors) will have the right to designate [NUMBER] directors, and the remaining [NUMBER] directors will be unaffiliated persons elected by the Common Stock and the Preferred Stock voting as a single class.

Stock Restriction Agreement	All present holders of Common Stock of the Company who are employees of, or consultants to, the Company will execute a Stock Restriction Agreement with the Company pursuant to which the Company will have an option to buy back at cost a portion of the shares of Common stock held by such person in the event that such stockholder's employment with the Company is terminated prior to the date of employment. [%] of the shares will be released each year from the repurchase option based upon continued employment by the Company.
Non-competition Proprietary Information	Each officer and key employee of the Company designated by the Investors will enter into a non- competition, proprietary information and Inventions agreement in a form reasonably acceptable to the Investors.
Expenses	The Company shall pay the reasonable expenses of legal counsel to represent the Investors in the completion of the Preferred Stock Agreement and the completion of all due diligence, up to a maximum of [AMOUNT].
Definitive Purchase & Due Diligence:	The purchase of the Series A will be made pursuant to negotiation of a definitive Series A purchase agreement. Additionally, the closing of this investment will be contingent on the satisfactory completion of VC's due diligence reviews and final investment committee approvals. Such due diligence reviews will include, but not be limited to, a professional review of all legal and financial contracts of the Company.
Closing	The Company and VC agree to use their best efforts to close the transaction on or about [DATE]. It is agreeable to have a first closing of the transaction for [AMOUNT] of Series A and leave the transaction open for an additional [NUMBER] days post first closing to close up to [NUMBER] of total Series A.

Other than that the Company hereby agrees to pay Investors' reasonable legal fees of up to [AMOUNT] in case a definitive agreement is not ultimately reached with VC (which agreement is legally binding) the undersigned acknowledge that this term sheet does not constitute a binding agreement, but expresses an agreement in principle covering the principal terms of an equity financing, and an undertaking to proceed in good faith to negotiate a definitive agreement.

This Term Sheet merely constitutes a statement of the present material intentions of the parties, but that except as set forth under the heading "Confidentiality," "Expenses" and "Exclusivity" above as to which the parties intend to be legally bound, no legally binding agreement or obligation of any party are covered by this Term Sheet. No oral modifications to this principle shall be valid.

This proposal remains open until [DATE], at which point it will be deemed to have been withdrawn.

[YOUR COMPANY NAME]   **VENTURE CAPITAL FIRM**

_____   _____

[REPRESENTED BY NAME & TITLE]   **[REPRESENTED BY NAME & TITLE]**

www.ingramcontent.com/pod-product-compliance
Lightning Source LLC
LaVergne TN
LVHW070525070526
838199LV00073B/6706